Lecture Notes in Computer S‹

T0237781

Commenced Publication in 1973
Founding and Former Series Editors:
Gerhard Goos, Juris Hartmanis, and Jan van Leeuwen

Serge Fdida   Kazunori Sugiura (Eds.)

Sustainable Internet

Third Asian Internet Engineering Conference, AINTEC 2007
Phuket, Thailand, November 27-29, 2007
Proceedings

 Springer

Volume Editors

Serge Fdida
University Pierre and Marie Curie
CNRS, LIP6 Laboratory
104, Avenue du Président Kennedy
75016 Paris, France
E-mail: Serge.Fdida@lip6.fr

Kazunori Sugiura
Communications Research Laboratory
4-2-1 Nukui-Kitamachi, Koganei
Tokyo, 184-8795, Japan
E-mail: uhyo@sfc.wide.ad.jp

Library of Congress Control Number: 2007939171

CR Subject Classification (1998): C.2, C.3, F.1, F.2.2, K.6

LNCS Sublibrary: SL 5 – Computer Communication Networks
and Telecommunications

ISSN   0302-9743
ISBN-10   3-540-76808-4 Springer Berlin Heidelberg New York
ISBN-13   978-3-540-76808-1 Springer Berlin Heidelberg New York

Springer is a part of Springer Science+Business Media

springer.com

© Springer-Verlag Berlin Heidelberg 2007
Printed in Germany

Typesetting: Camera-ready by author, data conversion by Scientific Publishing Services, Chennai, India
Printed on acid-free paper   SPIN: 12192373   06/3180   5 4 3 2 1 0

Preface

The 3rd Asian Internet Engineering Conference (AINTEC) followed the first two successful editions held in Bangkok, Thailand, and focused on developing synergies between researchers in Asia and worldwide, but was also a unique chance for young, talented regional scientists to meet and interact. AINTEC 2007 was therefore a major opportunity for presentations and discussions around these objectives. In particular, it aimed at addressing issues pertinent to the Asian region with vast diversities of socio-economic and networking conditions while inviting high-quality and recent research results from the global international research community to be presented. The conference is single-track to favor discussions among a diverse set of participants.

We want to thank the authors of the 66 papers submitted for considering AINTEC as the right target for their paper. The submissions came from 18 countries with, as expected, a majority from Asia. The program was composed of 14 accepted papers organized in 6 technical sessions including 7 invited talks by leading experts on innovative topics, presentations of papers, demos, posters and a pre-conference 18th Asian School on Computer Science (November, 25–26 2007).

You might think that AINTEC is yet another conference but it has different objectives and spirit, it offers a great opportunity to discuss future challenges for a sustainable Internet, and to get to know the local and regional researchers and enjoy the great hospitality of Thailand.

This edition was made possible thanks to many individuals. We want to warmly thank the Program Committee members for accepting to spend time in supporting the conference and carefully reviewing the submissions. We are very pleased with the support from Springer as a publisher for the proceedings and would like to thank them for their trust. Finally, our strong recognition goes to Apinun Tunpan, who took care of all the logistics in managing the review process and Kanchana Kanchanasut for perfectly orchestrating the event. We, personally, enjoyed being involved in this edition of AINTEC.

November 2007   Serge Fdida
                                                    Kazunori Sugiura

Organization

Sponsored By

Asia Pacific Network Information Centre (APNIC), French regional cooperation, National Electronic and Computer Center (NECTEC, Thailand), Thai Research and Education Network (ThaiREN) and T.H.NIC Co. Ltd.

Scientific Advisory Committee

Randy Bush	Internet Initiative Japan Inc., USA
Erol Gelenbe	Imperial College, UK
Jun Murai	WIDE Project and Keio University, Japan
Keith W. Ross	Polytechnic University of New York, USA
Surasak Sang-uanpong	Thai Research and Education Network, Thailand

Steering Committee

Kenjiro Cho	WIDE Project, Japan
Philippe Jacquet	INRIA, France
Kanchana Kanchanasut	Asian Institute of Technology, Thailand

General Chair

Kanchana Kanchanasut	Asian Institute of Technology, Thailand

Program Committee Co-chairs

Serge Fdida	University Pierre & Marie Curie, France
Kazunori Sugiura	Keio University / WIDE Project , Japan

Local Organizers

Dwijendra Kumar Das	Asian Institute of Technology, Thailand
Wit Hmone Tin Latt	Asian Institute of Technology, Thailand
Apinun Tunpan	Asian Institute of Technology, Thailand

Publicity Committee

Panita Pongpaibool	NECTEC, Thailand
Vasaka Visoothiviset	Mahidol University, Thailand

Program Committee

Khaldoun Al Agha	University of Orsay, France
Rui Aguiar	IT, Portugal
Georg Carle	Tuebingen University, Germany
Kenjiro Cho	IIJ, Japan
Marco Conti	IIT-CNR, Italy
Costas Courcoubetis	AUEB, Athens, Greece
Noel Crespi	INT, France
Marcelo Dias de Amorim	UPMC, France
Michel Diaz	LAAS, France
Christophe Diot	Thomson, France
Luigi Fratta	Politecnico di Milano, Italy
Silvia Giordano	SUPSI, Switzerland
Matthias Grossglauser	EPFL, Lausanne, Switzerland
Chalermek Intanagowiwat	Chulalongkorn University, Thailand
Philippe Jacquet	INRIA, France
Youki Kadobayashi	NAIST, Japan
Farouk Kamoun	ENSI, Tunisia
Jim Kurose	Umass, USA
Guy Leduc	University of Liege, Belgium
Laurent Mathy	Lancaster University, UK
Martin May	ET, Switzerland
Yoshifumi Nishida	Sony CSL, Japan
Anan Phonphoem	Kasetsart University, Thailand
Radu Popescu-Zeletin	Fokus, Germany
Jennifer Rexford	Princeton, USA
Simon Pietro Romano	University of Naples, Italy
Keith Ross	Polytechnic University, USA
Poompat Saengudomlert	AIT, Thailand
Teerapat Sa-nguankotchakorn	AIT, Thailand
Jochen Schiller	Freie Universität of Berlin, Germany
Aruna Seneviratne	NICTA, Australia
Jun Takei	Intel KK, Japan
Leandros Tassulias	Volos University, Greece
Yasuo Tsuchimoto	intERLab, AIT, Thailand
Rolland Vida	BUTE, Hungary

Yannis Viniotis	NCSU, USA
Ryuji Wakikawa	Keio University, Japan
Cedric Westphal	Nokia, USA
Lars Wolf	Braunschweig University, Germany
Artur Ziviani	LNCC, Brazil

Table of Contents

Invited Talk 3

Session 4: Applications and Services

Invited Talk 4

Invited Talk 5

Session 5: Network Monitoring

Invited Talk 6

Session 5: Routing

Invited Talk 7

Packet Forwarding in Pocket Switched Networks – An Empirical Characterization of Human Mobility

Christophe Diot

Thomson, France

Abstract. Pocket switched networks (PSNs) make use of human mobility and local forwarding in order to distribute data. Information can be stored and passed, taking advantage of the device mobility, or forwarded over a wireless link when an appropriate contact is met. Such networks fall into the fields of mobile ad-hoc networking and delay-tolerant networking. PSN are totally distributed and cannot rely on central services for issues such as naming, authentication, trustability. The direct consequence is that forwarding in PSN is non trivial. In order to better understand the challenges associated to PSN design, we have collected human mobility data.

We establish three fundamental properties of PSNs. First, the distribution of inter-contact time follows an approximate power law over a large time range in all data sets. This observation is at odds with the exponential decay expected by many currently used mobility models. Second, we establish that the diameter of PSNs is in the order of 10 hops, confirming the existence of the well know "small world" phenomenon in human mobility. Last, we show that all forwarding algorithms are equivalent from a delay and success rate standpoint due to a "path explosion" phenomenon that generally occurs a coupe of minute after the optimal path. We establish these three properties experimentally and give in each case a simple analytical model that explains our observations. We discuss the implications of these observations on forwarding algorithms in PSN. We conclude the talk by early results on the role of communities and interest in the PSN node population. These communities could be later used to optimize packet forwarding. We describe the on-going implementation of our PSN application.

S. Fdida and K. Sugiura (Eds.): AINTEC 2007, LNCS 4866, p. 1, 2007.

Mobility Versus Density Metric for OLSR Enhancement

Cholatip Yawut, Beatrice Paillassa, and Riadh Dhaou

IRIT laboratory – ENSEEIHT
Network & Telecommunication Department
Toulouse – FRANCE
{cyawut,Beatrice.Paillassa,Riadh.Dhaou}@enseeiht.fr

Abstract. In order to improve network performance, adaptive protocol would adapt to different aspects of the network dynamic exhibited by the wireless systems and more particularly by the ad hoc networks. In this paper we consider the adaptation to the ad hoc network dynamic through two parameters: mobility and density. We study the impact part of the density metric and of the mobility metric. Considering the Optimized Link State Routing protocol (OLSR), our work focus on the Multipoint Relays (MPR) selection. A new approach to select a MPR by using a simple modification and no additional packet header is proposed. It introduces the idea of Link Duration criterion as mobility metric for MPR selection. From simulation results it appears that the protocol performance can be enhanced by mobility adaptation after the density one. The proposed scheme outperforms the standard protocol for large number of nodes.

Keywords: OLSR, MPR Selection, Link Duration, Mobility Metric.

1 Introduction

Ad-hoc network are characterized by an absence of pre-existent infrastructure that can induce suddenly and unpredictably change of the network. A route can be broken by the move of an intermediate node or by the bad quality of a wireless link. Mobile nodes can enter or leave the network and thus modify the network density and the connectivity. So, to improve their performance, protocols would adjust their behavior to network conditions. Protocol adaptations would be based on metrics to capture mobility, node density or link quality.

A first question is: how to describe the mobility? It may be defined by different metrics. A metric is a probability, a direct or indirect measurement of mobility. A direct measurement is based on the position or the absolute or relative velocity of the nodes. It is thus necessary to associate this kind of metric to a positioning system. An indirect measurement of mobility is based on the assumption: if an increase in mobility degrades a metric, it is assumed that a degradation of this metric indicates an increase in mobility. The present study on mobility is based on indirect measurement of mobility.

A synthesis of mobility metrics is given in [1]. It indicates a classification based on the means of detection of the indicators and the functions which they influence. Metrics are obtained from different levels (i.e. at physical, logical link and network

S. Fdida and K. Sugiura (Eds.): AINTEC 2007, LNCS 4866, pp. 2–17, 2007.

level). In [2] we evaluate three mobility metrics: Frequency of Link State Changes (LC), Link Connectivity Duration (LD) and Link Stability Metric (LS). In [3], a mobile adaptive routing strategy is presented. Mobility metrics are used to select cluster head and to change the routing mode: in case of high network dynamic, the routing mode is flat, while it is hierarchical for low mobile environment. In a similar way, others protocols would be enhanced by knowing the *"less"* mobile element. Optimized Link State Routing (OLSR) protocol [4] is a well-known manet protocol based on specific nodes called *Multipoint Relays (MPRs)*. Because only the MPRs are in charge of the control traffic flooding, the control overhead is reduced. Furthermore, only a part of the topology information is exchanged through MPRs. To minimize the MPR set, the MPR Selection heuristic actually focuses on the density. The research of stable MPRs set would yield to better results [5].

We propose to take into account link duration criterion in MPR selection process. As a result, the network has a stable MPR set; it would also provide route stability because OLSR uses only MPRs in route calculation. So, by selecting stable MPR set, which we can observe by the number of MPR changes, we would improve the route stability, decrease the end-to-end delay and decrease the overhead for route maintenance. Meanwhile, because MPR stability is also related to the network density we propose to conserve the density criteria. In this paper we investigate the impact of the mobility compared to the density for the OLSR performance.

Paper organization is as follows: section 2 presents mobility metrics, section 3 depicts OLSR and MPR selection algorithm improvements, section 4 describes the proposed heuristic for MPR selection with mobility metric and section 5 indicates performance metrics and simulation models to evaluate density and mobility impact over OLSR and performance simulation results are discussed in the final of this section.

2 Mobility Metric

In this section, we present the study of mobility metrics. Good mobility metric characteristics [6] should to be: computable in a distributed way without global network knowledge, able to indicate or predict the protocol's performance, feasible to compute (in terms of node resources), independent of any specific protocol and computable in real network. According to these characteristics, Frequency of Link State Changes (LC) and Link Connectivity Duration (LD) metrics are studied in [6]. *LC* is the number of link state changes. When Node comes into the transmission range of another node, the value of this metric is increased by one indicating a link connection. When Node moves out of the transmission range, the value of this metric is increased by one indicating link breakage. The average LC is done over the number of considered nodes. *LD* indicates the period a link is in the transmission range of a determined node. Results show a better performance correlation with LD than with LC. Thus LD is considered to be better than LC. However, the connection period is not shown in LC and the frequency of link changes is not presented in LD. Hence, the authors in [7, 8] present *LS* that combines the information of both LD and LC. LS capture link longevity as well as frequency of link changes. It is defined as: LS = LD/LC. Meanwhile we do not consider LS as a *"good metric"* as explained in figure1.

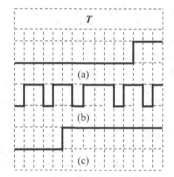

	a	*b*	*c*
LC	1/T	9/T	1/T
LD	T/5	2T/3	2T/3
LS	$T^2/5$	$2T^2/27$	$2T^2/3$

(d)

Fig. 1. Impact of mobility on three mobility metrics

As shown in figure1-a and 1-c, LC in both cases is equal but the link duration is different. The routing protocol may work better in the case 1-c than in the case 1-a because of the long duration connectivity which means that there is a route to the destination (if there is a route the protocol can find it). Average LC in figure1-b is more frequent than in figure1-a. However, the routing protocol can perform better in figure1-b than in figure1-a because of the long duration connectivity. Hence, the average LC is not the best mobility metric.

LS can indicate LD as well as LC. Nevertheless, LS is not really a good metric because it depends on LC. According to figure1-d, the value of LS, it ordered by $2T^2/3$ (c) > $T^2/5$ (a) > $2T^2/27$ (b). It appears that LS in figure1-a is more stable than in figure1-b. Indeed, the routing protocol can work better with LS in case 1-b than in case 1-a because of the long duration connectivity. Therefore, the average LS does not seem to be the best mobility metric.

As illustrated in figure1-b and figure1-c, LD in both cases is equal but the frequency of link change is different. Network goodput can probably be good in 2 cases because of the long duration connectivity. Although, the overhead is higher in figure1-b case than in figure1-c, because of LC value. The average LD in figure1-b is more stable than in figure1-a but it is more frequent too. However, the routing protocol can be more efficient in figure1-b than in figure1-a. Hence, the average LD would be the best mobility metric among all three mobility metric.

Considering by NS2 simulations the performance correlation with the three metrics, Figure 2 shows the pertinence of the LD metric compare with LC and LS, since the growth of the metric induces an increase of the packet delivery ratio for many routing protocols (AODV, DSR, OLSR) over different mobility models, such as Random Way Point (RWP) and Reference Point Group Mobility model (RPGM). For the results of LC and LS, there are no good relations between the packet delivery ratios with mobility metric.

Meanwhile the computation of LD is closely dependant of the node number. In case of low number of nodes, the number of neighbors for each node is not sufficient to obtain valuable value; the confidence interval is too large. Note that the confidence interval can be reduced by an increase of the observation period, but in this case the adaptation process would be too long to reflect the network dynamic.

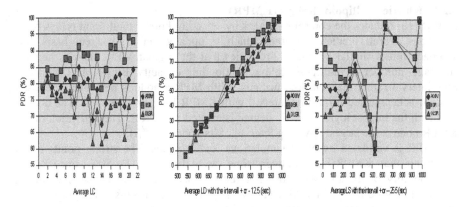

Fig. 2. Performances relative with different mobility metrics

As a conclusion it appears that even if the mobility metric, especially link duration, influences the protocol performance, density has not to be neglected.

3 Optimized Link State Routing Protocol (OLSR) and MPR Selection Algorithm

Many works have been done to improve OLSR such as increasing Hello message interval (Fast-OLSR) [9], increasing topology maintenance interval (OLSR-TM) [10], Multi-channel OLSR [11] and Link Buffering for OLSR [12]. As for us we focus on the MPR selection algorithm.

3.1 MPR Basics

The OLSR [4] main concept is Multipoint Relays (MPR). The idea of MPR is to reduce the information exchange overhead in the same region in the network. Each node periodically broadcasts HELLO messages, containing the information about its neighbors and their link status. From these messages nodes select MPR.

More precisely, the MPR set includes minimum number of one-hop symmetric neighbors from which it is possible to reach all the symmetrical strict two-hops neighbors. The node must have the information about one and two-hop symmetric neighbors to calculate for the MPR set. All the information exchanges are broadcasted using Hello messages. The symmetric neighbors who have indicated their interest in the Hello message can be selected to act as MPR.

The main criteria of Multipoint Relay selection algorithm is the reachability number of two-hop node, we can say that it is based on a *density metric*. The given node chooses the one-hop neighbor nodes that reach the maximum number of two-hops nodes as MPR.

3.2 MPR Modified Selection Algorithm

This sub-section presents works using different metrics to choose MPR set.

3.2.1 Kinetic Multipoint Relays (KMPR)

KMPR [13] reduces the control messages by selecting kinetic multipoint relays based on nodes overall predicted degree, which is updated on a per-event basis. The approach offers similar broadcast properties that the regular MPR, such as network coverage, number of multipoint relays, or flooding capacity. But, KMPR works on time interval rather than on time instants. With MPR a node is periodically chosen, while it is designated for a time interval with KMPR for a time interval. The node in $N(i)$ with the largest logical kinetic degree is elected as KMPR. The activation of this KMPR node is the largest covering interval of its nodes in $N^2(i)$.

KMPR is validated by NS-2 simulations for 20 nodes. The strong points of the results are that, KMPR has a delivery time faster than MPR by 50%, since KMPR uses mobility predictions and does not rely on periodic maintenance; the routing overhead may be reduced by 75%.The weak points of the results is to determine the influence of the mobility metrics compare to the density one, as there is a low network density, 20 nodes.

3.2.2 Link Stability Based Enhancements to OLSR (LS-OLSR)

LS-OLSR [5] introduces the statistical based link stability metrics [14] for selecting a MPR. *Link stability* is defined as link's probability to persist for certain span of time. *Residual Link lifetime* is the average amount of lifetime left in terms of probability for a link which has survived age *'a'*. Density (d_a) of residual link lifetimes for links of age *'a'* is derivated from density function, *'d'* and distribution of link lifetime duration function, *'D(a)'*. The average residual link lifetime is calculated from the equation of mean residual link lifetime of a link with age *'a'*.

The objective is to select a neighbor with maximum residual time as MPR until all the 2-hop neighbors are covered, thus ending up with a MPR set having maximum residual lifetime. In order to calculate the residual age or α-quantile, each node maintains a *Link_Life_Array* referred as *'d[t]'*. *Link_Life_Window* is the number of elements stored in array *'d[t]'* for maintaining the link duration distribution. Observation period is defined as a period of time during which node observes the link life duration and populates the array *'d[t]'*. The observation period should be set long enough to capture the data of longest link survived by the node. *Link set* which records the link information should be modified to carry information regarding the age *'a'*.

LS-OLSR is evaluated by NS-2 simulations for 75 nodes. The strong points of results are that, the average percentage increase of path duration and the average throughput are increased; the average of link changes and the packet loss are reduced. The weak points of this approach are that, the MPR set size is increased about 21%. As a result the end-to-end delay as well as the overhead is increased. Furthermore, it is difficult to set the observation period to set long enough to capture the data of longest link survived by the node.

4 OLSR with Link Duration

From works presented in section 2, we choose to introduce the Link Duration metric in the MPR selection algorithm. Our proposition differs from LS_OLSR by the way to compute the Link Duration and by the fact that Link Duration is not the only criterion for MPR selection. We propose to combine it with density criterion. Selection algorithm would be enhanced by, firstly, using the original density metric with the number of the reachability, secondly, by using the LD metric beyond the first consideration.

The simple way for a node to compute LD value is to use HELLO messages. When a node receives a HELLO from a neighbor, it checks to see if the HELLO contains the IP address of the interface on which the message was received. The link set is then updated as follows:

- If no link entry exists for the tuple (*originating IP, IP of received interface*) then such an entry is established. The originating IP is obtained from the IP header of the received packet. Whenever a link entry is established, a corresponding neighbor entry is initiated as well if no such entry exists.
- The validity time received is used to update an asymmetric timer. This timer indicates for how long the link entry is considered as asymmetric if the symmetric timer times out.
- If the address of the receiving interface is included in the received HELLO, the symmetric timer is updated. The status of the link and the status of the neighbor entries according to this link entry are updated if necessary.
- The maximum of the asymmetric timer and the symmetric timer is used to set the actual holding time for this entry.

Examining the Hello processing on an example (figure 3), we state the difficulty to compute directly the Link Duration from the HELLO message. At t = t1, node X first sends an empty HELLO message. Node Y receives this message and records X as an asymmetric neighbor, as it can not find its own address in the HELLO message. An asymmetric timer (*Asym*) and an actual holding time (*Time*) of this entry are set to t1 + V (Validity time). Then, at t = t2, Y sends a HELLO message declaring Y as an asymmetric neighbor. When X obtains this message it finds its own address in it and therefore sets Y as a symmetric neighbor. At t = t3, X includes Y in its HELLO message. Y records X as a symmetric neighbor upon reception of the HELLO message from X. Furthermore, the asymmetric timer, symmetric timer (*Sym*) and actual holding time of this entry are set to t3 + V. At t = t4, Y sends a HELLO message declaring Y as a symmetric neighbor. At t = t5, X transmits a HELLO message declaring Y as a symmetric neighbor. Upon reception of the HELLO message, Y then updates all the timer of this entry = t5 + v.

As shown in the example, when a node updates a link entry, it only records the time during which this link is considered valid. It can not find link duration because it did not record a time starting point. Thus we modify the OLSR procedure in the simplest way without any addition in the OLSR header packet. The element *"Start Connection Time"* (*Start_t*) is just added to the Link Tuple. When a node has to choose a MPR, it calculates LD by the difference between actual time and *Start_t*. It then can get LD of each node. Refer to MPR selection process, the MPR set is selected from one-hop symmetric neighbors from which it is possible to reach all the symmetrical strict two-hops neighbors. In our proposed solution, we think that Link Duration should to start since a node knows its neighbors. Therefore the started time is recorded since the node status is asymmetric. However the node is not selected as

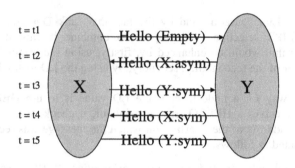

Link Tuple of Y

	NB_ID	Sym	Asym	Time	Start_t
t = t1	X	-	t1 + V	t1 + V	t1
t = t3	X	t3 + V	t3 + V	t3 + V	t1
t = t5	X	t5 + V	t5 + V	t5 + V	t1

V = Validity time

Fig. 3. Local LD calculation

MPR, if the link status is not asymmetric. In case of a node has the higher LD value but it is not in the transmission range, The LD of this node is deleted because of missing of the Hello message exchange (If a node is out of the transmission rage, it can not receive the Hello message). Thus only the node has the higher LD value and it is in the transmission range is selected as MPR.

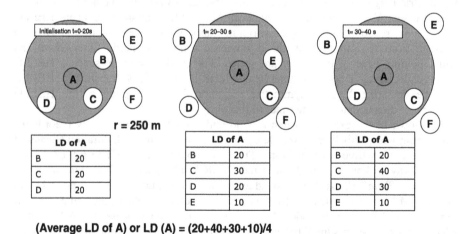

(Average LD of A) or LD (A) = (20+40+30+10)/4

Average LD of all = [LD (A) + LD (B) + LD (C) + LD (D) + LD (E) + LD (F)] /6

Fig. 4. Global LD calculation

Furthermore, there are 2 types of LD that can be deduced from HELLO message. There are *local* and *global LD*, When a node has to choose a MPR, it calculates LD by the difference between current time and Start_t. It then can get LD of each node, it is called the *"local LD"*. For the *"global LD"* the given node calculates all link duration with every neighbor nodes. Figure 4 illustrates the global LD calculation.

The mobile node A is a given node. Firstly, at t = 0-20s, the mobile node B, C and D are in the transmission range, the LDs with B, C and D are 20s. Secondly, at t = 20-30s, the mobile node B and D move out of the transmission range, the LDs with them do not change. The mobile node E comes in the transmission range and the mobile node C already stays there, the LD with E is 10 and the LD with C is added by 10. Thirdly, at t = 30-40s, the mobile node E moves out of the transmission range, then the LD with E do not modify. The mobile node D returns in the transmission range and the mobile node C already stays there, then the LD with C and D are increased by 10.

When the node have to send global LD to neighbor nodes, the header of HELLO message has to be modified in order to contain this LD. Consequently, the network overhead is increased. Hence, we select the local LD method.

Another question concerns the LD value selection: is it more valuable to select, the shortest or the longest LD ?. LS-OLSR uses the shortest LD, since it selects the longest residual life time. Authors believe when nodes have long connection, neighbor nodes have to move out of the transmission range. The validity of the assumption is function of the considered mobility model. Because the random way point mobility model is 'a worst case' we evaluate the hypothesis validity for this mobility model. The first hypothesis is that it is better to select a node with long connection duration: the oldest neighbor. As the opposite the second hypothesis is that it is better to select the newest neighbor.

If the pause time parameter of the mobility model is more than 0 s., when neighbor nodes stay in the transmission range until the pause time period, the nodes have to move again. When the pause time is null, it is not true that oldest node have to move out of the transmission range. They perhaps move in the same direction or inversely move with very low speed. We show the interest of the first hypothesis in simulation. Thus we use the longest LD value in our proposition (section 5).

Another reason to choose the longest LD rather than the lowest one concerns the observation period. LS-OLSR must define the observation period that should be set long enough to capture the data of the longest link survived by the node, so it may be difficult to achieve in practice. For our proposition, it is not required.

5 Simulation and Discussion

In this section, we present performance metrics that we use to evaluate the protocol performance. Next, simulation models are given in detail. Finally, the simulation results in average values on all the simulation scenarios are evaluated and discussed.

5.1 Performance Metrics

The performance metrics [2, 3, 15, 16] are used to evaluate protocol performances. There are:

• **Packet delivery ratio (PDR)** (%) is the ratio of the data packets delivered to the destination to those generated by the CBR sources.
• **Normalized routing overhead** (%) is the number of "transmitted" routing packets per data packet "delivered" to the destination. Each hop-wise, transmission of a routing packet is counted (in bytes). The routing overhead includes: a Routing Protocol Overhead Packet (in byte) such as Route Request, Route Reply, Route Error, and, a Routing Overhead on data packet (in byte) calculates by Packet transmission (RTR) – Packet Original (AGT). Normalized routing overhead = 100 * (Protocol Routing Overhead on data packet + Routing Protocol Overhead Packet) / Packet Original (AGT) transmitted on RTR).
• **Delay** (seconds) is time elapsing from a packet which is sent from the source (AGT) until it is received by the destination (AGT). It includes all delays caused by buffering, during route discovery latency, queuing at the interface queue, retransmission delays at the MAC, and propagation and transfer times.
• **Efficiency** (%) is the number of delivered packets which are transmitted (Data) / (Data + Routing Overhead)
• **Packet Collision** (packet numbers) is the number of packets which occurs collision in the network.
• **Number of MPR changes** (times) is the total number of MPR changes for each node in network. When each node first chooses MPRs, the counter is set to the number of MPRs chosen. Next, each node chooses again MPRs, the counter is added by the number of MPRs chosen which are different from the previous MPRs set.
• **All of the MPR numbers** (times) is the total number of MPR for each node in network. When each node first chooses MPRs, the counter is set to the number of MPRs chosen. Next, each node chooses again MPRs, the counter is added by the all number of MPRs chosen.

5.2 Simulation Models

Network simulator NS2.29 [17] is used with Random Waypoint (RWP) mobility model. The pause time is null and the maximum speed Vmax varies from 1.5 and 5 to 25m/s by step of 5m/s in order to generate different movement patterns. 15 scenarios for each speed of RWP are created. Data rate is 4 packets/sec and the packet size is 512 bytes. A nominal bit-rate of 2 Mb/sec. CBR sources are 3, 10 and 15 sources for 10, 50 and for since 100 nodes respectively. A radio range of 250 meters for 10 and 50 nodes and 150 meters for 100, 150 and 200 nodes are used. Simulation area is 1000m x 1000m. OLSR according UM-OLSR-0.8.8 [18] based on RFC 3626 is used. Simulation time is 1000s for 10 and 50 nodes Due to constraint of time and machine resources, it is 250s (the same simulation time with T. Clausen and P. Jacquet [16] who are ones of OLSR developers) for nodes superior to 100.

Firstly, in order to select a good LD to apply to MPR selection process, the shortest and longest LD are evaluated.

Secondly, in order to evaluate the importance of the density and the mobility over performance, we compare three methods of MPR selection:

- **OLSR 1D** is the standard OLSR, MPRs are selected from the number of neighbors criterion: a density metric (D).
- **OLSR 1D+2LD** selects at first MPR from the density criteria and then at the second it applies the LD criterion.
- **OLSR 1LD+2D** selects at first MPR from the link duration criterion (1LD) and in case of equality it applies at the second, the density metric (2D).

5.3 Simulation Results

A method is considered as good when it improves the protocol performance compared to the standard OLSR method (Table1).

Table 1. The meaning of used symbols

Symbol	Meaning
+	Improve the protocol performance when compare with OLSR RFC
-	Decrease the protocol performance when compare with OLSR RFC

5.3.1 Comparative the Shortest and Longest LD

The difference percentage of performance improvement, or decreasing, for the longest LD compared with the shortest LD for 10 and 50 nodes are represented in table 2 and 3 respectively.

Table 2. Comparative the shortest and longest LD performances for 10 nodes

Performance Metric	Protocols		*Longest LD* Improvement (%)
	Shortest LD	*Longest LD*	
PDR	41.800	41.796	**-0.010**
Normalized Routing Overhead	12.768	12.785	**-0.127**
End-to-end delay	0.0137	0.0113	**+17.673**
Efficiency	462.436	459.785	**-0.573**
Packet collision	129.800	132.783	**-2.298**
Number of MPR changes	35.315	38.738	**-9.694**
All of the MPR numbers	1242.447	1231.570	**+0.875**

As depicted in table 2, the longest LD for 10 nodes performs better than the shortest LD over a delay about 17.673 %. Also the results of longest LD for 50 nodes (table 3) perform better than the shortest LD in all the aspect. Therefore, we consider to apply the longest approach to MPR selection process.

Table 3. Comparative the shortest and longest LD performances for 50 nodes

Performance Metric	Protocols		Longest LD Improvement (%)
	Shortest LD	*Longest LD*	
PDR	81.640	81.988	+0.426
Normalized Routing Overhead	23.774	22.547	+5.161
End-to-end delay	0.4478	0.4254	+5.002
Efficiency	144.370	153.165	+6.092
Packet collision	238428	231058	+3.091
Number of MPR changes	562.718	566.574	+0.685
All of the MPR number	30267.691	26474.231	+12.533

5.3.2 Low Density

Although OLSR has been designed for large network configuration, we examine its performance over small configuration with low density : about 10 nodes over an 1000m x 1000m area, so that we can compare the mobility influence. The difference percentage of performance improvement, or decreasing, for *1D+2LD* and *1LD+2D* compare with *OLSR 1D* for 10 nodes is represented in table 4.

In table 4, results show that *1D+2LD* has nearly performance with *1LD+2D*. Due to the low number of nodes, a given node has a few one-hop neighbors which perhaps have to cover 1-2 two-hop neighbors. Therefore, it has high probability that one-hop

Table 4. Comparative performances for 10 nodes

Performance Metric	Protocols			Improvement (%)	
	1D	*1D + 2LD*	*1LD+2D*	*1D + 2LD*	*1LD+2D*
PDR	41.727	41.7376	41.7956	**+0.025**	**+0.164**
Normalized Routing Overhead	12.810	12.822	12.785	**-0.090**	**+0.202**
End-to-end delay	0.0137	0.0118	0.0113	**+13.899**	**+17.917**
Efficiency	463.625	461.143	459.785	**-0.536**	**-0.828**
Packet collision	126.117	127.817	132.783	**-1.348**	**-5.286**
Number of MPR changes	36.102	38.862	38.738	**-7.645**	**-7.303**
All of the MPR number	1223.970	1215.557	1231.570	**+0.687**	**-0.621**

neighbors have the same density. Thus LD is main parameters for the two selected methods. It has a little PDR improvement, but more improvement on the end-to-end delay. However, it has less performance when considering other performance metric.

Note that the higher number of MPR changes of *1LD+2D* does not relate with performance criteria. Because when node starts to choose MPR set in *1LD+2D*, it has more MPRs than in *1D*. For the next time, the node's MPRs have a same or higher change than with 1D due to the low node density. Hence, the number of MPR changes of *1LD+2D* is higher than 1D. Many MPRs send in the same time many messages in the network. As a result the packets collision increases. However, all of the MPR numbers in all the protocols are less significant (less than 1%).

Considering the influence of LD and D criteria over PDR overhead, delay and efficiency, LD is more influent than D since it has the best percentage improvement in term of delay. But other performance metrics are less sensitive (less than 1.0 %). These results are confirmed by those obtained with the Kinetic approach over 20 nodes (3.2.1). The results obtained with the simple Link Duration metric may be improved by a more sophisticated metric. Thus mobility metric is more influent than density metric in small environment.

5.3.3 Medium Density

Table 5 shows the different performance of *1D+2LD* and *1LD+2D* compared with *OLSR 1D* for 50 nodes. The obtained results show that *1D+2LD* has nearly the performance of *1LD*. A given node has several one-hop neighbors which perhaps have to cover few or several two-hop neighbors. Therefore, it has low probability that one-hop neighbors have the same density. Hence, the LD criterion has a low probability to improve the protocol performance.

Results for 50 nodes indicate that *1LD+2D* just increases the percentage of improvement of the number of MPR changes. But similarly to the previous low density case, the lower number of MPR changes does not relate with other performance criteria, as the number of MPR is increased. There is a lower percentage improvement for all other criteria. Also, *1LD+2D* defines more MPR than other criteria because it chooses more MPR when it starts to work.

Table 5. Comparative performances for 50 nodes

Performance Metric	Protocols			Improvement (%)	
	1D	1D + 2LD	1LD+2D	1D + 2LD	1LD+2D
PDR	83.020	83.113	81.988	+0.112	-1.244
Normalized Routing Overhead	20.185	20.232	22.547	-0.232	-11.703
End-to-end delay	0.3613	0.3478	0.4254	+3.726	-17.741
Efficiency	172.576	172.546	153.165	-0.017	-11.248
Packet collision	200157.250	203775.833	231058.208	-1.808	-15.438
Number of MPR changes	658.053	650.593	566.574	+1.134	+13.901
All of the MPR number	23875.575	23014.118	26474.231	+3.608	-10.884

Simulations show that the density is more influent than mobility metric when the node number increases. Therefore, our proposition to apply the Link Duration mobility metric above the density in the MPR selection process would presents some interest for larger configuration

5.3.4 High Density
We evaluate the interest to complete the density metric by mobility metric. Results for 150 and 200 nodes are respectively presented in Table 6 and 7. As OLSR *1D+2LD* perform better than 1D for all performance criteria.

Table 6. Comparative performances for 150 nodes

Performance Metric	Protocols		1D+2LD Improvement (%)
	1D	1D+2LD	
PDR	28.456	29.188	+2.571
Normalized routing overhead	122.039	116.407	+4.616
End-to-end delay	2.198	2.130	+3.069
Efficiency	9.418	10.010	+6.285
Packet collision	689055.5	668431.2	+3.00
Number of MPR changes	331.186	317.172	+4.231
All of the MPR number	9627.046	9249.385	+3.923

All performance criteria indicate that *1D+2LD* may improve the overall *1D* performance. *1D+2LD* has lower delay than *1D* due to the route stability improvement (number of MPR changes of *1D* is higher than *1D+2LD*). Considering the MPR stability, we note that for high density network, the protocol performance is inversely proportional to the number of MPR change. In *1D+2LD*, the number of MPR changes is lower; so the number of route changes decrease as well as the end-to-end delay is lower because of the route availability. The numbers of control messages, which are broadcasted, is reduced also. As a result, the number of packet collision decreases and PDR is improved. Finally, the efficiency of the network is significantly increased. Furthermore, *1D+2LD* use lesser MPR than *1D* because of mobility metric assistance.

For 200 nodes (Table 7) we see that, the *1D+2LD* performance gain is greater than with 150 nodes.

For the question: " why *1D+2LD* has higher performance for high density networks? ", there are two reasons. Firstly, for denser networks the numbers of MPR candidate nodes are higher and the probability for an available route is therefore also higher. Secondly, as the network becomes denser, stable MPRs are chosen due to the use of the mobility criteria. A given node has many one-hop neighbors which perhaps have to cover few or several two-hop neighbors. Therefore, it has high probability that one-hop neighbors have the same density. Hence, the LD has a high probability to improve the protocol performance. As only MPR nodes will retransmit topology control messages, the control overhead will drop quickly.

Table 7. Comparative performances for 200 nodes

Performance Metric	Protocols		1D+2LD Improvement (%)
	1D	1D+2LD	
PDR	16.667	18.192	**+9.15**
Normalized routing overhead	278.612	264.814	**+4.952**
End-to-end delay	3.221	2.908	**+9.715**
Efficiency	2.982	3.443	**+15.441**
Packet collision	1863030	1795068	**+3.648**
Number of MPR changes	434.685	404.632	**+6.914**
All of the MPR number	13817.04	13352.77	**+3.36**

Simulations highlight that for dense network the MPR selection process with LD contribution is more significantly improved for lower mobility than for higher mobility. *1D+2LD* performs better with all performance metrics because the MPR candidate nodes are higher and the probability for an available route is also higher. Results indicate that the number of MPR changes is reduced; it reduces the number of TC messages in the network and the delays because of stable MPR set as well as the number of packet collisions are reduced. Furthermore, the efficiency of the network is also enhanced.

The summarization of the applied metric methods interest is presented in table 8. For low density environment, the mobility metric (*1LD+2D*) is more significant than the density (*1D*). For low density environment, the density (*1D*) is more importance than the mobility metric (*1LD+2D*). For high density, firstly, the density is taken in to account; in the case of equality the mobility metric then is used (*1D+2LD*).

Table 8. Applied metric methods for different density

Density		
Low	**Medium**	**High**
Mobility	Density	Density + Mobility

It appears that *1D+2LD* can be self adaptive to low, medium and high density environments. It performs quite close to *1LD+2D* for low density as well as to 1D for medium density. Furthermore, it has the best performance in high density network for which OLSR is well adapted.

6   Conclusion

In this paper, we propose to introduce a mobility metric, "Link Duration" criterion, to improve MPR selection process. We study how to apply this mobility metric to the original MPR selection which is only based on a density metric. The influence of density and mobility metrics are observed in different density environment. The simulation results show that the mobility metric is more important in low density as well as the density is more important in medium density. For high density, the importance is firstly, the density; secondly, the mobility. We find that the method that selects the MPR firstly from the number of neighbor then in equality event from the link duration significantly improves the protocol performance in all the density cases because it can self adaptive. Hence, the LD mobility metric is considered beyond the density in the MPR selection process.

This study shows that the protocol performance can be enhanced by the contribution of the mobility metric but that it is not a major improvement. It is because the mobility is measured locally for each node so that it does not really reflect the state of connectivity graph between nodes. With an important number of nodes it will be more probable to find a route even if the local mobility may be important.

References

1. Yawut, C., Dhaou, R., Paillassa, B.: On Cross-Layer Mobility Indicators in Mesh Networks, Euro-NGI deliverable for the LEO-MESH-NET specific research project (November 2006)
2. Yawut, C., Paillassa, B., Dhaou, R.: On Metrics for Mobility Oriented Self Adaptive Protocols. In: ICWMC 2007. 3rd International Conference on Wireless and Mobile Communications, Guadeloupe, France (2007)
3. Jaddi, F., Paillassa, B.: Mobility and density self-adaptative routing strategies in adhoc Networks. In: 3rd IEEE International Conference on Mobile Ad-hoc and Sensor Systems, LOCAN, Vancouver, Canada (2006)
4. Clausen, T., Jacquet, P.: Optimized Link State Routing Protocol (OLSR). RFC3626 (2003), http://rfc.sunsite.dk/rfc/rfc3626.html
5. Obilisetty, S., Jasti, A., Pendse, R.: Link stability based enhancements to OLSR (LS-OLSR). In: Vehicular Technology Conference, 2005. VTC-2005-Fall. 62nd. IEEE, pp. 306–310 (2005)
6. Boleng, J., Navidi, W., Camp, T.: Metrics to enable adaptive protocols for mobile ad hoc networks. In: ICWN 2002. Proceedings of the International Conference on Wireless Networks, pp. 293–298 (2002)
7. Ghassemian, M., Friderikos, V., Aghvami, A.H.: A Novel Algorithm for Supervisory Control by Monitoring Mobility and Traffic in Wireless Ad-hoc Networks. In: Wireless World Research Forum 12 meeting (2004)
8. Ghassemian, M., Mostafavi, M., Friderikos, V., Aghvami, A.H.: On Mobility Applied for Ad-hoc Network Protocol Evaluation. In: MWCN 2005. The 7th IFIP International Conference on Mobile and Wireless Communications Networks (2005)
9. Benzaid, M., Minet, P., Agha, K.A.: RR-4510 - Integrating fast mobility in the OLSR routing protocol. INRIA research report, pages 12 (2002)
10. Ren, Z., Zhou, Y., Guo, W.: An adaptive multichannel OLSR routing protocol based on topology maintenance. In: Mechatronics and Automation, IEEE International Conference (2005)
11. Qu, Y., Lung, C.H., Srinivasan, A.: Multi-channel OLSR with Dedicated Control Interface. In: SPECTS 2006. Proceedings of the International Symposium on Performance Evaluation of Computer and Telecommunication Systems, pp. 155–162 (2006)

12. Goto, M., Yoshida, S., Mase, K., Clausen, T.: A Study of Link Buffering for OLSR. In: The OLSR Interop & Workshop 2004 (2004)
13. Haerri, J., Filali, F., Bonnet, C.: On the Application of Mobility Predictions to Multipoint Relaying in MANETs: Kinetic Multipoint Relays. Eurecom Technical Report, Institut Eurecom, France (2005)
14. Gerharz, M., de Waal, C., Frank, M., Martini, P.: Link Stability in Mobile Wireless Ad Hoc Networks. In: LCN 2002. Proceedings of 27th Annual IEEE Conference on Local Computer Networks, Tampa, Florida (2002)
15. Perkins, C.E., Loyer, E.M., Das, S.R.: Performance comparison of two on-demand routing protocols for ad-hoc networks. In: IEEE Personal Commun. Mag., pp. 16–28 (2001)
16. Clausen, T., Jacquet, P., Viennot, L.: Comparative study of routing protocols for mobile ad-hoc networks. In: Proceeding of the First Annual Mediterranean Ad Hoc Networking Workshop. MindPass Center for Distributed Systems, Aalborg University and Project Hipercom, INRIA Rocquencourt, The First Annual Mediterranean Ad Hoc Networking Workshop (2002)
17. The Network simulator-ns-2, http://www.isi.edu/nsnam/ns/
18. UM-OLSR, http://masimum.dif.um.es/?Software:UM-OLSR

DAD-MPR Flooding Protocol, Convergence Evaluation Through Simulation

Saadi Boudjit[1], Cédric Adjih[2], and Paul Muhlethaler[3]

[1] Institut Galilée - Université Paris 13, France
saadi.boudjit@l2ti.univ-paris13.fr
[2] INRIA, France
cedric.adjih@inria.fr
[3] INRIA, France
paul.muhlethaler@inria.fr

Abstract. In this paper, we present the convergence evaluation of DAD-MPR flooding protocol through simulation. DAD-MPR flooding protocol is the autoconfiguration protocol we proposed for OLSR (Optimized Link State Routing protocol) [1]. This autoconfiguration protocol comprises two parts: the first part [2] describes the autoconfiguration rules for OLSR nodes with single interfaces, and the second part [3] describes the autoconfiguration rules to handle OLSR nodes with multiple interfaces. In our simulation, the interesting performance metrics include the latency of address duplication detection and therefore, the convergence of the DAD-MPR flooding protocol.

Keywords: MANETs; Autoconfiguration; DAD; OLSR.

1 Introduction

In addition to the challenge of routing in ad hoc networks, the design of mobile ad hoc networks must be able to support mechanisms for autoconfiguration. A node in an IP-based network is configured with an IP address, a netmask and a default gateway (the node to which packets for destinations not having an explicit entry in the routing table are sent). These network parameters can be assigned manually to the node, however this procedure becomes impractical in a large scale MANET where hundreds of nodes constitute the network. Moreover, since an ad hoc network is an open system and due to frequent network partitioning and merging, address duplications may happen. Hence, there is a need for an efficient distributed dynamic host configuration mechanism to configure nodes in a MANET and to handle the problem of address duplications.

Several protocols were proposed, addressing the problems of autoconfiguration and duplicate address detection in ad hoc networks. These protocols differ in a wide range of aspects, depending on when and how duplicate addresses are detected. *Conflict-free* protocols are characterized by a set of nodes in the network responsible for address allocation. These nodes have disjoint address pools and when a new mobile node joins the MANET, an address pool is divided into

S. Fdida and K. Sugiura (Eds.): AINTEC 2007, LNCS 4866, pp. 18–32, 2007.
© Springer-Verlag Berlin Heidelberg 2007

halves between itself and a configured node. Examples of conflict-free protocols include the "Dynamic Configuration and Distribution Protocol" (DCDP) [4] and the "Prophet Allocation Protocol" [5]. *Conflict-detection* protocols are charcterized by all nodes performing the DAD (Duplicate Address Detection) to ensure the uniqueness of the allocated IP address. The general procedure is that a node generates a tentative address and then performs the DAD within its neighborhood (radio range of the node). If the address is unique, the DAD is performed again over the whole network and a unique IP address is constructed. Examples of such approaches include [6].

This paper is organized as follows: Section 2 gives a brief overview on OLSR protocol. A summary on the autoconfiguration protocol we have proposed for OLSR with single interfaces [2] is given in Section 3. The way this protocol is implemented and integrated with OLSR, is presented in Section 4. Section 5 is dedicated to the evaluation of the latency of address duplication detection. Finally, Section 6 concludes the paper.

2   OLSR Protocol

OLSR is a proactive routing protocol for mobile ad hoc networks which inherits from the *link state* functioning of the Interior Gateway Protocol *OSPF* (*Open Shortest Path First*) [7]. It has the advantage of having routes immediately available when needed due to its proactive nature. OLSR is an optimization of a pure link state routing protocol and it is based on the concept of *multipoint relays* (*MPRs*), to diffuse its control traffic in the network. *MPRs* are selected nodes which forward broadcast messages during the flooding process. The use of *MPRs* significantly reduces the control traffic overhead as compared to a classical flooding mechanism, where every node retransmits each message when it receives the first copy of the message. Indeed only *multipoint relays* forward control messages.

An heuristic for a simple selection of MPRs was proposed in [1]. It constructs a MPR-set that enables a node to reach any node in its symmetrical strict 2-hop neighborhood. However, this heuristic assumes that there is no address duplication in the 2-hop neighborhood of any node in the network. Hence, the presence of any address duplications in the 2-hop neighborhood of a node can impair the correct functioning of the heuristic.

In the following section we give an overview on the autoconfiguration protocol we have proposed for OLSR with single interfaces.

3   Autoconfiguration Protocol for OLSR

Our autoconfiguration protocol for OLSR is based on three principles:

a. *Initial address assignment*: an IP address is selected by the arriving node and the node can join the ad hoc network. Numerous schemes can be used to select this IP address. For instance the node can perform a random selection in a well known pool of addresses, without special message exchanges with its neighbors; another technique consists of one of its neighbors selecting the address on behalf of the arriving node.

b. *Duplicate Address Detection*: The aim of this step is to detect potential address duplications on run. To perform this task a *Duplicate Address Detection* algorithm is started on this newly configured node. This DAD algorithm allows the newly configured node to state whether the selected address is duplicated or not in a proactive manner. The proposed DAD procedure is based on a special control message called MAD: Multiple Address Declaration. This MAD message is periodically emitted by each node, and it includes the identifier of the node (ID_{node}) and all its addresses. The identifier of each node is assumed to be unique. It is a sequence of bits of fixed length L which is randomly generated. Hence we are using the standard idea that the probability of two nodes having the same node identifier is low, and the probability of at least one address collision with N nodes, which is the well known "birthday problem" [8], can be set arbitrarily low by choosing a value of L large enough[1].

The central idea is that if there is a conflict between two nodes:

– One of the nodes in conflict will receive the MAD message from the other node in conflict: the MAD message received will include the address of the receiving node but it will have the identifier of the other node.
– The receiving node will deduce that the MAD message is not its own message and was sent by another node, hence that there is a conflict.

c. *Conflict resolution*: when a node detects that another node is using the same address, it will select a new address.

Because MAD messages should be sent to the whole network, and because OLSR has an optimized mechanism, called MPR-flooding, to transmit information to the whole network, it is natural to reuse this mechanism for MAD messages. However, the presence of conflicts may introduce deficiencies in the mechanism. These deficiencies could result in failure to detect the duplication of addresses. As an illustration of such possible situations, we give the following example.

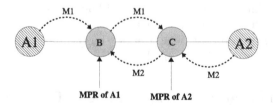

Fig. 1. An example of address duplication scenario

---

[1] Different birthday probability, denoted $Q_1(N, 2^L)$, can be estimated as $(1 - \frac{N}{2^{L+1}})^{(N-1)}$ with an error bound given by [8] for instance.

Figure 1 shows two nodes $A1$ and $A2$ sharing the same address A. Hence, nodes B and C see a 1-hop network and do not need to choose each other as a MPR to cover respectively their 2-hop neighbors $A2$ and $A1$. In this configuration, the MAD message of $A1$ can not reach node $A2$ and the MAD message of $A2$ can not reach $A1$. Consequently, nodes $A1$ and $A2$ will not detect the address conflict and the network remains corrupted.

Therefore, an important contribution of our work is to introduce changes to the MPR-flooding mechanism, so that MAD messages are propagated effectively, and, equally important, that these changes allow duplicate address detection in all possible cases of conflicts. This modified version of MPR flooding takes into consideration the possibility that MAD originator addresses might be duplicated. It is only useful for "Multiple Address Declaration" message, but could be used in general for any kind of message which includes the node identifier. This version of MPR flooding is called *Duplicate Address Detecting MPR Flooding* or *DAD-MPR Flooding*.

3.1   Special Rules of the DAD-MPR Flooding Protocol

Let us assume that there are only two nodes with a duplicated address in the network, and let us consider this pair of nodes with a duplicated address. Let us denote by $A1$ and $A2$ these two nodes with same address A, but different node identifiers ID_{A1} and ID_{A2} and let us assume that both of them send a MAD message $M1$ and $M2$.

We intend to add special rules to the classical MPR-flooding algorithm to handle the MAD messages diffusion. Then several cases can occur, depending on the distance d, in number of hops, between $A1$ and $A2$.

Fig. 2. *Distance ≥ 5*   **Fig. 3.** Distance $= 4$

$d \geq 5$: In Figure 2, nodes $A1$ and $A2$ have the same address, and they are 5 hops away from each other. In this case nodes $A1$ and $A2$ and all the intermediary nodes do not have duplications in their 1-hop and 2-hop neighbors according to our assumption of only two nodes with a duplicated address. Hence all the intermediary nodes calculate their MPR set properly. So, using the MPR-flooding the messages $M1$ and $M2$ will be correctly propagated to the nodes $A2$ and $A1$ respectively and the conflict will be detected. With the same consideration we can show that, in this case, all the MAD messages will reach all the nodes in the network.

$d = 4$: In Figure 3, nodes $A1$ and $A2$ do not have duplications in their 1-hop and 2-hop neighbors according to our initial assumption. Therefore, the MAD messages diffused by $A1$ and $A2$ will reach node C. Node C can detect the conflict by examining the node identifiers contained in the received MAD messages. These messages should be relayed by C, because it has been chosen as a MPR by B and D. In our case, this is not trivial. In fact, messages generated by $A1$ and $A2$ may have close sequence numbers, which may prevent one of the two sets of messages from being relayed by C (due to possible existence of a duplicate tuple indicating that such a message having the same sequence number and originator, has been received and processed). We need here to add an extra rule to allow MAD message relaying. We modify the MAD duplicate message detection, which will be based on the node originator address, the message sequence number, plus the node identifier. Hence, $A1$ and $A2$ MAD messages will be forwarded by C in all cases and reach B and D. Notice here that the MPR calculation of C is affected due to the presence of duplicated addresses in its 2-hop neighbors ($A1$ and $A2$). C chooses only one node between B and D as a MPR to cover its 2-hop neighbors. The chosen MPR, should act like node C as described before to relay the MAD messages. Following this rule, we are sure that one of the two nodes ($A1$ and $A2$) receives the MAD messages generated by the other node and hence can detect the conflict. We call this rule *Rule 1*.

$d = 3$: In case of distance $d = 3$, nodes B and C (Figure 4) do not need to choose a MPR to cover respectively their 2-hop neighbors $A2$ and $A1$ since they have the same address. Address A is considered as a one hop neighbor. In contrast, $A1$ chooses node B as a MPR to reach node C, and node $A2$ chooses C as a MPR to reach node B. In this situation, and thanks to the new rule described previously, the $A1$ MAD messages will reach node C, and the ones generated by $A2$ will arrive at node B. But, B and C do not choose each other as a MPR, consequently, $A1$ can not receive MAD messages coming from $A2$, and $A2$ MAD messages will never reach $A1$ node. To tackle this problem, we add another rule that we call ,*Rule 2*, to enable MAD relaying for such situations, as follows: if a given node N receives a MAD message from a neighbor M, and M did not select N as a MPR, then, node N will repeat this message if it detects that one of its 1-hop neighbors has the same address as the one contained in the MAD message. The MAD TTL value is put to 1 to avoid the transmission of the MAD message beyond the conflicting nodes.

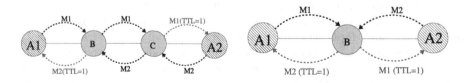

Fig. 4. Distance = 3   **Fig. 5.** Distance = 2

$d = 2$: In Figure 5, the node B detects the duplication because the nodes $A1$ and $A2$ are in its 1-hop neighborhood, it proceeds by the same manner as in the case of $d = 3$. Thus node $A1$ will receive the MAD message of $A2$; and node $A2$ will receive the MAD message of $A1$.

$d = 1$: This is the simplest case and because nodes $A1$ and $A2$ are in the radio range of each other, the conflict will be detected by both nodes.

In this analysis, we have considered the case of a unique couple of nodes having the same address in the network. The general case of multiple conflicts is treated in the following section.

Case of multiple conflicts: By multiple conflicts we mean, that we may have more than a single duplicated address in the network, knowing that a duplicated address, could be shared by several nodes at the same time. In the case of a duplicated address shared by more than two nodes in the network, conflicts are detected and fixed couple by couple by applying the previous rules. Eventually, this kind of conflict is resolved. Nevertheless, the previous rules are not sufficient for the special case of loops as depicted in Figure 6. In fact, in Figure 6, each node considers that it has only two neighbors at 1-hop distance and no 2-hop neighbors (i.e the network seen by node A is composed by direct neighbors B and C). None of the nodes present in this network will be elected as a MPR. Hence, MAD messages will not be relayed and never reach other conflicting nodes or at least a neighbor of a conflicting node. In that case the previous rules will not ensure the relaying of MAD messages between nodes in conflict.

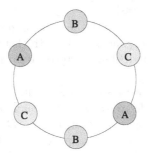

Fig. 6. Case of multiple conflicts

To handle multiple conflicts, we add a third rule to the classical MPR-flooding mechaninsm. We weaken the relaying condition for nodes who are in the 1-hop neighborhood of a node who is sending a MAD message. When these neighbor nodes receive a MAD message, they must relay it irrespectively of the relaying conditions of the OLSR MPR-flooding algorithm. We call this rule *Rule 3*.

With these three rules, and in the absence of packet loss a MAD message will reach all the nodes in the network.

In the following, we give the specifications of the DAD-MPR flooding protocol we proposed for OLSR with single interfaces. The formal proofs of its correct functioning and other details of the protocol can be found in [2].

3.2   DAD-MPR Flooding Algorithm

We assume that each node A periodically sends a MAD message M including:

- The originator address of A, $Orig_A$, in the OLSR message header.
- The message sequence number, $mssn$, in the OLSR message header.
- The node identifier ID_A (a string of bits) in the message itself.

The message is propagated by MPR flooding to the other nodes; but for DAD-MPR Flooding, the duplicate table of OLSR is modified, so that it also includes the node identifier list in the duplicate tuple. That is, a duplicate tuple, includes the following information:

- The originator address (as in OLSR standard duplicate table).
- The message sequence number (as in OLSR standard duplicate table).
- The list of node identifiers.

The detailed algorithm for DAD-MPR Flooding is the following:

- When a node B receives a MAD message M from node C with originator $Orig_A$, with message sequence number $mssn$, and with node identifier ID_A, it performs the following tasks:
    1. **If** a duplicate tuple exists with the same originator $Orig_A$, the same message sequence number, and ID_A is in the list of node identifiers, **Then**, the message is ignored (it has already been processed). The algorithm stops here.
    2. **Else** one of the following situations occurs:
        (a) A duplicate tuple exists with the same originator $Orig_A$ and the same message sequence number, but ID_A is not in the list of node identifiers: then, a conflict is detected (address $Orig_A$ is duplicated). ID_A is added to the list of node identifiers.
        (b) No duplicate tuple exists with the same originator $Orig_A$, and the same message sequence number $mssn$. A new one is created with the originator address, message sequence number and list of node identifiers containing only ID_A.
    3. The MAD messages should be relayed if one or more of the following rules are met:
        (a) C had chosen this current receiving node, B, as a MPR (as in normal MPR flooding).
        (b) The node B has a link (symmetric or asymmetric) with the originator address, $Orig_A$, contained in the MAD message M (*Rule2* and *Rule 3*).

4   Implementation of the DAD-MPR Flooding Protocol

DAD-MPR flooding protocol is implemented as an extention to OLSR to support autoconfiguration. This implementation is based on the implementation of NOA-OLSR [9], a totally different autoconfiguration algorithm that was developed at Niigata University, itself based on OOLSR[2] the INRIA object oriented re-implementation of OLSR protocol in the C++ programming language. The generation and processing of MAD (Multiple Address Declaration) message is mainly based on the implementation of OLSR MID (Multiple Interface Declaration) message. Only the autoconfiguration rules related to single interfaces [2] are implemented.

5   Convergence of the DAD-MPR Flooding Protocol

To evaluate the latency of address duplication detection using our DAD-MPR flooding protocol, we have simulated the merger of more than two networks generating massive address duplications. The nodes in each network are randomly placed in a square area of 1.0 x 1.0. The simulations were performed on MANETs with nodes moving from their starting points to a chosen destination in such a way that the length of the intersection area after merge is equal to a given value l (see Figure 7).

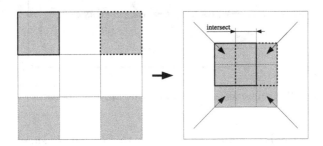

Fig. 7. Length of the intersecting area after merge

As an illustration, Figure 8 and Figure 9 show the positions of the nodes of 3 networks of 40 nodes each before and after the merger. The length of the intersection square area l is equal to 0.70.

The code used for simulations is compiled in a specific library (*libolsr_static_plugee.a*). It contains the core files for the OLSR protocol implementation with autoconfiguration and a simple simulator support. The code used for running simulations is composed of three modules, *oolsrsimple.cc*, *liboolsr.py*, and *madAutoConfSimul.py* (see Figure 10). The module *oolsrsimple.cc* is a wrapper used to use *libolsr_static_plugee.a* library and the *Python* functions there.

---

[2] http://hipercom.inria.fr/OOLSR/

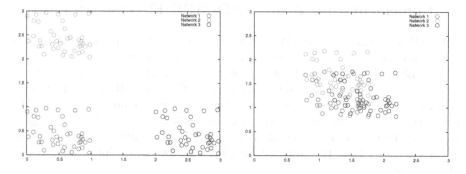

Fig. 8. Before the merger   **Fig. 9.** After the merger

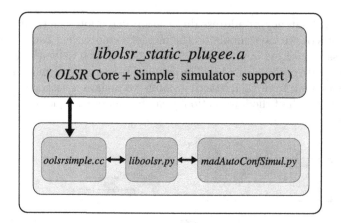

Fig. 10. Components of the autoconfiguration simulator

The library *liboolsr.py* is a small *Python* library to create basic simulations, and *madAutoConfSimul.py* is the *Python* program used to make simulations.

The simulations were run for a period of 100 s. No mergers were simulated in the first 30 seconds to allow the pre-configured nodes in each network to calculate their MPR sets and to set up their routing tables. There is no MAC, hence no contention or collision, the transmission delay is uniform, and there is no mobility after merge. The parameters of the simulation are: the radio range (R: 0 to 1) of each node, the number of nodes (N) in each network, the number of networks merging (*nb-part*: 1 to 4), and the length of the intersecting square (l: 0 to 1) after merge. In the following, we discuss the challenge of detecting all duplicated addresses in a reasonable time when a merger of several networks containing duplicates occurs. The main parameter to compute is the duration our DAD-MPR flooding algorithm takes to detect all address conflicts after the merger. We discuss several merger scenarios by varying the values of the simulation parameters cited above.

At the begining each network is a copy of each other and every node x of each network m, m≥2, has the same address as the node x of the network 1 and has the same position but translated.

Figure 11 shows the duration of address duplications detection, when 2, 3, and 4 networks merge by varying the number of nodes in each network. The radio range R of each node is set to 0.40 and the length of the intersecting area l is set to 0.70. We notice here that all the durations of address conflicts detection are ≤ 5s (one period of MAD message). In this case, either the networks form a 1-hop network after merge (all nodes are 1-hop neighbors of each other) and one period of MAD message suffices to the MAD messages to reach all the nodes, or the MPR sets in the networks computed before the merger continue to cover all the nodes after the merger. These situations occur when the radio range of the nodes and the length of the intersecting area are relatively high as it is the case here.

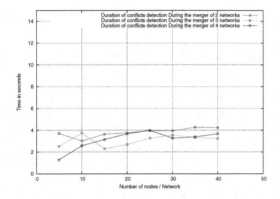

Fig. 11. Duration of conflicts detection/Number of nodes

Figure 12 shows the duration of address duplications detection during the merger of two networks of 50 nodes each, by varying the radio range of the nodes. The length of the intersecting area l is set to 0.70. As we can see on this figure, there exist address conflicts detection durations > 5s. This happens when the resulting network after the merger is a multi-hop network and the MPR sets in the original networks do not cover all the nodes after the merger. In fact, some of the MAD messages need to wait for the recalculation of the MPRs in the resulting network and hence to wait, at least, for the second period of MAD message after the merger to be propagated to the whole network. In addition, when a node detects an address conflict and changes its address, it must declare itself with the new address to the other nodes. Consequently, the neighbor tables, the MPR sets, and the topology tables are updated by at least its neighbors taking into account this new address, and therefore generating more latency in propagating the MAD messages and detecting the remaining address conflicts. That is why the duration of duplicate addresses detection can be more than 10s (two periods of MAD message) in some conflictual cases. Finally, when the radio range of the nodes is high enough, the network tends to become a 1-hop network and the address duplications are detected during the first MAD message period.

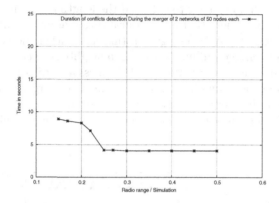

Fig. 12. Duration of conflicts detection/Radio range R

To get more accurate results by simulations and confirm the robustess of our autoconfiguration protocol, it is better that the resulting network after the merger contains at least 5 hops. That way, our DAD-MPR flooding protocol can be faced to more complicated scenarios depending on the distance d between the nodes in conflict [2]. For this purpose we set the length of the intersecting area l to 0.0, in such a way that there exists at least a link between the original networks after the merger (see Figure 13 and Figure 14).

Also, it was not easy in our simulations to generate connected network topologies because of the random character of the positions of the nodes in the square area of 1.0 x 1.0. Therefore, to increase the chances to get a connected network topology, we vary the number of nodes N in each network and the radio range of the nodes R in such a way that the density of neighbors D in the network is kept equal to 10^3. Let us denote by S the surface of the square area where the nodes are randomly placed, and by S_x the surface of the area covered by the radio range R of node x (see Figure 15). Hence, we have $S_x = \pi R^2$ and $\frac{S}{\pi R^2} D = N$. Therefore, since the surface of the square area where the nodes are placed is of size 1.0x1.0, the interaction between the radio range R and the number of nodes N in the network to keep the value of D equal to 10 is expressed as $R = \sqrt{\frac{D}{\pi N}}$.

---

[3] An approach to topology control based on the principle of maintaining the number of neighbors of every node equal or slightly below a specific value k, was proposed in [10]. The value of k that guarantees connectivity of the network with high probability was estimated. Setting $k = 9$ produces a network which is connected with probability at least 0.95 for numbers of nodes in the range 50-500. The sizes of the networks in our simulations belong to this range.

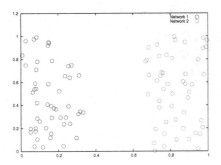

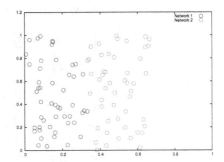

Fig. 13. Position of the nodes before the merger ($l = 0.0$)

Fig. 14. Position of the nodes after the merger ($l = 0.0$)

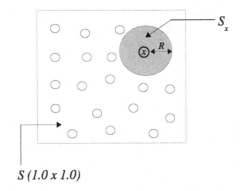

Fig. 15. The area covered by the radio range R

The numbers of nodes used in the following simulations and their corresponding values of the radio range parameter R for $D=10$ are presented in Table 1.

Figure 16 shows the durations of address duplications detection during the merger of two networks with a density of neighbors $D=10$ and by varying the radio range of the nodes. The length of the intersecting area l is set to 0.0. Here the durations of conflicts detection vary from 10.59s for $R=0.15$ to 3.59s for $R=0.50$ which are reasonable values. One can notice that the only difference between this figure and Figure 12 is that in this figure the durations of address conflicts detection for the values of $R \leq 0.35$ are a little bit higher than those reported in Figure 12. This is due to the fact that the numbers of nodes after the merger in this figure vary from 280 nodes to 100 nodes for $R \leq 0.25$ and are higher than the one in Figure 12 which is fixed and equal to 100 nodes. However, the durations of conflicts detection for $R>0.35$ are almost the same in both figures because the networks tend to become a 1-hop networks and the address duplications are detected during the first MAD message period.

Table 1. Correspondance between R and N

Radio range R	Number of nodes N
0.15	140
0.17	110
0.20	79
0.22	65
0.25	51
0.27	44
0.30	35
0.35	25
0.40	20
0.45	15
0.50	10

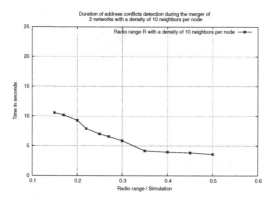

Fig. 16. Radio range R (density of neighbors $D = 10$)

Now rather than considering fully duplicated networks, we compute the durations of address duplications detection by varying the number of duplicated addresses after the merger.

Figure 17 shows the durations of address duplications detection during the merger of 2 networks of 50 nodes each. The radio range R is set to 0.25 and l is set to 0.0. The number of address conflicts vary from 5 to 50 addresses. In this figure the durations of conflicts detection vary from 3.14s for 5 address conflicts to 5.80s for a network containing 50 address conflicts.

The same simulation parameters as in Figure 16 are used in Figure 18; however, the durations of address conflicts detection reported in Figure 18 are function of the approximative number of hops in the network after the merger. This number of hops is calculated by dividing the length of the square area where the nodes are placed by the radio range R. We see here that even for networks containing more than 6 hops, the duration of address conflicts detection remains limited (≈ 10.5s).

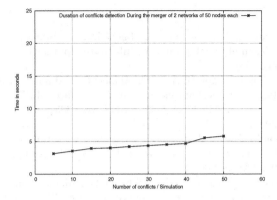

Fig. 17. Duration of conflicts detection/Number of conflicts

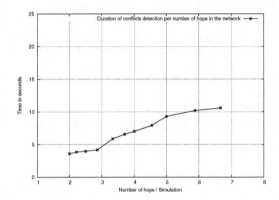

Fig. 18. Duration of conflicts detection/Number of hops

6   Conclusion

In this paper we have presented how our autoconfiguration protocol is implemented and integrated with OLSR. In order to test the convergence of our protocol, we have simulated the merger of more than two networks generating massive address duplications. The main parameter of interest is the duration our DAD-MPR flooding algorithm takes to detect and resolve all address conflicts after the merger. The results of the simulation experiments show that DAD-MPR flooding protocol can efficiently detect and resolve address duplications within seconds, even if the addresses in the networks are fully duplicated.

References

[1] Adjih, C., Clausen, T., Jacquet, P., Laouiti, A., Muhletaler, P., Minet, P., Qayyum, A., Viennot, L.: Optimized Link State Routing Protocol, IETF RFC 3626 (October 2003)

[2] Boudjit, S., Adjih, C., Laouiti, A., Muhlethaler, P.: A duplicate address detection and autoconfiguration mechanism for a single-interface OLSR network. In: Cho, K., Jacquet, P. (eds.) AINTEC 2005. LNCS, vol. 3837, pp. 128–142. Springer, Heidelberg (2005)

[3] Adjih, C., Boudjit, S., Muhlethaler, P., Laouiti, A.: Autoconfiguration protocol for a multiple interfaces OLSR Network. In: Proceedings of European Wireless 2007 conference (April 2007)

[4] Misra, A., Das, S., McAuley, A., Das, S.K.: Autoconfiguration, Registration, and Mobility Management for prevasive Computing. IEEE Personal Communication, 24–31 (August 2001)

[5] Zhou, H., Ni, L.M., Mutka, M.W.: Prophet Address Allocation for Large Scale MANETs. In: IEEE INFOCOM 2003 (March 2003)

[6] Weniger, K.: PACMAN: Passive AutoConfiguration for Mobile Ad hoc Networks. In: Proceedings of IEEE WCNC 2003 (March 2003)

[7] Moy, J.: Open Shortest Path First Version 2, IETF RFC 2328 (April 1998)

[8] Sayrafiezadeh, M.: The Birthday Problem Revisited. Math. Mag. 67, 220–223 (1994)

[9] Mase, K., Adjih, C.: No Overhead Autoconfiguration OLSR, IETF Draft (work in progress) (May 2005)

[10] Blough, D.M., Resta, G., Leoncini, M., Santi, P.: The K-Neighbors Protocol for Symmetric Topology Control in Ad Hoc Networks. In: MobiHoc 2003 (June 2003)

A Prototyping Environment for Wireless Multihop Networks

Fehmi Ben Abdesslem[1], Luigi Iannone[2], Marcelo Dias de Amorim[1],
Katia Obraczka[3], Ignacio Solis[4], and Serge Fdida[1]

[1] Université Pierre et Marie Curie – Paris 6
`{fehmi,amorim,sf}@rp.lip6.fr`
[2] Université Catholique de Louvain
`luigi.iannone@uclouvain.be`
[3] University of California at Santa Cruz
`katia@cse.ucsc.edu`
[4] Palo Alto Research Center
`isolis@parc.com`

Abstract. Relative to the impressive number of proposals addressing
the multitude of challenges raised by IEEE 802.11-based wireless networks, few have known real implementation. In wireless networks, due
especially to the unpredictable nature of the wireless channel, bridging
theory and practice is far from trivial. In this paper, we advocate including prototyping in the design process of wireless protocols. The goal is
to speed up the design process and to help validating novel solutions under real conditions. To this end, we introduce *Prawn*, a tool that allows
rapid prototyping of wireless network protocols. The basic idea behind
Prawn is to provide a set of basic building blocks that implement common
functionalities needed by a wide range of wireless protocols (e.g., neighbor discovery, link quality assessment, message transmission and reception). Besides these ready-to-use blocks, Prawn also provides a standard
API that allows protocol designers easy access to the Prawn primitives.
Through a number of examples, we showcase Prawn as a simple, yet
powerful tool for fast prototyping of wireless network protocols.

1 Introduction

Designing protocols for wireless networks poses countless technical challenges
due to a variety of factors such as node mobility, node heterogeneity, and power
limitations. Furthermore, the characteristics of the wireless channel are non-
deterministic and can be highly variable in space and time. This implies that
testing and evaluating such protocols under real operating conditions is crucial
to ensure adequate functionality and performance.

In fact, the networking research community has already acknowledged the
importance of testing and evaluating wireless protocol proposals under real-
world conditions. As a result, over the last few years, a number of testbeds, such
as Orbit [1], Roofnet [2], and MiNT-m [3], as well as implementation tools, such

S. Fdida and K. Sugiura (Eds.): AINTEC 2007, LNCS 4866, pp. 33–47, 2007.

Table 1. Introducing a prototyping step

	Implementation	*Emulation*	*Simulation*	*Prototyping*
Code	Real	Real	Synthetic	Synthetic
Medium	Real	Synthetic	Synthetic	Real
Examples	Click, Roofnet	Empower	NS-2	**Prawn**

as Click [4] and XORP [5], have been developed to support the deployment and evaluation of wireless protocols under realistic scenarios.

When designing communication systems, and before the final version, there are mainly three evaluation methodologies commonly used, namely mathematical analysis, simulation, and emulation, all of them using a synthetic virtual environment. Evaluation in real environment is done by producing a real implementation of the protocol, with or without the help of implementation tools. Moving to this second step requires non-negligible programming skills and time.

In this paper, we go a step further and advocate including *rapid prototyping* as an integral part of the design process (cf., Table 1). We postulate that what is needed is a tool that makes prototyping as quick, easy, and effortless as possible. To this end, we introduce *Prawn* (PRototyping Architecture for Wireless Networks), a novel software environment for prototyping high-level (i.e., network layer and above) wireless network protocols.[1] On the one hand, rapid prototyping is complementary to current testbeds and tools, which are typically used to produce a beta version of the final implementation. On the other hand, rapid prototyping enables performing correctness verification, functionality, and performance tests under real operating conditions early enough in the design cycle that resulting feedback and insight can be effectively incorporated into the design.

Prototypes implemented with Prawn are not expected to be optimized, offering edge performance. Rather, our focus with Prawn is on obtaining, quickly and with little effort, a complete and fully functional instantiation of the system, in order to gain a first insight into its behavior in real conditions. Prawn makes prototyping as simple as writing network simulation scripts, with the difference that testing is done under realistic conditions. Assessing these conditions is done through the Prawn Engine, which runs as a background process that proactively performs tasks such as neighbor discovery and link quality assessment. This feature allows Prawn to provide accurate and up-to-date feedback from the wireless interface.

As shown by the several case studies presented in this paper, Prawn prototypes can be used for functional assessment as well as both absolute and comparative performance evaluation. Once the prototype has been extensively tested and thoroughly validated, and its functional design tuned accordingly, it is then ready for final implementation (which is out of the scope of Prawn).

---

[1] Currently, Prawn targets IEEE 802.11 networks, although its design can be extended to run atop other wireless network technologies.

The remainder of this paper is organized as follows. We put our work on Prawn in perspective by reviewing related work in the next section. Section 3 provides an overview of Prawn, while in Sections 4 and 5 we describe Prawn's two main components in detail. Then we present in Section 6 a number of case studies showing how Prawn makes prototyping rapid and simple. Finally, we present our concluding remarks and directions for future work in Section 7.

2   Related Work

Simulations are perhaps the most widely used methodology for evaluating network protocols. They allow designers to evaluate the system at hand under a wide range of parameters like different mobility models and node heterogeneity, but only under synthetic channel models. Simulation has the advantage of allowing the exploration of the design space by enabling designers to vary individual protocol parameters (e.g., timers) and combinations thereof. Finally, they are instrumental for scalability analysis and they offer reproducibility. Examples of well-known simulation platforms include NS-2 [6], GloMoSim [7], and OPNET [8].

Emulation tries to subject the system under consideration to real inputs and/or outputs. Environments like EMPOWER [9] or Seawind [10] emulate the wireless medium by introducing packet error rates and delays. Other emulators like m-ORBIT [11] also emulate node mobility by space switching over a testbed of fixed nodes. A key advantage of emulation in the context of wireless/mobile networks is to facilitate testing by avoiding, for example, geographic and mobility constraints required for deployment.

More recently, a number of projects have pioneered the field of wireless protocol evaluation under real conditions. They include testbeds such as Orbit [1], and Roofnet [2] as well as tools that support protocol implementation like Click [4] and XORP [5]). As previously pointed out, such tools and Prawn have different goals, address different phases of the design process, and are therefore complementary. While tools like Click and XORP targets the implementation at the final stages of protocol design, Prawn focuses on prototyping a research proposal at the very early stages of the design process. Therefore, through Prawn, protocol designers can very quickly and easily generate a fully functional, although non-optimized, implementation for live testing in real scenarios.

3   Basic Design

Prawn targets prototyping protocols and services at the network layer and above. Simplicity was a major goal we had in mind when designing Prawn; we wanted to ensure that learning how to use Prawn would be as intuitive and immediate as possible requiring only basic programming expertise. Our focus was to provide: (1) a concise, yet complete set of functions to realize high-level protocols and (2) a simple, easy-to-use interface to provide access to Prawn's functionalities.

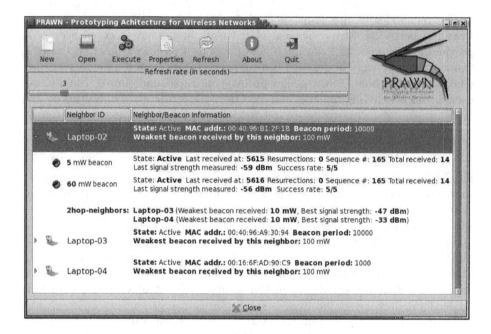

Fig. 1. Prawn graphic user interface

Architecture. Prawn consists of two main components: (i) the Prawn Library (cf., Section 4), which provides high-level primitives to send and receive messages, retrieve information from the network, etc; and (ii) the Prawn Engine (cf., Section 5), which implements the primitives provided by the Prawn Library.

Prawn is distributed under GPL license. The current implementation runs on Linux atop IP for backward compatibility with the global Internet. The interaction between the Prawn Engine and the physical wireless device relies on the Wireless Tools [12]. This set of tools allows retrieving information from most wireless devices as well as setting low-level parameters. Furthermore, it is available with most Linux distributions.

Prawn's functionalities are accessible through the Prawn Library. Messages and requests received from the library are then processed by the Prawn Engine. The Prawn Library and the Prawn Engine communicate with each other through the loop-back interface using a simple request/reply mechanism. This choice simplifies modularity and portability.

Using Prawn. Running Prawn requires only few basic steps. First, it needs to be configured and installed on the machines that will be used in the experiments. In particular, in the Prawn configuration file it is necessary to set the names of the wireless interface and network (e.g., the ESSID). Optionally an IP address can be specified. Otherwise, Prawn will randomly generate an IP address in a default subnetwork.

Using Prawn itself only requires two operations: executing the Prawn Engine and including the Prawn Library in the prototype code. The Prawn Engine (described in detail in Section 5) is launched as a command line program on machines connected in "ad hoc" mode. Prawn is supposed to run in daemon mode, but can run in console mode for debugging purposes. As stated before, Prawn provides a number of options that can be set/configured at the execution of the Prawn Engine. They are listed in Table 2. Other options are tunable in the prawn.cfg configuration file.

The Prawn Library (described in detail in Section 4) is composed of a set of primitives that are linked to the prototype through standard include files. Currently, prototypes can be developed either in C, Perl, or Java. For C development, the file prawn.h should be included in the header of the prototype code. Similarly, the file prawn.pl is to be included for prototypes developed in Perl, and the Prawn class methods can be used for prototypes developed in Java.

A graphic user interface is also available to monitor the neighborhood and to edit/run Perl scripts of Prawn prototypes (Figure 1).

Example. To illustrate the use of Prawn, we describe how to implement a simple "hello world" prototype using Prawn's Perl library. In this example we send a message from Bob to Alice.

1. Launch Prawn with "prawn -d -N Bob" in the first machine and "prawn -d -N Alice" in the second machine.
2. Get the first machine ready to receive messages by executing the following Perl script:

```
require "prawn.pl";
while(!@Message){
@Message=Prawn_Receive();
}
print 'Received : '.$Message[4].' from '.$Message[2]."\n";
```

3. On the other machine launch the following Perl script:

```
require "prawn.pl";
Prawn_Send("Hello World!","Bob");
```

The result is trivial: Alice sends a "Hello World" message to Bob, and Bob prints "Received: Hello World from Alice" on the screen. This simple example aims at showing the level of abstraction provided by Prawn, where low-level system knowledge (e.g., sockets, addressing) is not required. More elaborated examples, using the advanced features of Prawn, will be presented in Section 6.

4   The Prawn Library

The Prawn Library, currently implemented in C, Perl and Java, provides a set of high-level communication-oriented functions. They hide from protocol

Table 2. Prawn's command line options

Option	Parameter	Default
-N name	node ID	hostname
-b period	beacon period in ms	10000
-h	help	–
-d	daemon mode	–
-v	verbose mode	–
-vv	more verbose	–
-p port	neighbor port	3010
-c port	client port	3020
-i I	uses wireless interface I	ath0
-P	set transmit power level	–
-n	no power control features	–
-W window	window size for PER	5
-V	version	–

designers lower-level features such as addressing, communication set-up, etc. Their syntax is quite simple and intuitive. Prawn's current set of primitives addresses basic functions required when prototyping a high-level communication protocol. Nevertheless, Prawn was designed to be easily extensible allowing new primitives to be implemented and integrated. The primitives currently available are:

- **Prawn_Info**(): Returns information on the configuration of the local Prawn Engine. Basically, it consists of the list of settings chosen when launching the daemon (cf., Table 2). Some examples are the node's ID, interface port number, and beacon period.
- **Prawn_Neighbors**(): Returns the list of the node's one-hop and two-hop neighbors as well as statistics concerning the quality of the respective links. In Section 5, a thorough explanation of the information returned by the Prawn Engine will be given.
- **Prawn_Send**(**Message**, **ID**, **TX_Pwr**): Sends **Message** to node **ID**; the optional argument **TX_Pwr** can be used to explicitly set the transmit power to be used during the transmit. **Message** can be a string, a number, a data structure, or any other data or control message, depending on the prototyped protocol
- **Prawn_Send_Broadcast**(**Message**, **TX_Pwr**): Sends a broadcast message containing **Message**; in a similar way to **Prawn_Send**(), the optional argument **TX_Pwr** allows to set the transmit power.
- **Prawn_Receive**(): Checks if a message has been received; if so, the message is returned. This primitive is non-blocking: if no message has been received, it just returns zero.

5 The Prawn Engine

The Prawn Engine is event-driven, i.e., its main process remains asleep waiting for an event to occur. An event can be triggered by a request from the Prawn Library (coming through the loop-back interface) or by a message received on the wireless interface. Meanwhile, local neighborhood discovery is performed through beacon and feedback packets.

5.1 Beaconing

To build and maintain the list of neighbors, each node running Prawn broadcasts 24-byte beacons periodically. The beacon period is configurable depending on the requirements of the prototype under development. By default, the Prawn Engine is configured to test connectivity under different power levels (useful for instance to prototype topology control algorithms based on power control [13, 14]). The Prawn Engine applies a round-robin policy to continuously change the transmit power. A beacon is first broadcast with the lowest power value. The transmit power level is successively increased for each beacon; up to the maximum transmit power. We call this sequence of beacons a *cycle*. The different values of the transmit power are either obtained from the interface or set by the user. This cycle is then repeated at every beacon period. This way, the time elapsed between two beacons sent with the same transmit power is equal to the beacon period.

The power control feature is optional, depending on the designer's needs. If this feature is disabled, each cycle is then composed of only one beacon, sent at the default transmit power level. The number of transmit power levels and their values are customizable, depending on the power control features provided by the wireless interface under utilization.

The beaconing packet format, which is illustrated in Figure 2, includes the following fields:

- Type: This field is set to '1'.
- Transmit Power: Transmit power used to send the beacon.
- Transmitter ID: Sender identifier.
- Beacon Period: Time period between two beacons transmitted with the same power level.
- MAC Address: MAC address of the transmitter.
- Sequence Number: Sequence number of the beacon.

Upon the reception of a beacon (or sequence of beacons if different transmit powers are used), various statistics can be derived. For instance, a node A can determine, at a given point in time, the minimum transmit power that B should use to send messages to A. This value corresponds to the lowest transmit power among all the beacons received by A from B. Of course, the minimum transmit power may change over time, and will be updated along the successive cycles.

Configuring Prawn is important to achieve an adequate balance between performance and overhead. For example, sending beacons too frequently would

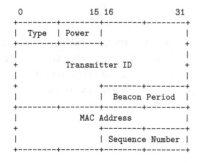

Fig. 2. Prawn beacon packet format

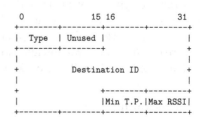

Fig. 3. Prawn feedback packet format

generate high overhead. On the other hand, limiting the number of beacons is likely to result in out-of-date measures. For these reasons, the beaconing period is one of Prawn's customizable parameters and its value is carried in the header of each beacon sent. A beacon is considered lost when the beaconing period (included in previous received beacons) times out. By default, a neighbor is removed from a node's neighbor table when three consecutive beacons from this neighbor have been lost (or when three consecutive beacons for every transmit power have been lost).

5.2   Replying to Beacons

Nodes reply to beacons using 16-byte feedback packets, as shown in Figure 3. Feedback packets summarize neighborhood– and link quality information as perceived by the receiver of the beacons. This feature allows verifying the bidirectionality of links. Feedback packets are sent to every neighbor after a complete cycle.[2] Prawn keeps sending feedback packets also in the case where a neighbor is considered lost (a unidirectional link may still exist between the two nodes). Feedback packets contain the following fields:

- **Type:** This field is set to '3'.
- **Destination ID:** Identifier of the neighbor concerned by the feedback.
- **Minimum Received Transmit Power:** Is the transmit power of the beacon received with the weakest signal strength from that particular neighbor.
- **Maximum Received Power Strength** (in dBm): Is the maximum signal strength measured when receiving beacons from that particular neighbor.

The rationale for reporting the transmit power of the weakest beacon received from a particular neighbor is that it allows to roughly characterize the quality of the corresponding link. This estimation is also confirmed using the maximum received signal strength measured within a cycle.

---

[2] Note that if the power control feature is disabled, then the cycle is unitary.

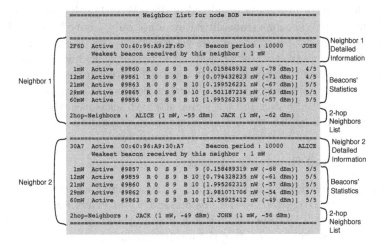

Fig. 4. Information provided by Prawn for a node whose ID is "BOB"

Although destined to a single neighbor, feedback packets are broadcast and thus overheard by all one-hop neighbors. This way, nodes can obtain information on two-hop neighborhood (cf., Figure 4).

5.3   Getting Information from Prawn

When a node calls the Prawn_Neighbors() primitive, the Prawn Engine returns a data structure with information about the node's neighborhood. This information can be also obtained by running Prawn in console mode, e.g., for debugging purposes. Figure 4 shows a snapshot of the information returned by the Prawn Engine running in console mode on a node named "Bob". This snapshot shows a list of Bob's neighbors, along with statistics on last beacons received by each neighbor for every transmit power. Basically, Bob has two active neighbors, John and Alice. The link between Bob and Alice has, on average, better quality than the one between Bob and John; indeed for beacons sent at 1 mW and 12 mW, only 4/5 of them have been received.

As previously described, neighborhood information is obtained through beacons and feedback packets. More specifically, broadcast beacons are used to build the list of direct neighbors. This list is established by gathering the transmitter ID of each received beacon. Moreover, data included in beacons and feedback packets inform each node what is the minimum transmit power required to reach a neighbor. Such information is of primary importance in assessing link quality. Another prominent link characteristic is the error rate, which is determined according to the beacon period included in each beacon transmitted. The Prawn Engine considers a beacon as lost when it is not received within the beacon period indicated by the corresponding neighbor. The size of the receiving window used to compute the error rate is customizable. For instance, in Figure 4, the error rate for John's packets transmitted at 12 mW is 1/5, because over the 5 most recent 12 mW beacons transmitted by John, only 4 have been received.

When receiving a beacon, the Prawn Engine stores the received signal strength. Along with the transmit power of the beacon (which is also included in the beacon), the received signal strength returned by the Prawn Engine helps to evaluate the signal attenuation. The difference between the transmitted power level indicated in the beacon and the signal strength measured when the beacon is received can also be used by a protocol to characterize link quality.

5.4   Sending and Receiving Messages

Two other key functions performed by the Prawn Engine are transmission and reception of data (triggered by the Prawn_Send() and Prawn_Receive() primitives, respectively). The Prawn Engine is in charge of the communication set up, namely opening sockets, converting the receiver identifier to a valid IP address, encapsulating/decapsulating packets, and adjusting the transmit power before transmission. Figure 5 shows the structure of the data packets, which contain the following fields.

- Type: This field is set to '2'.
- Transmit Power: Power used to send the packet.
- Payload Size: Size of the payload field.
- Payload: Data being sent.

```
0                15 16            31
+--------+--------+--------+--------+
|  Type  |  Pwr   |  Payload Size  |
+--------+--------+--------+--------+
|               Payload            |
~                                  ~
|                                  |
+--------+--------+--------+--------+
```

Fig. 5. Prawn data packet

```
require "prawn.pl";
while(1){
    while(!@Message){
        $Message = Prawn_Receive();
    }
    $msgID = unpack("N",$Message[4]);
    if (!grep(/$msgID/,@ID_list)){
        push(@ID_list,$msgID);
        Prawn_Send_Broadcast($Message[4]);
    }
    @Message = ();
}
```

Fig. 6. Perl code of a flooding prototype

Data packets are sent using UDP to the corresponding IP address. This explains why their header does not need to include the destination ID.[3] On the receiver side, the Prawn Engine listens on an open socket for any incoming packets. Packets are then decapsulated and sent to the prototype, which retrieves them by using the Prawn_Receive() primitive.

---

[3] Note that the same method cannot be used for beacons, since beacons are always sent broadcast at IP level and thus contain the broadcast address.

6   Prototyping with Prawn

Prawn is intended to be a tool for prototyping a wide range of communication algorithms for heterogeneous wireless networks. In this section, we first illustrate the use of Prawn through a number of case studies, highlighting its range of applicability and ease of use as well as how it can be employed to evaluate and test protocols.

6.1   Example 1: Flooding

Flooding is the simplest possible routing algorithm. Its basic operation is as follows: upon receiving a packet, each node sends it once to all its neighbors.[4] Thus the only requirement to implement this algorithm is to be able to receive and broadcast packets.

Prawn makes this algorithm easier to implement even for inexperienced programmers, since they do not need to know lower-level functions like sockets, ports, addressing, etc. Flooding can be implemented simply by using the Prawn_Receive() and Prawn_Send_Broadcast() functions.

Figure 6 shows how short and simple the flooding prototype using the Prawn Library is. This 12-line piece of code has been running successfully on our testbed. The behavior of the flooding algorithm is very different from simulations. Even more, Cavin et al. [15] tried to simulate the flooding algorithm using three different simulators namely, NS-2, OPNET, and GloMoSim, with exactly the same parameters and scenarios. Surprisingly, the results were considerably different, depending on the simulator used.

6.2   Example 2: Network Coding

While the previous section illustrates the use of Prawn to prototype one of the simplest protocols, we show, in this section, that Prawn can also be used to prototype more complex protocols. In particular, we show case the use of Prawn to prototype the COPE [16] network coding algorithm. Our goal here is to show that some evaluation of network coding proposals could be easily done without requiring a fully functional implementation of the algorithm.

For clarity, we briefly explain the essence of network coding through a very simple example. In traditional forwarding, when a node A and a node B want to exchange data via a third node C, both send their packets to C, and then C forwards the packets to A and to B. Exchanging a pair of packets requires 4 transmissions. Using network coding, instead of sending separate packets to A and B, node C combines (using the XOR function) both packets received from A and B, and broadcasts the encoded packet. Since A knows the packet it has sent, it can decode the packet sent by B (applying again the XOR function) from the encoded packet received from C. Similarly, B can decode the packet

---

[4] Of course, more elaborated variations of flooding exist, but here we consider it in its simplest form.

```
require "prawn.pl";
my @Stdby=();
my @Msg=();

while(!@Stdby) {@Stdby = Prawn_Receive();}
while(1){
 @Msg = Prawn_Receive();
 if (@Msg){
  if ($Msg[2] ne $Stdby[2]){
   $xored="";
   for ($i=0;$i<=1400;$i++){
    substr($xored,$i,1,substr($Msg[4],$i,1)^substr($Stdby[4],$i,1));
   }
   Prawn_Send_Broadcast($xored);
   @Stdby=();
   while(!@Stdby) {@Stdby = Prawn_Receive();}
  }
  else{
  if ($Stdby[2] eq "NodeA") {Prawn_Send($Stdby[4], "NodeB");}
  else {Prawn_Send($Stdby[4],"NodeA");}
   @Stdby=@Msg;
  }
 @Msg=();
 }
}
```

Fig. 7. Perl code of a network coding algorithm

sent by A from the same packet received from C. Thus, with this method, only 3 transmissions, instead of 4, are required.

Using Prawn, we implemented a prototype of the algorithm described above. As shown in the Perl code running on node C (Figure 7), the first received packet is stored in a standby variable ($Stdby), then the next packet is stored as $Msg. If the two stored packets are not received from the same node, then they are XORed and broadcast. If, instead, both packets are from the same node, it does not make sense to XOR them. In this case, the packet stored in standby is sent as a normal unicast packet, and the latest packet goes to the standby queue.

We also implemented a prototype of a traditional forwarding algorithm. We compare both implementations to measure the performance gains achieved by network coding when A sends 10,000 packets of 1,400 bytes each to B and vice-versa. Without network coding, the amount of data transmitted was 54 MB on both links. With network coding, only 44 MB were sent. With this code as a starting point, network coding protocol designers can test and tune their algorithms on real platforms under real conditions.

6.3   Example 3: Topology Control

Topology control algorithms require updated information about neighbors. Selecting good neighbors is often beneficial for the whole network. Prawn supports varied neighbors selection criteria relying on cross-layer information. For instance, in order to save energy and reduce interference, neighbors with lowest

```
require "prawn.pl";
$Neighbor = Prawn_Neighbors();
for ($i=1; $i<=$Neighbor[0]; $i++){
    push(@rx_power_list, [$i,$Neighbor[$i]{MAX_POW}]);
}
@sorted_list = sort {($b)->[1]<=>($a)->[1]} @rx_power_list;
@Selected_Neighbors=@sorted_list[0..1];
```

Fig. 8. Perl code of a topology control prototype

required transmit power can be selected. Conversely, neighbors with the highest signal strength received could be chosen. Many recent research efforts relying on cross-layer approaches would benefit from Prawn's lower layer information.

The code in Figure 8 shows how to get in 7 lines a list of neighbors sorted according to their receive signal strength. This code is running successfully on our testbed consisting of heterogeneous nodes. An important point here is that the received signal strength value retrieved from the wireless driver can be different depending on the wireless device model. If the neighbors do not have all the same wireless cards, the selection could be biased. This is an example of practical issue that cannot be taken into account from simulations. Using Prawn, designers can evaluate their proposal taking into account the features and performance of off-the-shelf hardware and drivers.

7 Summary and Outlook

In this paper we proposed Prawn, a novel prototyping tool for high-level network protocols and applications. Prawn's main goal is to facilitate the prototyping of wireless protocols so that prototyping becomes an integral part of the design process of wireless systems.

Prawn is not an alternative to simulation or any other evaluation method. Instead, it stands as a complementary approach that goes beyond simulation by taking into account real-world properties. Prawn surfs the wave of recent research efforts toward making implementation easier (e.g., Click and XORP), but as a preliminary phase in this process. The designer has to keep in mind, however, that the performance of a prototype does not always match exactly with the performance of a final and optimized implementation. Specifically, Prawn performs operations that may not appear in the final implementation (e.g., beacons, feedbacks, data encapsulation). However, first measures of this overhead incurred by Prawn are encouraging. For instance, using a Pentium M 733 (1.1 GHz) laptop, the additional delay to send a packet when using Prawn is only 140 μs (averaged over 10,000 packets), whereas the bandwidth loss is around 1.8 percent.

Through several case studies, we showcased the use of Prawn in the context of a wide range of network protocols. But the possibilities of Prawn are not restricted to the examples given in this paper. Other experiments where Prawn can be useful include: evaluating existing protocols for wired networks in the wireless context, implementing new routing protocols, testing overlay approaches in wireless multi-hop networks, evaluating distributed security algorithms, testing new naming mechanisms over IP, testing incentive mechanisms for communities, implementing localization algorithms, measuring wireless connectivity in both indoor and outdoor scenarios, evaluating peer-to-peer algorithms, testing opportunistic forwarding mechanisms.

We hope our work will provide a starting point for an improved design methodology as prototyping provides both easy and accurate evaluation of wireless protocols and services under real conditions. This paper has demonstrated that this is feasible – Prawn is a fully functional tool that responds to the needs of early protocol evaluation. Finally, we expect that Prawn's simplicity will allow researchers to adopt it. To help this becoming true, ongoing work includes adding new prototyping facilities (TCP data packets, automatic update of the OS routing table, more physical values retrieved from the driver, etc) and porting Prawn to other operating systems such as FreeBSD and Microsoft Windows.

References

1. Raychaudhuri, D., Ott, M., Seskar, I.: Orbit radio grid tested for evaluation of next-generation wireless network protocols. In: Proceedings of Tridentcom, pp. 308–309 (2005)
2. MIT Computer Science and Artificial Intelligence Laboratory (CSAIL). MIT roofnet, Available http://pdos.csail.mit.edu/roofnet/doku.php
3. De, P., Raniwala, A., Krishnan, R., Tatavarthi, K., Modi, J., Syed, N.A., Sharma, S., cker Chiueh, T.: Mint-m: an autonomous mobile wireless experimentation platform. In: Proceedings of ACM/USENIX Mobisys, pp. 124–137 (2006)
4. Kohler, E., Morris, R., Chen, B., Jannotti, J., Kaashoek, M.F.: The Click modular router. ACM Trans. Comput. Syst. 18(3), 263–297 (2000)
5. Handley, M., Hodson, O., Kohler, E.: XORP: an open platform for network research. Computer Communications Review 33(1), 53–57 (2003)
6. The Network Simulator NS-2, Available http://www.isi.edu/nsnam/ns/
7. Zeng, X., Bagrodia, R., Gerla, M.: GloMoSim: a library for parallel simulation of large-scale wireless networks. In: Proceedings of Workshop on Parallel and Distributed Simulation, Banff, Canada (May 1998)
8. OPNET Modeler, Available http://www.opnet.com/products/modeler/
9. Zheng, P., Ni, L.: EMPOWER: A network emulator for wireless and wireline networks. In: Proceedings of IEEE Infocom, San Francisco, CA (April 2003)
10. Kojo, M., Gurtov, A., Manner, J., Sarolahti, P., Alanko, T.O., Raatikainen, K.E.E.: Seawind: a wireless network emulator. In: GI/ITG Conference on Measuring, Modelling and Evaluation of Computer and Communication Systems, Aachen, Germany (September 2001)
11. Ramachandran, K., Kaul, S., Mathur, S., Gruteser, M., Seskar, I.: Towards large-scale mobile network emulation through spatial switching on a wireless grid. In: Proceedings of ACM Sigcomm, Philadelphia, PA (August 2005)
12. Wireless Tools for Linux, Available
    http://hpl.hp.com/personal/Jean_Tourrilhes/Linux/Tools.html

13. Blough, D.M., Leoncini, M., Resta, G., Santi, P.: The k-neighbors approach to interference bounded and symmetric topology control in ad hoc networks. IEEE Transactions on Mobile Computing 5, 1267–1282 (2006)
14. Li, N., Hou, J.: Localized topology control algorithms for heterogeneous wireless networks. IEEE/ACM Transactions on Networking 13, 1313–1324 (2005)
15. Cavin, D., Sasson, Y., Schiper, A.: On the accuracy of manet simulators. In: proceedings of POMC 2002, Toulouse, France (October 2002)
16. Katti, S., Rahul, H., Hu, W., Katabi, D., Médard, M., Crowcroft, J.: XORs in the air: practical wireless network coding. In: Proceedings of ACM Sigcomm, Pisa, Italy (2006)

Efficient Selection of Multipoint Relays in Wireless Ad Hoc Networks with Realistic Physical Layer

Dhavy Gantsou and Patrick Sondi

University of Valenciennes
LAMIH/ROI
Le Mont Houy – ISTV2
59313 Valenciennes cedex 9, France
{Dhavy.gantsou, Patrick.sondi}@univ-valenciennes.fr

Abstract. Much of the schemes for Multipoint Relay (MPR) selection in wireless ad hoc networks have been studied using the unit graph model, under the assumption that packets are always received without any error. As this model does not reflect the real scenario of transmissions, recent studies propose heuristics which enable selecting MPR under realistic assumptions. For this, they use redundancy to maximize the probability of delivery. But redundancy can increase the size of the MPR set, and therefore generating amounts of retransmissions and collisions, which can lead to degradation of the MPR protocol performance. Using reversible marking, a mechanism we presented in a previous study, we propose two heuristics which efficiently compute MPR. One of them resorts to redundancy and both compute a MPR set which size is at most *log m* greater than the optimum.

Keywords: Wireless ad hoc network, multipoint relay selection, probability of delivery, reversible marking.

1 Introduction

To broadcast a packet to all the nodes of a wireless network, the most obvious means is basic flooding. This technique implies the participation of the whole nodes, thus increasing packet collisions and retransmissions. To optimize the diffusion in mobile ad hoc networks (MANET) [1], several techniques have been proposed. One of them is the multipoint relay or MPR [2], [3], [4], [5].

The idea of this technique is that each node has to choose a subset of its one-hop neighborhood referred to as MPR in order to cover the entire two-hop neighborhood. The efficiency of this technique is straightly related to the size of the MPR set. Garey and Johnson [6] shown that the problem of computing a MPR set of minimal cardinality is NP-hard. That's why heuristics are commonly used to perform MPR selection. The simple greedy proposed in [4] is one of these heuristics. It provides a size of the MPR set which is at most *log m* larger than the optimum, while computation takes $O(m^2)$ in time. However, it uses the unit disk graph to model physical layer in wireless networks. The unit graph model assumes that transmitted

S. Fdida and K. Sugiura (Eds.): AINTEC 2007, LNCS 4866, pp. 48–59, 2007.
© Springer-Verlag Berlin Heidelberg 2007

messages are received without error: it does not reflect real radio transmission conditions. These limitations were recently emphasized in [7].

Contrary to the approaches based on unit disk graph, the study presented in [8] uses the lognormal shadowing model. This model allows a more realistic representation of the transmission conditions [7]. Assuming a realistic physical layer, the study shows how the simple greedy heuristic [4] has been adapted in order to maximize the probability of delivery. To achieve this goal, the heuristic resorts to the redundancy of MPR. Unfortunately, this is done in a manner which increases the size of the MPR set. More messages are generated, thus introducing additional overhead that can affect the performance of the MPR protocol. Indeed, evaluations carried out by Ge [12] show that, in situations where several MPR cover the same node, the error rate increases due to collisions occurring on the receiver's interface.

In this article, we adopt an approach assuming probabilities of loss on the links. This has the advantage to conceive MPR selection heuristics which are still efficient under realistic conditions. However, unlike the heuristic proposed in [8], ours focus on how to maximize the probability of delivery without increasing the size of the MPR set. In other words, our heuristics aim at maximizing the probability of delivery, and keeping the size of the MPR set close to the minimum. To achieve this goal, we use two concepts proposed in Gantsou et al. [9]:

- the first is the mathematical model whose resolution provides an exact lower bound of the size of the MPR set. The results of our heuristics are closed to that lower bound.
- the second is the reversible marking mechanism. It consists in exploring a graph in order to satisfy two requirements: 1) finding a subset of nodes which offer a good coverage according to a specified criterion and 2) keeping the size of the MPR set close to the optimum.

This enables both to improve the probability of delivery, and to guarantee a size of MPR set that is at most *log m* larger than the optimum. One of our heuristics does rely on redundancy, and the other does. Thanks to the aforementioned concepts, redundancy can be used without negative effects on the performance of the MPR protocol.

In section 2, we overview some work aiming at maximizing the probability of packet delivery in wireless networks. We then present our heuristics in section 3. In section 4, we compare the performance of our heuristics and those of the heuristic presented in [8]. These evaluations show that our heuristics outperform the latter. Section 5 concludes this article and presents future work.

2   Related Works

Many studies are devoted to broadcasting in wireless ad hoc network. We use the following notations presented in [5] for the description of the problem.

Let $N(E)$ be the set of all the nodes of E or having some neighbor in E. We say that E covers F if $F \subseteq N(E)$. Let $N_1(E)=N(E)-E$ be the set of all the nodes in the one-hop neighborhood of E, and $N_2(E)=N(N(E))-N(E)$ the set of all the nodes in the two-hop neighborhood of E. We are interested in the particular case where $E=\{u\}$. $N_1(\{u\})$ is the one-hop neighborhood of the node u which computes its MPR set and $N_2(\{u\})$, its two-hop neighborhood. For each edge (v_1,v_2) in the graph representing the network, we denote $P(v_1,v_2)$ the probability of delivery on that edge. Its value is supposed to be known. The set of MPR selected by u is denoted by M_u. It is a subset of $N_1(\{u\})$ such that $N_2(\{u\}) \subseteq M_u$. We use the term *Minimum* for the size of the minimal covering set, i.e the one obtained by an exact algorithm without taking into account any criterion. The fewer the size of M_u, the fewer retransmissions will occur.

2.1 The Simple Greedy

Since all heuristics which will be presented in this article are inspired from the simple greedy [4], we believe it is important to present it first.

In the simple greedy, the node chooses a MPR according to the number of its neighbors in $N_2(\{u\})$ which not yet covered.

The heuristic starts with an empty MPR set M_u.

- Step 1: Add in M_u all nodes in $N_1(\{u\})$ which are the single neighbor of a node in $N_2(\{u\})$.
- Step 2: Add in M_u that node of $N_1(\{u\})$ which is the neighbor of most uncovered nodes in $N_2(\{u\})$.
- Repeat step 2 until all nodes in $N_2(\{u\})$ are covered.

The designers of the simple greedy show that this heuristic provides a number of MPR that is at most *log m* greater than the Minimum, where m is the greatest degree of a node in the network. Adjih et al. [5] mention that the simple greedy heuristic computation takes $O(m^2)$ time.

2.2 Heuristic Improving Robustness

Among the heuristics proposed in [8], we decided to consider the one which uses the redundancy of MPR. To our knowledge, it is the only heuristic which adopts this approach to improve the probability of delivery. We refer to this heuristic as lns_*mpr_select*. It is quite similar to the simple greedy from which it is inspired. Both heuristics are different essentially because lns_*mpr_select* introduces two changes:

At the step 2, instead of choosing a node x as MPR according to the number of its uncovered neighbors in $N_2(\{u\})$, the heuristic computes a score. For example, for a node $v \in N_1(\{u\})$ having 3 uncovered neighbors v_1, v_2 and v_3 in $N_2(\{u\})$, the heuristic computes the following score: $P(u,v)*((P(v,v_1)+P(v,v_2)+P(v,v_3))/3)$.

When an MPR is selected among its uncovered successors in $N_2(\{u\})$, only those which are covered with a probability of delivery greater than a given threshold are considered as definitively covered. For remaining nodes, the heuristic will add nodes in the MPR set until the threshold is reached or until no more selection is possible. As an example, for a node v_l in $N_2(\{u\})$ for which the threshold is reached after the selection of two MPR v and v' in M_u, the value of the probability compared to the threshold is: $1-((1-P(v,v_l))*(1-P(v',v_l)))$.

More formally, according to [8], we have:

- $S_u(v)$, the score of a node v which can be selected as MPR,
- $C_u(v)$, the set of uncovered successors of v in $N_2(\{u\})$,
- $t_u(z)$, the current value of the probability provided to a node z in $N_2(\{u\})$,
- z_i, the node at rank i in $C_u(v)$,
- v_i, the node at rank i in M_u, and,
- $MPR(u)$, the MPR set of u, also denoted by M_u.

Considering these notations in the equations below, we have respectively:

- the formula to be used for computing the score for each node in $N_1(\{u\})$ during MPR selection process.

$$S_u(v) = P(u,v) * \sum_{i=1}^{i=|C_u(v)|} (P(v,z_i)/|C_u(v)|). \tag{1}$$

- The formula for computing the value of the probability of delivery provided to a node $N_2(\{u\})$ and which is compared to the threshold before considering that it is definitively covered [8].

$$t_u(z) = 1 - \prod_{i=1}^{i=|MPR(u)|} (1 - P(v_i,z)) \tag{2}$$

3 Contribution

We carried out performance evaluation showing that the heuristic proposed in [8] outperforms the simple greedy [4] regarding the probability of delivery. However, we also made following observations:

1. By prioritizing the probability of delivery, the first improves the quality of coverage. The resulting robustness is an important asset for satisfying parts of the QoS constraints. But, as stated by the designers of the heuristic, this robustness introduces an additional cost: the resulting MPR set is larger than that computed by the simple greedy heuristic.
2. The enlargement of the size of the MPR set is partly due to the fact that the relative degree of the nodes is not taken into account during the MPR selection.

3.1 First Heuristic: GS_mpr_select_1

The main idea of this heuristic is to find a subset of $N_1(\{u\})$ that offers nodes in $N_2(\{u\})$ the best probability of delivery. As a consequence, this subset is chosen among all the subset of $N_1(\{u\})$ which have a size that is at most $\log m$ greater than the *Minimum*. This is achieved by introducing following changes in the simple greedy:

- At step 2, each MPR j is selected according to the number of its successors in $N_2(\{u\})$ not yet covered. If several nodes reache the maximum number of successors, the node j such that $P(u,j)$ has the highest value is selected as MPR.
- Each time a node is inserted in M_u, the reversible marking mechanism is performed to all its successors in order to select those of its successor nodes which ensure the best coverage: this improves the probability of delivery. Given a MPR v relaying packets from a node u to the covered node j, the coverage is the probability of delivery $P(u,v)*P(v,j)$. At the end, all nodes in M_u which don't cover any node in $N_2(\{u\})$ are removed. This contributes to reduce the size of M_u. Gantsou et al. [9] showed that heuristics using the reversible marking mechanism in this way provides more often MPR set which size is smaller than those computed using the simple greedy [4].

In practice, the reversible marking mechanism works as follows: once a node j is chosen as MPR, the heuristic visits all its successors. Each of them which is not yet covered is assigned to j. For each other node s in $N_2(\{u\})$ which is a successor of j and is already covered by another node k in M_u, if j offers s a better quality of coverage than k, then s is taken out from k and added to j. At the end, all nodes which were inserted in M_u and which does not cover any node in $N_2(\{u\})$ are removed from the MPR set. This keeps the entire graph until the computation ends, so as to allow the heuristic to change previous decisions when a better solution is found.

3.2 Second Heuristic: GS_mpr_select_2

This heuristic is quite similar to GS_*mpr_select_1*, but like *lns_mpr_select* it uses redundancy of the MPR to improve robustness. While trying to maximize the probability of delivery, the *lns_mpr_select* heuristic leads to performance degradation of the MPR protocol. This is due to large amount of retransmissions and collisions introduced by the enlargement of the size of the MPR set [12]. Does this imply that the MPR selection cannot be improved when considering realistic physical layer? Not necessarily, we believe that it is possible. Our approach is guided by following aspects:

- It is mandatory to ensure the size of the MPR set close to the optimum when using MPR redundancy in order to maximize the probability of delivery. To build a MPR set that is at most $\log m$ larger than the optimum, we resort to the reversible marking mechanism presented in [9].
- Setting a threshold on the number of MPR which can cover simultaneously each node in $N_2(\{u\})$.

This second heuristic modifies slightly *GS_mpr_select_1* as follows:

- At step 2, each MPR j is selected according to the number of its successors in $N_2(\{u\})$ not yet covered. If several nodes reache the maximum number of successors, the node j with the highest value of $P(u,j)$ is selected as MPR.
- When a node j is inserted in M_u, the first is added in the lists of MPR of its successors which have not yet reached the threshold (*coverage*). Those of its successors which have reached the threshold perform the reversible marking. This enables these successors to determine if j can replace a node in their list of MPR. As a consequence, useless nodes are removed from the MPR set.

4 Evaluation of Proposed Heuristics

We used the same data structures to implement all the heuristics. Experimentations have been carried out on a personal computer with an Intel Pentium 4 (3.00 GHz) processor and 512 Mo of RAM running Linux.

The graphs were generated randomly, our main objective being not to simulate a real mobile ad hoc network but to compare the performance of the heuristics. Each value presented in the graphics is an average of 4 values obtained on a graph with the same number of nodes in $N_1(\{u\})$ and $N_2(\{u\})$ but generated differently. As an example, to have statistics on a graph such that $| N_1(\{u\}) | = 120$ and $| N_2(\{u\}) | = 380$, with a growing average of neighbors ranging from 10 to 100, we have generated 40 graphs. Varying the mean number of neighbors allowed us to test the heuristics on sparse networks so as on very dense ones. We distinguish between small and large networks. Small networks are networks where $|N_1(\{u\})|=120$ and $| N_2(\{u\})|=380$, and large networks, those where $|N_1(\{u\})|=250$ and $| N_2(\{u\}) |=750$.

On all figures bellow, the density of the network refers to the mean number of neighbors around a node.

Concerning *lns_mp_select*, we have fixed the threshold to 0.5 as done in [8]. To perform evaluation of *GS_mpr_select_2,* and as this is done concerning coverage in Optimized Link State Routing protocol OLSR [13], we set a threshold on the number of MPR covering simultaneously the same node. In order to enable the variation of this value according to the density of the network, we use the integer part of $1+log(K)$ as threshold, where K is the mean number of neighbors around a node. The list of MPR covering each node is sorted. This allows each MPR to compute a retransmission delay according to its range, and to take into account the need to minimize the risks of collisions on the receiver's interface [12].

To evaluate the probability of delivery, we use following formulas. When transmitting from the node u to a node z in $N_2(\{u\})$ using the node v in M_u as relay, the probability of success of the transmission is computed as follows: $P(u,z) = P(u,v)*P(v,z)$. This is obtained easily from the general formula below [11] (each a_i is an edge):

$$P(a_1 a_2 ... a_n) = \prod_i P(a_i)$$ (3)

The formulas for evaluating the probabilities in the case of *GS_mpr_select_1* are simple due to the fact that only one MPR is considered for each node. They are a little more complex for *lns_mpr_select* and *GS_mpr_select_2* because of redundancy.

Let's consider that z in $N_2(\{u\})$ is reached from u by using the nodes v_i in M_u as relays. If we fraction virtually u into several nodes u_i (see Fig. 1 below), we obtain i two-length chains arriving at z.

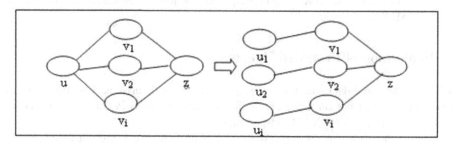

Fig. 1. Transforming the graph for probabilities computation

Applying the formula used to compute $t_u(z)$ (Equation 2), we obtain:

$$t_u(z) = 1 - \prod_{i=1}^{i=|MPR(u)|} \left(1 - P(u_i, v_i) * P(v_i, z)\right)$$ (4)

Since $P(u_i, v_i) = P(u, v_i)$ for each i, we can simplify:

$$t_u(z) = 1 - \prod_{i=1}^{i=|MPR(u)|} \left(1 - P(u, v_i) * P(v_i, z)\right)$$ (5)

One can notice that if we apply the equation (5) to the case where only one MPR is allowed for each node in $N_2(\{u\})$, we then find:

$$t_u(z) = P(u, v_1) * P(v_1, z)$$ (6)

This is exactly the formula used for *GS_mpr_select_1*.

4.1 Comparison of Computation Time

Fig.2 and Fig.3 show clearly that *GS_mpr_select_2* has the best computation time. On small networks (Fig.2), *lns_mpr_select* is slightly faster than *GS_mpr_select_1* but its execution time increases considerably on large networks. On the contrary, the computation time of the latter becomes more stable be it on small or on large network (Fig.3).

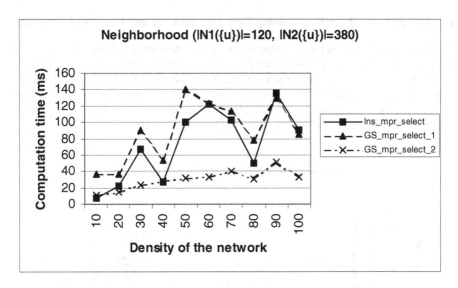

Fig. 2. Computation time of the heuristics on small networks

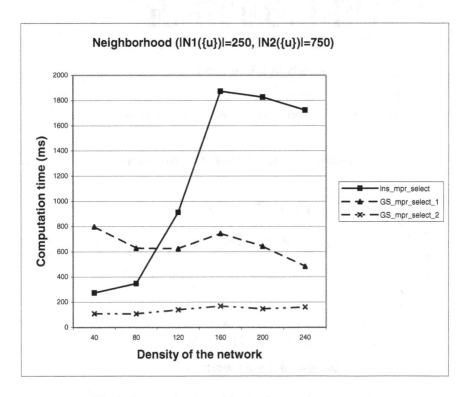

Fig. 3. Computation time of the heuristics on large networks

4.2 Comparison of the Relationship Between MPR Set and Quality of Coverage

The size of the MPR set M_u computed using our heuristics *GS_mpr_select_1* and *GS_mpr_select_2* is always lower than that computed using *lns_mpr_select* (Fig.4 and Fig.6). Moreover the number of selected MPR is always very close to the optimum (Fig.4) which is the size of the minimal covering set computed by *mprmodeleMIP*. The latter is an exact algorithm which solves the mathematical model we proposed in [9]. It is computed using the CPlex solver [14].

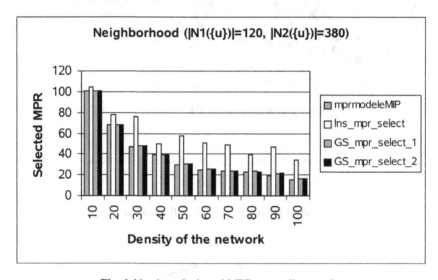

Fig. 4. Number of selected MPR on small networks

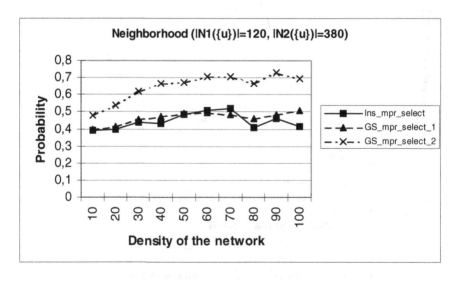

Fig. 5. Probability of delivery on small networks

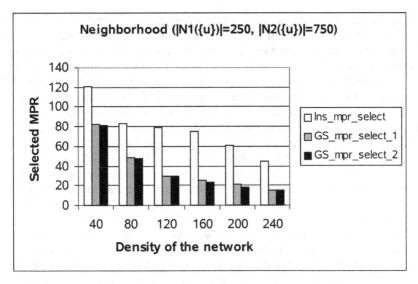

Fig. 6. Number of selected MPR on large networks

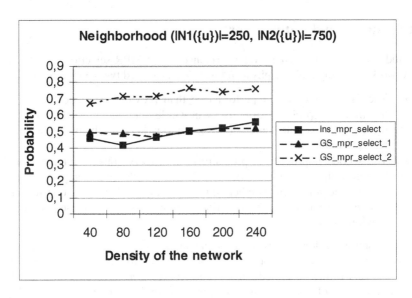

Fig. 7. Probability of delivery on large networks

Regarding the probability of delivery, Fig.5 and Fig.7 confirm that *GS_mpr_select_1* ensures nodes in $N_2(\{u\})$ a quality of coverage overall better than *lns_mpr_select*.

Although resorting to MPR redundancy allows the heuristics proposed in [8] to provide better probability of delivery than the simple greedy [4], the first introduces additional costs: 1) computation time, and 2) the high number of selected MPR which can have negative effects on the global performance of MPR protocol. Indeed, evaluations carried out by Ge et al. [12] show that, in a situation where several MPR cover the same node, the error rate increases because of collisions occurring on the receiver's interface. For avoiding these collisions, the authors suggest to introduce a temporization between the retransmissions of the various MPR. Each redundant MPR has a level of priority to transmit to the receiving node and compute the latency it has to observe before transmission. To solve these problems, we adopted a strategy based on the reversible marking mechanism. Indeed, rather than adding additional MPR in M_u, reversible marking explores all possibilities offered by the graph. This enables guarantee a size of the MPR set that is close to the optimum. In other words, redundancy is interesting for the robustness if one takes care to preserve the size of the MPR set close to the *Minimum*. Thanks to reversible marking and redundancy, *GS_mpr_select_2* provides a better quality of coverage than both *GS_mpr_select_1*, and *lns_mpr_select* (Fig.5 and Fig.7).

In their evaluations [8], the designers of *lns_mpr_select* showed that for a threshold that is higher than 0.5, the probability of delivery may be a little higher. Nevertheless, the number of MPR selected in these cases is too high. One can see that our heuristics ensure higher probability of delivery than does *lns_mpr_select* without introducing negative effect.

5   Conclusion and Future Work

This study aimed at improving the performance of the MPR selection in wireless ad hoc network assuming realistic physical layer. We proposed two heuristics:

- The first enables better performance than previous heuristics dedicated to maximize the probably of delivery in wireless ad hoc networks. Contrary to these heuristics, ours relies on reversible marking mechanism and does not resort to redundancy.
- The second improves the probability of delivery considerably. Although it combines the reversible marking mechanism with redundancy, this heuristic prevents negative effects inherent to redundancy. Moreover, it ensures a size of MPR set and a computation time that are lower than those computed by previous heuristics.

Redundancy is particularly important in situations where most of the links present high probability of loss. Therefore, it becomes essential to have more than one MPR relaying packets to the same node. This aspect is referred to as *coverage* in OLSR. Our future work will focus on investigating the impact of our proposals on the performance of this protocol.

References

1. Corson, M.S., Macker, J.: Mobile ad hoc networking (MANET): Routing protocol performance issues and evaluation considerations, IETF, RFC 2501 (1999)
2. ETSI STC-RES10 Committee, Radio equipment and systems: High performance radio local area network (hyperlan) type 1, functional specifications, ETS 300-652 (June 1996)

3. Jacquet, P., Minet, P., Muhlethaler, P., Riviere, N.: Increasing reliability in cable-free radio lans: Low level forwarding in hiperlan, Wireless Personal Communications (January 1997)
4. Laouiti, A., Qayyum, A., Viennot, L.: Multipoint Relaying: An Efficient Technique for Flooding in Mobile Wireless Networks. In: HICSS 2001. 35th Annual Hawaii International Conference on System Sciences (2001)
5. Adjih, C., Jacquet, P., Viennot, L.: Computing connected dominated sets with multipoint relays. Ad Hoc & Sensor Wireless Networks (March 2005)
6. Garey, M.R., Johnson, D.S.: Computers and intractability. A Guide to the Theory of NP-Completeness. Freeman, Oxford, UK (1979)
7. Stojmenovic, I., Nayak, A., Kuruvila, J.: Design Guidelines for Routing Protocols in Ad Hoc and Sensor Networks with a realistic Physical layer. IEEE Communication Magazine 43(3), 101–106 (2005)
8. Ingelrest, F., Simplot-Ryl, D.: Maximizing the Probability of Delivery of Multipoint Relay Broadcast Protocol in Wireless Ad Hoc Networks with a Realistic Physical Layer. In: Cao, J., Stojmenovic, I., Jia, X., Das, S.K. (eds.) MSN 2006. LNCS, vol. 4325, pp. 143–154. Springer, Heidelberg (2006)
9. Gantsou, D., Sondi, P., Said, H.: Revisiting Multipoint Relay Selection in Optimal Link State Routing Protocol. Submitted for Publication in International Journal of Communication Networks and Distributed System
10. Härri, J., Bonnet, C., Filali, F.: OLSR and MPR: mutual dependences and performances. Med-Hoc Net 2005. In: 4th IFIP Mediterranean Ad Hoc Networking Workshop, Île de Porquerolls, France (June 21-24, 2005)
11. Wang, Z., Crowcroft, J.: Quality of Service Routing for Supporting Multimedia Applications. IEEE Journal of Selected Areas in Communications 14(7) (1996)
12. Ge, Y., Kunz, T., Lamont, L.: Proactive QoS Routing in Ad Hoc Networks. In: Pierre, S., Barbeau, M., Kranakis, E. (eds.) ADHOC-NOW 2003. LNCS, vol. 2865, Springer, Heidelberg (2003)
13. Clausen, T., Jacquet, P.: Optimized Link State Routing Protocol (OLSR), RFC 3626, IETF (October 2003)
14. ILOG. CPLEX 9.0 (user's manual) (2003)

Mobile Hotspots

Aruna Seneviratne[1,2], Eranga Perera[1], and Henrik Petander[1]

[1] NICTA, ATP Laboratory, NSW 1430, Australia
[2] School of Electrical Engineering and Telecommunications, UNSW, NSW 2056, Australia
{Aruna.Seneviratne, Eranga.Perera, Henrik.Petander}@nicta.com.au

Abstract. The unprecedented proliferation of wireless networking services and products has taken the notion of hotspots a step further to accommodate "mobile hotspots". The deployment of hotspots in trains, ships, planes, buses etc. would certainly change the way we travel. In this article we will first discuss the reasons as to why the current host mobility protocols such as MIPv6 are inadequate to handle the mobility of an entire network. We will then present an overview of the current standard protocol, NEMO Basic Support protocol that was designed to handle the mobility of networks. By way of network mobility scenarios, shortcomings of this protocol that need to be addressed for network mobility to be a truly ubiquitous experience will be identified. Some solutions that have been proposed and implemented in order to handle the identified issues will be presented. Further we present a bandwidth fueling architecture for mobile networks which addresses the challenge of providing continuous high-performance service over wireless networks at a reasonable cost.

Keywords: IP Mobility, Network Mobility, Mobile Routers, Handoff Management, Route Optimization.

1 Introduction

The deployment of wireless networks have progressed to the point, it is now becoming available everywhere, including in moving vehicles such as in buses, cars and airplanes. We believe that this will lead to new services which will use the unique features especially of moving networks. There have already been several proposals for using moving vehicles for collecting data from sensors [1], and the use of vehicular communication for opportunistic networking [2]. In this paper we focus on the provision of communication services between devices in moving networks (which we refer to as mobile hotspots) and devices outside it.

IETF has in recent years developed protocols such as Mobile IP (MIP) [3] and Mobile IPv6 [4] for providing mobility support in IP networks. These mobility support protocols however on their own do not address the needs of mobile hotspots to provide services to potentially a large number of users. One of the major draw backs is the overhead of handling the mobility of each of the devices within a mobile hotspot. The obvious solution to this is to employ one device to handle mobility for all the devices within the mobile hotspot. The IETF's Network Mobility Working

S. Fdida and K. Sugiura (Eds.): AINTEC 2007, LNCS 4866, pp. 60–69, 2007.

Group [5] has recognized this and an architecture, where a *Mobile Router (MR)* is used to handle the mobility of the devices within the mobile hotspot has been standardized. Although the IETF's basic network mobility support protocol, NEMO [6], handles the mobility of a set of nodes moving as a unit, the defined mechanism has certain limitations that need to be addressed in order for devices within mobile hotspots to seamlessly communicate with the world outside. This paper proposes an architecture which extends NEMO to provide efficient seamless communication for devices within mobile hotspots.

The rest of the paper is organized as follows. Section 2 justifies the need for a new network mobility architecture by considering the limitations of the host mobility protocols in handling the mobility of entire networks. In section 3 a brief overview of the NEMO Basic Support protocol is given. By utilizing a few scenarios the problems with current standard network mobility (NEMO) architecture is highlighted in section 4. In sections 5 and 6 two optimizations that address the issues highlighted in section 4 are presented. In section 7 an enhanced network mobility architecture that takes into consideration the scarceness and high cost of Wireless Wide Area Network (WWAN) bandwidth when providing Internet connectivity from public transportation systems is given. Section 8 provides the conclusion to the paper.

2   Need for a New Architecture

Host mobility protocols such as MIP are not sufficient to handle network mobility due to a number of reasons. As mentioned earlier, these can be addressed by employing a *Mobile Router* to act as a gateway; all devices within the network can be provided connectivity irrespective of their capabilities. A number of researchers have been working towards developing mechanisms that provide permanent Internet connectivity to all mobile network nodes via their permanent IP addresses as well as maintain ongoing sessions as the mobile network changes its point of attachment to the Internet [6], [7].

The benefits of using *Mobile Routers* are summarized in the following subsections. For a detailed study on design requirements for network mobility refer to [8].

2.1   Reduced Transmission Power

For devices within a mobile hotspot (Mobile Network Nodes), such as those on ships and aircrafts, the radio transmission distance to the *Mobile Router* is potentially much shorter than to another access router on the Internet. Therefore, the mobile network nodes need not be equipped with high-power communication capabilities and even if they are, utilize the minimum of power for transmission.

2.2   Reduced Hand-Offs

Once the mobile network nodes have established a link with the *Mobile Router*, the link does not need to be torn-down as the mobile hotspot moves. Since all external communication is via the *Mobile Router*, only the *Mobile Router* needs to handle link layer hand-offs. This reduces the complexity and cost of mobile network nodes as described below.

2.3 Reduced Complexity

Once a mobile network node joins a mobile hotspot, it would not have to keep changing its IP address since this functionality would be performed by the *Mobile Router*. When the mobile hotspot moves and changes its point of attachment to the Internet the *Mobile Router* auto configures itself with a location specific address. This reduces the need for the mobile network nodes having to perform link layer handoffs as well as the need for auto configuring a new address. By having the *Mobile Router* perform these actions on behalf of the network nodes, the software and hardware complexity on the network nodes could be greatly reduced.

2.4 Reduction in Bandwidth Consumption and Location Update Delays

When a mobile hotspot changes its point of attachment to the Internet mobile network nodes in the mobile hotspot may need to send registration messages to their *Home Agents*, potentially inundating the *Home Agent* on the home network. By having the *Mobile Router* send the registration updates on behalf of the mobile network nodes within the mobile hotspot, a single message to the *Home Agent* of the *Mobile Router* will be sufficient to register the whole network, thus offering a reduction in time and bandwidth consumption. Although the visiting mobile network nodes (i.e. nodes that do not belong to the same home network as the Mobile Router) would still need to send periodic registration messages to their respective *Home Agents* these nodes too benefit by not having to change their address whilst within the mobile hotspot.

2.5 Increased Manageability

The *Mobile Router* offers an easy central point in managing the mobility features of the mobile hotspot. When protocol updates or additional features were to become necessary, it is much easier to carry out the updates, as it only need to be done on the *Mobile Router* than on each of the network nodes.

2.6 Economic Incentive

From the point of view of transportation systems, it is often commercially lucrative to provide and charge for global connectivity to passengers' mobile devices through a *Mobile Router* installed in the vehicle, as is being currently done by airlines.

Host mobility can be handled on multiple protocol layers: link, network, transport, and application layer. Managing the mobility above the link layer is required when mobility takes place between multiple access network types. Managing mobility at a layer above the network layer has its own advantages and disadvantages for a mobile host [9]. However, we believe that a *Mobile Router* can best manage the mobility of mobile hotspots at the network layer since it allows the mobile nodes to be mobility unaware, and is efficient and provides easier management as described above.

The IETFs NEMO Basic Support protocol is a well defined mechanism that employs a *Mobile Router* for mobility management of mobile networks at the network layer. It can cater for any type of node present in the network irrespective of their capabilities. In the next section we give an overview of NEMO by discussing how this protocol handles different types of nodes that could be present in the mobile network.

3 NEMO Basic Support Protocol

NEMO allows a *Mobile Router* to manage the mobility of the nodes inside a mobile hotspot, with the help of a fixed mobility anchor point, namely the *Home Agent*. When the *Mobile Router* is in its home network it is connected directly to the *Home Agent*, so all traffic to and from the mobile hotspot is delivered via the *Home Agent* and *Mobile Router*. Also, when the *Mobile Router* is away from its home network and connected to a foreign network, the *Mobile Router* hides its mobility from the mobile network nodes, so that mobile hotspot is connected to the Internet via a one hop virtual link between the *Mobile Router* and the *Home Agent*. This is achieved by the MR and the *Home Agent* maintaining an IPv6 tunnel between the current location of the *Mobile Router*, i.e. its care-of-address and the *Home Agent's* address. The *Mobile Router* and its *Home Agent* then deliver all traffic between the mobile hotspot and the Internet via this tunnel. This overlay routing hides the mobility of the *Mobile Router* from correspondent nodes and also from mobile network nodes. Consequently, even the nodes without any mobility capabilities would be able to take advantage of the mobile Internet access provided via a *Mobile Router*.

3.1 Mobility Management for Visiting Mobile Nodes

A MIPv6 node entering a mobile hotspot (referred to as a Visiting Mobile Node) will send a binding update to its own *Home Agent* informing it to deliver all traffic to its

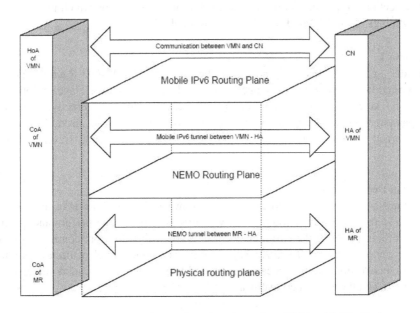

Fig. 1. NEMO and Mobile IPv6 routing planes for a Visiting Mobile Node

new care-of-address using IPv6 tunneling. This results in two levels of mobility management for Visiting Mobile Network nodes even if they are capable of handling their own mobility. The routing planes for such nested mobility are illustrated in Figure 1. The virtual routing plane created by the NEMO tunnel makes the network between the *Mobile Router* and its *Home Agent* to appear as a single routing hop logically connecting the mobile network through the *Home Agent* of the *Mobile Router* to the Internet. The tunnel between the care-of-address of Visiting Mobile Node and its *Home Agent* connects the Visiting Mobile Node logically with its home network, creating a second logical routing plane. This hides the mobility of the Visiting Mobile Node from applications and correspondent nodes.

Mobile IPv6 allows a mobile node and the corresponding node to communicate more directly. Mobile node can send a binding update to the corresponding node to inform corresponding node of its current care-of-address. This route optimization adds an IPv6 extension header to data packets to carry the home address of mobile node between the base IPv6 header and any transport protocol header. In the case of Visiting Mobile Node the Care-of-Address is from mobile network prefix, which belongs topologically to the home network of mobile node. Hence, Mobile IPv6 route optimization can not remove the extra routing leg, since all traffic between the corresponding node and the Visiting Mobile Node is still routed via the tunnel between the Care-of-Address of the *Mobile Router* and its *Home Agent*.

4   Network Mobility Scenarios and Problem Descriptions

In this section we present 3 different network mobility scenarios which highlight the shortcomings of the NEMO Basic Support protocol.

Scenario 1
Consider a case of a passenger accessing the Internet via a *Mobile Router* deployed on an aircraft. Although the passenger's mobile device has network layer capabilities it has no layer 2 capabilities in order to access the Internet directly. Therefore the passenger depends on the *Mobile Router* deployed on the aircraft to access the Internet. Figure 2 illustrates the routing path a packet would traverse in this case.

Problem Description
With the NEMO Basic Support protocol, as shown in Figure 2, leads to high delays because of the non optimal routing via two home networks. The performance would be severely impacted if the two home networks are in two different continents due to indirect routing via two *Home Agent*s. Further each added level of nested mobility requires an additional tunnel encapsulation, and these extra IPv6 headers increase the packet size and the associated overheads.

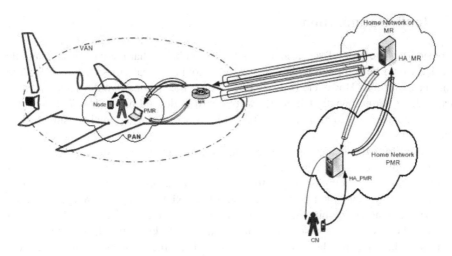

Fig. 2. Bidirectional Tunneling of packets to and from a Visiting Mobile Node to a Correspondent Node

Scenario 2
In the second scenario we attempt to highlight the importance of the *Mobile Router* performing seamless handoffs by considering a mobile hotspot aboard a train. In this case, the *Mobile Router* would have to potentially handle many mobile nodes that have active sessions. Further the *Mobile Router* would have to make handoffs more frequently due the speed of the train and due to cell sizes being relatively small unlike the case of Mobile Routers deployed on aircrafts (typically a Mobile Router on an aircraft would connect via satellite networks which have large coverage areas thus the handoff frequency would be much less).

Problem Description
As a *Mobile Router* would be responsible for the mobility management of potentially many nodes that have active sessions, handoff latency would have a significant impact [13].

Scenario 3
Consider the case of a passenger connecting to the office VPN via a *Mobile Router* in order to download a file.

Problem Description
Although this would be possible, downloading bandwidth intensive files would incur a high cost to the passenger if the *Mobile Router* is providing connectivity solely via a wireless wide area network.

In the next 3 sections we present 3 solutions proposed and implemented by us in order to handle the problem of non optimal routing, effects of handoff latencies and the cost of bandwidth.

5 Route Optimization

Considering the case of scenario 1, it is highly probable that the passenger's mobile device would be equipped with network layer mobility capabilities such as MIPv6 in the near future. However it is unlikely that the device would have satellite capabilities. Consequently the device would need to depend on the *Mobile Router* for layer 2 connectivity but would be able to perform routing optimally using MIPv6 capabilities.

The NEMO Basic Support protocol has been designed with the assumption that nodes within the mobile network have no mobility capabilities such as MIPv6. It is evident that this assumption has restricted the more capable nodes within the mobile hotspot from getting better performance out of the NEMO protocol. With the NEMO protocol the nodes within the network would not get a location specific care of address. For example a passenger on an aircraft would know that it is within the air craft's mobile hotspot but would not know where the network is at the current moment. According to the MIPv6 protocol standard it is not possible for a mobile node to achieve route optimization without having a location specific care-of-address. Therefore even though the passenger device has the MIPv6 route optimization capability it will not be able utilize it. To overcome this we have proposed an optimal routing architecture [12] for network mobility, namely OptiNets which exploits the desirable characteristics of both MIPv6 and NEMO protocols.

NEMO achieves this by requiring the *Mobile Router* to perform a layer 2 handoff on behalf the entire network and advertising the prefix of the foreign network to the nodes within the mobile hotspot. This enables the MIPv6 equipped nodes to configure an address specific to its current location and perform the route optimization procedure using the standard MIPv6 mechanisms. By getting the *Mobile Router* to play the role of an access router and advertising the foreign network prefix to the nodes within the network alleviates the need for these nodes to perform a layer 2 handoff. The nodes which are running on battery power need not communicate with an access router beyond the scope of the mobile hotspot in order to obtain the foreign network prefix. In enables more capable nodes within the network to perform optimal routing with minimal participation in the mobility management process.

In Table 1 shows a comparison, and as can be seen with OptiNets, that the mobile network nodes need only change its prefix in order to obtain optimal routing.

Table 1. Comparison of proposed architecture to MIPv6 and NEMO basic support

	Route Optimization (RO)	Layer 2 Handoff	Prefix Change
MIPv6	✓	✓	✓
NEMO Basic Support	✗	✗	✗
OptiNets	✓	✗	✓

6 Seamless Handoff

Over the years many researchers have developed methods of mitigating the effects of handoff latency on a Mobile Host [10], [11]. This research mainly focused on mitigating latency in systems where the mobile host is connected to only one access point at a time which results in the device having to break the connection to the current network before reattaching itself to the new network (Break-Before-Make handoffs). The reason for this is because most mobile devices currently are equipped with only one wireless interface of a given type which is incapable of listening to multiple base stations. Nevertheless, networks such as the newer cellular CDMA networks provides the capability to listen to multiple base stations simultaneously and for the synchronization of the traffic from the multiple base stations. It allows the mobile device to connect to the new network before breaking the current connection during a handoff (Make-Before-Break handoff). Make-Before-Break handoff can be achieved without support from the access network in the current non cellular networks by using multiple interfaces of the same type on the mobile device. Including two radio interfaces for a given type of network on a chip set is technically feasible today. However the major drawbacks of using multiple interfaces in this manner are the increase in power consumption, the interference caused by usage of multiple interfaces and the overall decrease in the network capacity. Use of the multiple interfaces at the *Mobile Router* will provide all the benefits associated with Make-Before-Break handoffs but will not suffer from the drawbacks of extra power usage, interference and loss of capacity because of the benefits of aggregation. Therefore it is justifiable to introduce a multiple interface, Make-Before Break handoff mechanisms for a network mobility environment.

In a network mobility setting a *Mobile Router* with multiple interfaces can perform a Make-Before-Break handoff as follows. It will be connected to the current network with one interface, which we refer to as the active interface. Any other available interfaces, referred to as scanning interfaces will be used for scanning and performing handoffs. With this arrangement the handoff delay will not affect the active data connection because a separate interface is used to scan for new access networks and when a suitable access network is found the scanning interface performs the handoff procedure. Such a mechanism would enable a *Mobile Router* to perform soft handoffs in a non cellular environment such as WiMax, WLAN as in a cellular environment such as CDMA. We have implemented [13] the above described seamless handoff mechanism on a network mobility setting and have shown that it is a feasible and a positive approach towards seamless network mobility.

7 Low Cost Bandwidth

Use of a Wireless Wide Area Network (WWAN) connection provides continuous connectivity for on board devices. However, the high cost of bandwidth these networks make the use of bandwidth intensive services less attractive. In order to make these services more attractive for the users the cost of the communications need to be minimized. Although in some environments it may be possible to use high bandwidth low cost wireless local area network connections, in most cases it is necessary to use wireless wide area networks due to their larger coverage areas. Therefore, for the foreseeable future, mobile networking environments will consist of high bandwidth wireless local area networks, overlaid with wireless wide area networks. It would be desirable to use the low cost wireless local area networks at all possible times to increase the bandwidth of mobile networks. In order to use the sporadically available low cost wireless local area networks we have proposed and carried out a prototype implementation of a bandwidth fueling architecture which uses the idea of pre-fetching and caching.

Caching exploits the characteristic of locality, i.e. the fact that a number of people will want access to the same information, by storing data locally. Pre-fetching anticipates the demand for data and downloads the information in advance when the bandwidth costs are minimal. In order for caching to work, it is crucial for the caches to be updated frequently. However, updating of the cache server within a mobile hotspot would be slow, potentially costly and would compromise the real-time services, if it was done indiscriminately. Furthermore, due to mobility management overheads specific to the NEMO Basic Support Protocol such as non optimal routing, performing frequent cache updates in a mobile network setting is challenging.

However, it will be possible to use localized roadside cache servers which allow cache servers within mobile hotpots to be updated whenever their *Mobile Routers* are within the coverage area of the roadside wireless local area networks. The roadside wireless local area network infrastructure would simply consist of one or more roadside routers connected to a roadside cache server. Figure 4 depicts the proposed bandwidth fuelling network mobility architecture with the Roadside WLAN networks. In updating the Mobile Cache Servers we use the optimizations proposed for NEMO for routing (section 5) and seamless handoffs (section 6). Details of technical aspects of this architecture can be found on [14]. Update of the cache servers within mobile hotspots would take place when the mobile network is in the vicinity of a roadside network. We have shown via a real implementation that the relative TCP performance of a Mobile Cache update using the NEMO protocol with the proposed optimizations is very close to a static cache update [14].

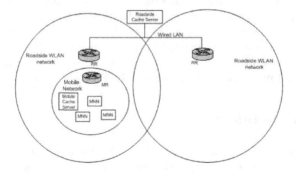

Fig. 3. Bandwidth Fueling Network Mobility Architecture

8 Conclusions

On-board communication has recently become an increasingly popular research topic. The performance of an onboard mobile network depends on the performance of the *Mobile Router* and the mobility management protocols. In this paper we presented an overview of the current standard protocol to handle mobile hotspots and highlighted their shortcomings. Then a new architecture which builds on the standard protocols and overcomes these limitations was presented. We believe the new architecture will enable the provision of services via mobile hotspots in the same manner as WiFi hotspots in the near future.

References

1. Marques, L., Nunes, U., Almeida, T.: SpreadNose: Distributed Agents for Environmental Monitoring. In: Siciliano, P. (ed.) Sensors for Environmental Control, pp. 234–238. World Scientific Pub., Singapore (2003)
2. Pelusi, L., Passarella, A., Conti, M.: Opportunistic Networking: Data forwarding in disconnected mobile ad hoc networks. IEEE Communications Magazine issue on Ad hoc and Sensor Networks 44(11) (November 2006)
3. Perkins, C.: IP Mobility support for IPv4. RFC 3344, IETF (August 2002)
4. Johnson, D., Perkins, C., Arkko, J.: Mobility Support in IPv6, RFC3775, IETF (June 2004)
5. http://www.ietf.org/html.charters/nemo-charter.html
6. Devarapalli, V., Wakikawa, R., Petrescu, A., Thubert, P.: Network Mobility (NEMO) Basic Support Protocol, RFC 3963 (January 2005)
7. Hager, R., Klemets, A., Maguire, G.Q., Reichert, F., Smith, M.T.: MINT- A Mobile Internet Router. In: 1st International Symposium on Global Data Networking, Cairo, Egypt, pp. 13–15 (December 1993)
8. Perera, E., Sivaraman, V., Seneviratne, A.: Survey on Network Mobility Support. ACM SIGMOBILE Mobile Computing and Communications Review 8(2) (April 2004)
9. Bhagwat, P., Perkins, C., Tripathi, S.: Network Layer Mobility: An architecture and Survey. IEEE Personal Communications 3(3), 54–64 (1996)
10. Hsieh, R., Zhou, Z.G., Seneviratne, A.: S-MIP: A Seamless Handoff Architecture for Mobile IP. In: Proceedings of the Infocom, San Francisco, USA (2003)
11. Koodli, R.: Fast Handovers for Mobile IPv6., RFC 4168 (July 2005)
12. Perera, E., Seneviratne, A., Sivaraman, V.: OptiNets: An architecture to enable optimal routing in network mobility. In: IWWAN 2004. International Workshop on Wireless Ad-Hoc Networks, Oulu, Finland (May 2004)
13. Petander, H., Perera, E., Lan, K., Seneviratne, A.: Measuring and Improving Performance of Network Mobility Management in IPv6 Networks. IEEE Journal on Selected Areas of Communications (JSAC), Special Issue on Mobile Routers and Network Mobility 24(9) (September 2006)
14. Perera, E., Petander, H., Seneviratne, A.: Bandwidth fuelling for Network Mobility. In: WOCN 2006. Proceedings of the 3rd IEEE and IFIP International Conference on Wireless and Optical Communications Networks, Bangalore, India, pp. 11–13 (April 2006)

Extending Home Agent Migration
to Mobile IPv6 Based Protocols

Guillaume Valadon[1] and Ryuji Wakikawa[2]

[1] Université Pierre et Marie Curie-Paris 6
`guillaume.valadon@lip6.fr`
[2] KEIO University
`ryuji@wide.ad.jp`

Abstract. Defined at the IETF, the Mobile IPv6 protocol allows a single mobile node to keep the same IPv6 address independently of its network of attachment. It was recently enhance so as to augment its applicability. One of these extensions, NEMO, NEtwork MObility makes it possible to move a whole network, such as sensors deployed in a car, in the Internet topology. On the other hand, Proxy Mobile IPv6 provides Mobile IPv6-like services to standard IPv6 nodes. While these three protocols are actually heavily supported by the industry and deployed in 3GGP2, WiMAX and ITS, they suffer from several performances issues. Most of them are caused by the Home Agent, a specific router located on the home network, that hides movements of mobile nodes to their correspondents. The restricted position of the home agent is responsible for longer communications delays and higher path lengths. In one of our previous work, Home Agent Migration, we described how to significantly reduce these issues by deploying multiple home agents in the Internet topology. In this paper, we discuss the possible extensions to this specific architecture in order to support and enhance NEMO and Proxy Mobile IPv6. Furthermore, we analyze Home Agent Migration in terms of security so as to provide detailed guidance for secure real life deployments and safe usages.

1 Introduction

Mobile phones are entirely part of our daily life. We use them not only for work but also to communicate with friends, access the Internet or play games. They are slowly changing the way people interact with each other [1] and how we access the information. Indeed in 2006, mobile devices in Japan represents 57%[1] of all user access to the Internet. Moreover, usages of mobile phones have recently changed thanks to dual-mode GSM/WiFi handsets and Voice over IP services. Customers are now used to make cheap phone calls wherever they are. Therefore, mobility is one of the key feature for future Internet based technologies. Following these trends, we expect that the next evolution of customers' usages will likely require

---

[1] Owned by approximately 48 million people, according to The Japanese Ministry of Internal Affairs and Communications.

S. Fdida and K. Sugiura (Eds.): AINTEC 2007, LNCS 4866, pp. 70–85, 2007.

vertical handovers to provide seamless voice calls between access technologies such as WiFi and HSDPA. Consequently, there is a need to develop efficient mobility services at the IP layer so as to keep phone calls valid after a change of IP address.

While not extensively deployed yet, mobility protocols were already standardized at the Internet Engineering Task Force (IETF). Here, we focus on the Mobile IPv6 [2] protocol. It provides a permanent IP address to a mobile node independently of its network of attachment thanks to a home agent, a dedicated Mobile IPv6 router. Several extensions such as NEMO [3] and Proxy Mobile IPv6 [4] were also normalized. They respectively delivered Mobile IPv6-like mobility service to whole networks, such as sensors deployed in a car, and to standard IPv6 nodes that do not implement Mobile IPv6 on the client side[2]. However, the base Mobile IPv6 protocol is inappropriate for efficient deployments as it has several issues. One of them, called dogleg routing, is especially important as it induces longer path and higher communications delays.

In our previous work, Home Agent Migration [5], we introduced a distributed architecture of home agents that effectively solves the dogleg routing in Mobile IPv6. Using anycast routing, home agents are distributed in the Internet topology, and advertise a unique IPv6 prefix from these different locations. Therefore, a mobile node is always associated with its closest home agent in terms of the network topology, reducing the effects of the dogleg routing. In this paper, we describe how Home Agent Migration could be extended to support both NEMO and Proxy Mobile IPv6 so as to enhance their performances. It is an important contribution as these two protocols are currently being studied to provide IP layer mobility to WiMAX networks [6]. Moreover, we also provide a comprehensive discussion on security related issues from an operator perspective. This is the second contribution of this paper that could be used to achieve efficient deployments of Mobile IPv6 based protocols that fulfills real life usages.

This paper is organized as follows. Section 2 presents the Mobile IPv6 protocol and its extensions NEMO and Proxy Mobile IPv6. In Section 3, we first introduce Home Agent Migration, then describe two typical deployments and finally discuss its use with the two extensions. Finally, in Section 4, security implications of Mobile IPv6 and Home Agent Migration concerning mobile, correspondent nodes and the network infrastructure are given.

2   Mobile IPv6 and Its Extensions

In this section, the Mobile IPv6 protocol is first described in details. Then, its two major extensions, NEMO, and Proxy Mobile IPv6, and their common uses are discussed. Finally, the limitations of these three protocols are given so as to understand what is the benefit of extending our previous work, Home Agent Migration, to enhance them.

---

[2] Referred as mobile node in the Mobile IPv6's terminology.

2.1   Mobile IPv6

On the Internet, the location of a node is strongly constrained by the routing architecture. An IPv6 address that belongs to an IPv6 prefix allocated to a French Internet Service Provider cannot be used to receive packets in Japan. Consequently, the current Internet architecture makes it impossible to keep the same address when a nodes move. This problem is linked to the dual function of the IP address. First, it implicitly provides the position of a node on the globe; this role is called *locator*. Then, it uniquely identifies the node in the whole Internet topology; this second role is called *identifier*. The Mobile IPv6 protocol provides a solution to separate this two functions. From now on, a mobile node uses two different IP addresses: the Home Address, HoA, and the Care-of Address, CoA.

1. the CoA changes when the mobile node moves; it is the *locator*. This is an IPv6 address belonging to the network where the mobile node is physically located. It allows IP packets to be routed to the mobile node.
2. the HoA is a fixed address that belongs to the home network of the mobile node; it is its *identifier*. It is transparently used by the upper layers, such as TCP and UDP, that do not perceive that Mobile IPv6 is used to communicate with correspondents nodes over the Internet.

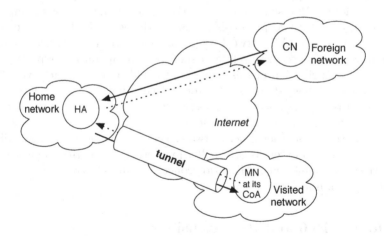

Fig. 1. Mobile IPv6

Correspondents of the mobile node are not aware of these two addresses, neither of its movements, and always communicate with the mobile node using the Home Address. A router called the Home Agent, HA, specific to Mobile IPv6, is located in the home network and performs the relation between the CoA and the HoA. As shown in Figure 1, the packets destinated to the HoA of the mobile node are routed to the home network. The goal of the home agent is therefore to intercept and forward them to the current location of the mobile node, its CoA, using and IPv6-in-IPv6 tunnel. Note that packets sent by the mobile node to its correspondent must go to the home agent before being routed to the Internet. When the mobile node moves to a new visited network, it notifies its home agent of this change using a packet called Binding Update containing the permanent Home Address and the recently acquired Care-of Address. Packets are then forwarded from the home agent to the new CoA using the tunnel. Unlike other mobility protocols, like HIP [7] or LIN6 [8], Mobile IPv6 only requires to modify the IPv6 stacks of the mobile nodes, and to deploy the home agent in the home network. This is the fundamental aspect of this protocol that makes its uses transparent regarding correspondent nodes, and the Internet architecture.

2.2 NEMO

Defined at the IETF in RFC 3963 [3], NEMO[3] is an extension to Mobile IPv6 that allows a whole network to move and change its point of attachment to the Internet as would a mobile node. A new entity similar to the mobile node and called a Mobile Router implements the NEMO protocol. Its goal is to hide the effect of mobility to the nodes connected to its ingress interface. The main concept of NEMO is to provide a mobility service to IPv6 nodes that do not implement Mobile IPv6 using an IPv6 prefix delegated from the home network. A typical usage scenario for this protocol is public transportation systems such as trains where end-nodes are connected to the Mobile Router using 802.11b.

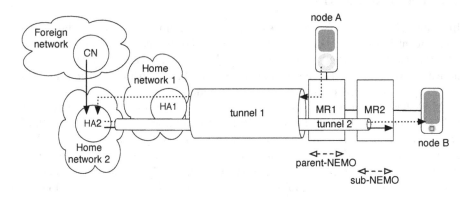

Fig. 2. Nested NEMO

Like a Mobile Node, the Mobile Router have a permanent Home Address that remains the same wherever it moves. In addition, it also manages a Mobile Network Prefix delegated from the home network. This is the IPv6 prefix used by

---

[3] NEtwork MObility.

end-nodes connected to its ingress interface. In NEMO, the home agent is slightly modified so as to delegate home addresses as well as mobile network prefixes, and to process dedicated Binding Update messages. It does not only intercept packets destinated to the home address of mobile nodes and mobile routers but also intercepts packets sent to nodes belonging to the mobile network prefix. For example, with the home network's prefix *2001:db8::/48*, a network administrator could delegate the prefixes *2001:db8:0:1::/64* and *2001:db8:0:2::/64* to two different mobile routers MR1 and MR2.

As defined by the NEMO terminology [9], a mobile network is said to be nested (sub-NEMO) when it is directly attached to another mobile router (parent-NEMO). Figure 2 shows a simple case of nested mobile network where a mobile router, MR2, is connected to another mobile router, MR1; the networks interconnecting MR1 and HA1, and HA1 and HA2 are not represented. We consider that Binding Update messages were respectively send and receive by the mobile routers and their corresponding home agents. When node A in the parent-NEMO sends packets to a node B located in the sub-NEMO, they are forwarded to MR1 which encapsulates packets into tunnel 1. Then, HA1 decapsulates and routes them to the home network 2 which is the correct destination regarding the routing system. When packets reach this network, they are intercepted by HA2, immediately forwarded to MR2 via tunnel 2, and delivered to node 2. This is a typical use of NEMO that presents some performance issues. They will be described later in Section 2.4. This scenario is likely to happen when a passenger brings its own mobile router, MR2, into a train, and use it to provide access Internet access to its devices such as its laptop and its smart-phone.

2.3   Proxy Mobile IPv6

In Mobile IPv6, a mobile node is responsible for sending a Binding Update to the home agent in order to achieve its own sessions continuity. IPv6 stacks of legacy nodes must be modified to support Mobile IPv6 and turn them into mobile nodes. However, there is a need to provide IP mobility without any modification to legacy nodes. This could for example provide seamless sessions continuity to WiMAX based devices while roaming between base stations. Network based mobility protocol has been discussed in IETF and supported by several Standards Development Organizations such as WiMAX and 3GPP2. Proxy Mobile IPv6 is an extension to Mobile IPv6 that achieves network based mobility support. As shown in Figure 3, a Local Mobility Anchor, LMA, is placed in a network and acts as a home agent. Mobility Anchor Gateway, MAG, are located in every access networks. Their goal is to send Binding Update messages to the LMA on behalf of IPv6 nodes. As soon as an IPv6 node roams into its access network (arrow 1), the MAG detects it and sends a proxy Binding Update message to the LMA (arrow 2). The binding registration is then performed and the Binding Acknowledgment sent by the LMA (arrow 3). An IPv6-in-IPv6 tunnel is consecutively established between the MAG and the LMA and is used to carry the traffic of the IPv6 node. The IPv6 node will obtain and keep the same IP address wherever it moves within the same administrative domain (arrow 5).

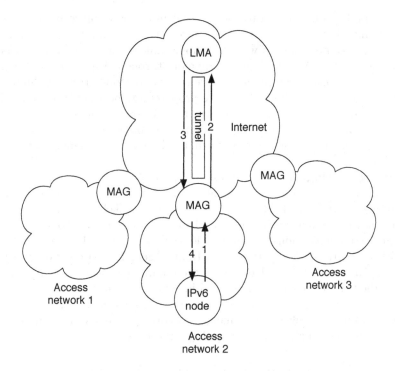

Fig. 3. Proxy Mobile IPv6

2.4 Limitations of Mobile IPv6 Based Protocols

The Mobile IPv6 protocol suffers from the following three problems. Specifically, they are related to the use of the home agent to intercept packets sent to the mobile node. These problems weaken both the protocol scalability and the performance of the communications.

1. **Limitation for the home link.** In order to intercept packets sent to the mobile node, the home agent acts as a neighbor discovery protocol proxy (Proxy NDP [10]). This represents a severe scalability issue as the number of neighbor discovery packets sent by the home agent is equivalent to the amount of mobile nodes it serves. Likewise, the individual bandwidth allocated to each mobile node is proportional to this number. Therefore, a home agent will possibly serve a fairly limited number of mobile nodes. Classic deployments of Mobile IPv6 are thus problematic as they can lead to limited performance. Partial solutions to these issues are available, and consist of suppressing the Proxy NDP using a virtual home link, as well as limiting the number of mobile nodes served by each home agent. However, they are cumbersome and inconvenient to use in an operational network.
2. **Restricted location of the home agent.** The position of the home agent is strictly limited by the routing architecture. It must be deployed where the

home prefix is advertised to the Internet in order to intercept packets sent to its mobile nodes. This strong requirement on the home agent's location is especially problematic when the home link becomes unreachable as the mobile nodes cannot be reached anymore through their home address. Solutions to provide redundancy and reliability to Mobile IPv6 by duplicating home agents on the home link were proposed at the IETF [11,12,13]. They ensure that when a home agent fails, another one automatically takes over to guarantee the continuity of mobile node's communications. However, the main problem of these solutions is that only one home agent is activated at a time.

3. **Dogleg routing.** As shown in Figure 1, a mobile node communicates with a correspondent via its home agent. All packets, sent and received, must go through the IPv6-in-IPv6 tunnel. Therefore, it is likely that the packets will take a non-optimal path. This problem, known as dogleg routing, induces higher communications delays, and longer paths when the mobile interacts with its correspondents. Preceding Home Agent Migration, works in route optimization [14,15] involve caching the binding between the Home Address and the Care-of Address on-demand in routers and in correspondent nodes. However, these solutions are not transparent to end-nodes and the Internet architecture as they require changes to correspondent's and router's IPv6 stacks, as does the Return Routability Procedure [2].

NEMO. As described in the NEMO problem statement document [16], along with the previous Mobile IPv6 issues, this protocol also suffers from the nested mobile network scenario described in Section 2.2. This is an important problem as all of the packets exchanged between correspondents and nodes behind the mobile router must go through the tunnel. Figure 2 shows a typical worst case scenario: two nodes A and B respectively attached to MR1 and MR2 exchange packets. As the mobile routers are not managed by the same home agent, the communication's path and delay are altered by the mandatory derivation to the home agents HA1 and HA2. Moreover, the bandwidth usage increases as the number of nested networks, wasting network resources and augmenting the probability of the tunnel congestion. The impact of this problem is even more serious when the home agents are far away, for example if HA1 is located in Tokyo and HA2 located in Paris. In addition to this first issue, if the egress interface of MR1 fails, node A can no longer send packets to node B. In other words, the egress interface of the root mobile router, here MR1, limits communications from all sub-NEMOs in terms of bandwidth and stability.

So far, the NEMO working group at the IETF did not come up with a solution to these issues. The only consensus is that the Routing Routability Procedure of Mobile IPv6 can not be used with NEMO. However, the most advanced works concern another scenario in which two mobile routers located in different vehicles try to communicate directly using a wireless interface instead of the tunnel. Solutions to this problem are actually discussed in the MANET[4] and NEMO

---

[4] Mobile Ad-hoc Network.

working groups and labeled as MANEMO [17]. They tend to use well-known MANET routing protocols such as OLSR [18] to discover direct routes to other mobile routers. The goal of MANEMO based solutions is therefore to use a free wireless-based *MANET interface* when mobile routers are in communications range, and use the tunnel otherwise.

Proxy Mobile IPv6. Unlike Mobile IPv6, this protocol do not suffer from issues previously described as *limitation for the home link*. Indeed, due to its design, the notion of home link disappeared from Proxy Mobile IPv6. However, communications between nodes located behind the Mobile Anchor Gateway, and their correspondents are still targeted by the dogleg routing. None of the previously detailed solutions can be applied to solve this issue. The location of the home agent is also limiting the performance of the protocol. However, if it fails, the consequence are more serious than with Mobile IPv6: nodes can not communicate at all as they only reveal their home address to their correspondents. In a regular deployment, the redundancy of home agents is therefore critical. Finally, the Mobility Anchor Gateway brings an issue similar to the mobile router's one: it limits communications from all nodes behind it.

Like the mobile router NEMO the Basic Support, the LMA must process the traffic of each mobile node and transmit it over the tunnel. Therefore Proxy Mobile IPv6 and NEMO share the same problems. The LMA is located where the home prefix is advertised to the Internet and acts as the default router for this prefix consequently it represents a single point of failure. This is a critical issue for a real life deployment as it directly targets the availability of the Proxy Mobile IPv6 architecture.

3 Home Agent Migration

In this section, concepts behind Home Agent Migration are first described so as to understand which issues of Mobile IPv6 it solves and how. Typical deployments of this architecture are then discussed for a single Autonomous System and for the whole Internet. Finally, we consider NEMO and Proxy Mobile IPv6 and explain in which ways they can also benefit from Home Agent Migration while not being modified.

3.1 Conceptual Description

Home Agent Migration is a network-based solution to the dogleg routing issue that also solves limitations for the home link. It is able to optimize the routes while remaining fully compatible with existing Mobile IPv6 implementations. This key feature is especially important as many networking vendors had already integrated the Mobile IPv6 protocol into their products. Moreover, correspondents of mobile nodes can benefit of this route optimization without any modification of their IPv6 packets nor communication performances. In Home Agent Migration, home agents are distributed in the network so as to disengage

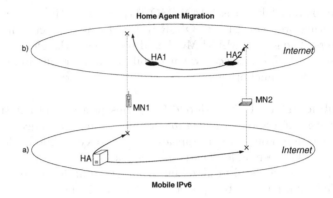

Fig. 4. Mobile IPv6 and Home Agent Migration architectures

them from the home link. Unlike in regular Mobile IPv6 deployments, several home agents are serving the same home prefix, as shown in Figure 4. To do so, the home prefix, also referred as mobile prefix, is advertised at diverse locations around the network in an anycast [19] fashion so as to create routing *shortcuts*.

Anycast is a common routing based mechanism that associates an IPv6 prefix to a dedicated service such as a DNS servers, or in this discussion home agents. Therefore when a mobile node sends a packet to the home agent IPv6 address, the routing plane decides which incarnation of the home agent will receive it. As a result, the mobile node is always associated with the closest incarnation of the home agents in terms of the routing topology.

In order to correctly deliver packets to mobile nodes, distributed home agents must also share the same information about received Binding Update messages in a unique Binding Cache. For every mobile node, this cache maintains the relationship between the Care-of Address, the Home Address and the home agent associated with a mobile node. The home agent associated with a mobile node is called the primary home agent. As a means to synchronize the Binding Cache, each home agent establishes a secured tunnel with the other home agents and uses it to exchange signaling and traffic of mobile nodes.

3.2 Typical Deployments

There is two possible deployments for the Home Agent Migration architecture. They are linked to the protocol operated to perform the anycast routing and advertise the mobile prefix. When an Interior Gateway Protocol, IGP, is used, the scope of Home Agent Migration is limited to a single Autonomous System, AS. The achieved route optimization concerns communications destinated to mobile or correspondent nodes associated to the AS. When an Exterior Gateway Protocol, EGP, is used, the prefix is distributed globally on the Internet. The optimization therefore concerns nodes located all over the Internet topology.

In an Autonomous System. In this deployment, the mobile prefix is picked up from the set of IPv6 prefixes associated with the AS. This mobile prefix is advertised from different locations in the network using an IGP such as OSPF. The choice of these locations and their numbers is left to network administrators. However, so as to provide an effective route optimization, the prefix should be advertised from routers with the highest centrality in terms of graph theory as shown in our on-going studies. Routers with high centrality are gathering most of the shortest paths in the network, and are therefore on the path to most of the communications. The home agents are placed close to these routers. Depending on the Autonomous System, home agents could be interconnected using direct links or VLAN, so as to provide a fast and reliable distribution system to synchronize the Binding Cache and exchange mobile node's data traffic. This IGP based deployment is more flexible than the EGP based one as network administrators are able to efficiently place the home agent in the locations that provide the best performance within their network.

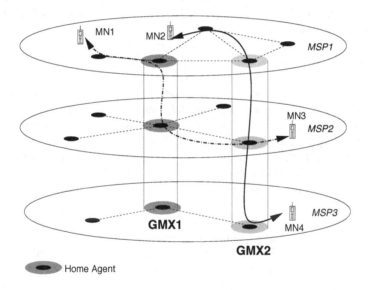

Fig. 5. Global Mobile eXchange

In the Internet. Compared to the Autonomous System' one, this deployment is more difficult to achieve due to its bigger scale. The mobile prefix must be associated to a dedicated AS number. The Home Agent Migration architecture would therefore look like a distributed AS regarding the Internet topology. The mobile prefix will be advertised from many different locations around the globe using an EGP such as BGP. This deployment relies on Internet Exchange Points (IXPs) to locate the distributed home agents. They are operated with a concept similar to IXP; therefore we call this architecture Global Mobile eXchange (GMX). The primary goals of GMX are to decrease the cost of the transit traffic related to mobile nodes and to allow Internet-Scale Mobility services. In Figure 5, there are three Mobile Service Providers managing different sets of home agents, MSP1, MSP2 and MSP3. All of them are interconnected by home agents located in GMX1 and GMX2. In a GMX, a home agent exchanges traffic and routing information as a regular router would do in an IXP. However, this EGP based deployment could be difficult to achieve as it requires peering agreements with Internet Service Providers located in IXPs where home agents are located.

3.3   In Details

Mobile IPv6. Figure 6 represents flows of packets generated when a mobile node, MN, associates with the Home Agent Migration system and communicates with its correspondents, CN1 and CN2. A mobile node (MN) first registers to its primary home agent (Seq1). The primary home agent then creates a binding for the Home Address of the mobile node, and subsequently distributes a copy to other home agents to synchronize the Binding Cache. When a mobile node communicates with a correspondent node, outgoing packets from the mobile node are tunneled to the primary home agent, here HA1 (Seq4). Then, as it is not possible to know which home agent is closer to the MN, the packets are simply routed to CN1 using the regular routing system. Incoming packets to the mobile node are intercepted by the home agent HA2, which is closer to the correspondent node. Intercepted packets are then tunneled to the primary home agent. The primary home agent delivers the packets to the mobile node through the tunnel (Seq5). If the mobile node decides to switch its primary home agent because of its movement, it sends a Binding Update to the new primary home agent (Seq7). The new primary home agent then synchronizes the binding with other home agents (Seq8). After receiving the Binding Update copy, all the home agents update the binding as well as the new primary home agent address.

NEMO. Home Agent Migration could easily be extended in order to provide route optimization to NEMO. Small modifications to the shared Binding Cache are sufficient so as to also take mobile network prefixes into account. Moreover, the network prefixes associated with mobile routers must belong to the IPv6 prefix advertised by the distributed home agents using anycast. However, the sub-NEMO scenario, described in Section 2.2, can not fully benefit from our proposal. In Figure 2, with Home Agent Migration, when node B wants to communicate with node A in the parent-NEMO, the performance is similar to the performance of two mobile nodes communicating together: packets are not anymore routed to a distant home agent as both tunnels terminates on the closest home agent. The overhead is thus equivalent to the round trip time between the parent mobile router and the home agent. While this could be considered as huge in environments sensible to delay, our proposal do not alter the privacy and the security of the communications as the packets are protected by IPsec between the home agent and the two mobile routers.

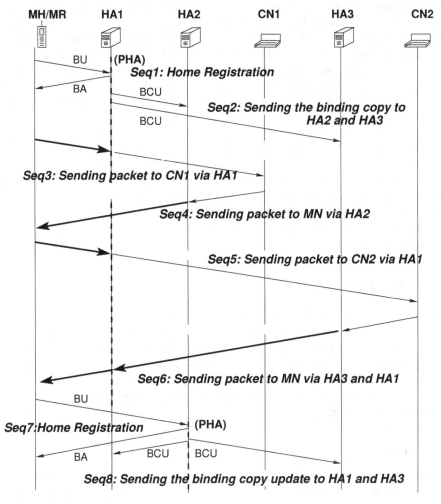

Fig. 6. Multiple Home Agents

Proxy Mobile IPv6. In order to use Proxy Mobile IPv6 with Home Agent Migration, both protocols need to be modified. Indeed, this is not a problem as the former protocol do not require any specific implementation on the client's side, and as the later one only specifies changes on the home agent. Therefore, modifications to these protocols are transparent to clients. First of all, we propose to merge Mobility Anchor Gateway and Local Mobility Anchor functions into a single entity, called LMAG. The LMAG are deployed in the access networks, as a MAG would. Their are interconnected using IPsec tunnels, like home agents in Home Agent Migration. Using these tunnels, the LMAG are able to exchange and synchronize information about the Binding Cache. As they are co-located in the access routers, there is no need to use anycast routing to intercept packets send from the nodes. Moreover, LMAG are not sending Binding Update messages anymore. They are only required to maintain the Binding Cache. As LMAG are now distributed in the network, if one fails, only nodes connected to it will be affected. Nodes in different access networks will still be able to communicate. As LMAG are part of the access routers, they are always on the shortest communication paths between nodes and their correspondents. The route optimization is therefore optimal. Concerning communications from the Internet, one LMAG must be colocated in the network's access router so as to intercept and forward packets destinated to IPv6 nodes behind LMAGs. This architecture is somehow simpler than Home Agent Migration from an operational point of view, however it is able to solve issues related to Proxy Mobile IPv6. Furthermore, it provides an efficient network based mobility solution that only requires modifications on the access routers.

4 Security

Mobile IPv6, its extensions, and Home Agent Migration should not bring new security related issues into the Internet architecture. From its conception, the Mobile IPv6 protocol was developed to limit its impacts on the network and the correspondents. This section initially describes the protection of the communications that should be performed in real life deployments. Moreover, it discusses the security implications of Mobile IPv6, and Home Agent Migration for the network infrastructure.

4.1 IPsec

The communications between a mobile node and its home agent are interesting targets for an attacker. If she manages to inject fake Binding Update messages, he can control the Binding Cache of the home agent, and alter the relation between the Care-of Address and the Home Address. As a result, she is able to retrieve the traffic sent to the mobile node, forbid it to communicate, or redirect its traffic to a target to perform a Denial of Service attack. In order to be protected from this injection, the RFC 3776 [20] defines how IPsec must be used to protect signaling messages[5] as well as the tunnel between the mobile node and the home agent. Real life deployments of Mobile IPv6 outside closed networks can not be done without using IPsec.

In a simple Home Agent Migration deployment, each home agent generates a distinct home agent address from the same home network prefix. Concerning the protection provided by IPsec, this means that every mobile node is pre-configured with four security policies for each Home Agent. Two ensures the

---

[5] Binding Update and Binding Acknowledgment messages.

protection of Binding Update and Binding Acknowledgment, and two others one the protection of the tunnel. The pre-configuration of these policies could be problematic, and could lead to operational issues if home agents are added after the first deployments of mobile nodes.

An advanced deployment of Home Agent Migration could solve this problem. If all the Home Agents share the same IPv6 address, only two security associations must be pre-configured for each mobile node. While promising, this architecture could lead to problems concerning the interaction of the IPsec and Mobile IPv6 stacks especially on the home agent side. In fact, so as to keep the IPsec sessions alive after a movement, the home agent would have to synchronize information about the negotiated security associations. The use of IPsec to secure the distribution system is however much simpler. In order to synchronize the Binding Cache, home agents are interconnected using IPv6-in-IPv6 tunnels in a mesh like fashion. Consequently, if the distribution system includes N home agents, each home agent must be pre-configured with $N-1$ security associations to the other home agents.

Concerning the integration of Mobile IPv6 in the 3GPP2 architecture, a simple authentication mechanism [21] modeled from Mobile IPv4 is preferred to IPsec. Indeed, the implementation and use of IPsec and IKE is considered as being too heavy to be integrated into small devices such as mobile phones. This mechanism is promoted by telecommunications operators as it simplifies the billing when roaming occurs between them. Moreover, operators considers that IPsec is not mandatory in their core networks IPsec if efficient packets filtering is performed.

4.2 Protection of the Infrastructure

The deployment of Mobile IPv6-based protocols is related to their performances as well as their impacts on the network infrastructure. From a security point of view, Mobile IPv6 integrates protection against denial of services, easier filtering capabilities and prevents problems associated with bypassing the ingress/egress filtering [22]. For a network administrator, Mobile IPv6 is a protocol that allows a node to send packets from his network using a source address that do not belong to the prefix of the site. While this could look like a perfect way to bypass filtering that prevents address spoofing, it do not work in practice. Indeed, as the traffic of the mobile node is always transferred via the tunnel, no spoofing occurs and Mobile IPv6 remains compatible with filtering policies.

Amongst the IPv4 options, the ones concerning *source routing* have always be considered as dangerous as they provide easy methods to discover network topologies, or divert firewalls. With IPv6, a similar source routing option is available as a specific extension called Routing Header Type 0 which was recently deprecated as it leads to serious amplification attacks [23]. Mobile IPv6 also uses a routing header, Type 2, that includes limitations that makes it safe[6]. The difference between Type 0 and Type 2 allows a specific filtering on firewalls. A

---

[6] The same discussion applies to the Home Address Option.

network administrator can therefore decide to protect his infrastructure against Type 0 related attacks, and authorize Mobile IPv6 as well. The semantic of the routing header Type 2 was limited: only one address is carried by this extension, and it must correspond to the Home Address of the destination. Moreover, this routing header is not examined by nodes that do not support Mobile IPv6, and its usage is limited to specific packets such as Binding Acknowledgments. Independently of these extensions, specific headers or ICMPv6 codes were defined for Mobile IPv6 to enable a simplified and dedicated filtering.

5   Conclusion

In this paper, we provided detailed descriptions of Mobile IPv6 and its two extensions NEMO and Proxy Mobile IPv6. We have also shown that Home Agent Migration could be reshaped so as to enhance these extensions with no modification of their implementations. We explained that using distributed home agents might not fully optimize every possible scenario deployments of these extensions. However, the achieved performances are sufficient for most customers as optimizations concerns typical uses of these technologies. Furthermore, unlike other proposals, ours remains fully compatible with the use of IPsec with Mobile IPv6 based protocols. Considering network operators, this is an important feature as it allows safe and secure deployments of mobility services on the Internet, as well as billing possibilities.

Future work based around the ideas described in this paper will focus on practical experiments. So far, we only focused our tests on Mobile IPv6, and we would like to perform them with NEMO at first; and then with Proxy Mobile IPv6. In fact, we would like to efficiently quantify the impact of the IPsec on the latency of handovers. Experiments using regular Mobile IPv6 already showed that it is possible to minimize this latency, but more tests need to be performed.

Acknowledgment

The authors would like to thank Arnaud Ebalard for his valuable discussions on IPsec and security related topics.

References

1. Mizuko, I., Okabe, D., Matsuda, M.: Portable, pedestrian: Mobile phones in Japanese life. MIT Press, Cambridge (2005)
2. Johnson, D., Perkins, C., Arkko, J.: Mobility Support in IPv6. RFC 3775, (Proposed Standard) (June 2004)
3. Devarapalli, V., Wakikawa, R., Petrescu, A., Thubert, P.: Network Mobility (NEMO) Basic Support Protocol. RFC 3963, (Proposed Standard) (January 2005)
4. Gundavelli, S., Leung, K., Devarapalli, V., Chowdhury, K., Patil, B.: Proxy mobile ipv6 (work in progress, draft-sgundave-mip6-proxymip6-02). Internet Draft, Internet Engineering Task Force (March 2007)

5. Wakikawa, R., Valadon, G., Murai, J.: Migrating home agents towards internet-scale mobility deployments. In: CoNext06, Lisbonne, Portugal (December 2006)
6. Jang, H., Jee, J., Han, Y., Park, S., Cha, J.: Mobile ipv6 fast handovers over ieee 802.16e networks. Internet Draft, Internet Engineering Task Force (January 2007)
7. Moskowitz, R., Nikander, P.: Host Identity Protocol (HIP) Architecture. RFC 4423, (Informational) (May 2006)
8. Kunishi, M., Ishiyama, M., Uehara, K., Esaki, H., Teraoka, F.: Lin6: A new approach to mobility support in ipv6. In: Wireless Personal Multimedia Communication (WPMC) (November 2000)
9. Ernst, T., Lach, H.: Network Mobility Support Terminology (work in progress, draft-ietf-nemo-terminology-06). Internet Draft, Internet Engineering Task Force (December 2006)
10. Narten, T., Nordmark, E., Simpson, W.: Neighbor Discovery for IP Version 6 (IPv6). RFC 2461 (Draft Standard) Updated by RFC 4311 (December 1998)
11. Wakikawa, R.: Home Agent Reliability Protocol (work in progress, draft-ietf-mip6-hareliability-01.txt). Internet Draft, Internet Engineering Task Force (March 2007)
12. Chambless, B., Binkley, J.: Home agent redundancy protocol (harp) (expired, draft-chambless-mobileip-harp-00.txt). Internet Draft, Internet Engineering Task Force (October 1997)
13. Faizan, J., El-Rewini, H., Khalil, M.: Virtual Home Agent Reliability Protocol (VHAR) (expired, draft-jfaizan-mipv6-vhar-02.txt). Internet Draft, Internet Engineering Task Force (April 2004)
14. Myles, A., Johnson, D.B., Perkins, C.: A Mobile Host Protocol Supporting Route Optimization and Authentication. IEEE Journal on Selected Areas in Communications, special issue on Mobile and Wireless Computing Networks 13(5), 823–849 (1995)
15. Wakikawa, R., Koshiba, S., Uehara, K., Murai, J.: ORC: Optimized Route Cache Management Protocol for Network Mobility. In ICT 2003. IEEE 10th International Conference on Telecommunication, pp. 119–126 (February 2003)
16. Ng, C., Thubert, P., Watari, M., Zhao, F.: Network mobility route optimization problem statement (work in progress, draft-ietf-nemo-ro-problem-statement-03). Internet Draft, Internet Engineering Task Force (September 2006)
17. Ng, C., Thubert, P., Watari, M., Zhao, F.: Analysis of manet and nemo (work in progress, draft-boot-manet-nemo-analysis-01). Internet Draft, Internet Engineering Task Force (June 2007)
18. Clausen, T., Jacquet, P.: Optimized Link State Routing Protocol (OLSR). RFC 3626 (Experimental) (October 2003)
19. Abley, J., Lindqvist, K.: Operation of Anycast Services. RFC 4786 (Best Current Practice) (December 2006)
20. Arkko, J., Devarapalli, V., Dupont, F.: Using IPsec to Protect Mobile IPv6 Signaling Between Mobile Nodes and Home Agents. RFC 3776 (Proposed Standard) Updated by RFC 4877 (June 2004)
21. Patel, A., Leung, K., Khalil, M., Akhtar, H., Chowdhury, K.: Authentication Protocol for Mobile IPv6. RFC 4285 (Informational) (January 2006)
22. Ferguson, P., Senie, D.: Network Ingress Filtering: Defeating Denial of Service Attacks which employ IP Source Address Spoofing. RFC 2827 (Best Current Practice) Updated by RFC 3704 (May 2000)
23. Biondi, P., Ebalard, A.: IPv6 Routing Header Security. In: CanSecWest Security Conference (April 2007)

Experimental Evaluation of EAP Performance in Roaming Scenarios

Saber Zrelli and Yoichi Shinoda

Japan Advanced Institute of Science and Technology
School of Information Science
zrelli,shinoda@jaist.ac.jp

Abstract. The Extensible Authentication protocol (EAP), is the main component of the standard AAA (Authentication Authorization and Accounting) framework for network access control. AAA frameworks support cross-domain authentication that enables a certain access network to authenticate a roaming client that belongs to a remote network. The cross-domain authentication requires message exchange between the AAA server of the visited network and the AAA server of the client's home network. Because these inter-domain exchanges occur over the Internet, they are subject to degradations such as packet loss and network delays thus increasing the overall authentication time. When the client changes of access point, the same authentication procedure takes place again, disrupting the user traffic at each hand-off.

In this paper, we examine the performance of inter-domain EAP authentication in terms of authentication delay using an emulated environment. Moreover, in an effort to understand the performance of Inter-domain authentication over the Internet, we model the authentication time using mathematical approach and we define basis of future research items focusing on the estimation of inter-domain EAP authentication delays.

1   Introduction

Network access control is the process through which network access providers authenticate and authorize users before granting them the service which generally consists of Internet connectivity. In wireless access networks this process takes place during the hand-off which involves three main steps. First, network selection, during which the client discovers access networks and selects the one it wants to use. Second, the authentication takes place using the EAP [1] protocol. Finally, security associations are established between the client and the edge routers of the access network using keying materials resulting from the authentication phase. The EAP authentication thus takes a central part and its performance directly impacts the performance of the overall hand-off process.

S. Fdida and K. Sugiura (Eds.): AINTEC 2007, LNCS 4866, pp. 86–98, 2007.

Authentication of roaming users

If the client has authentication credentials provided by the local access network network, then the authentication of the client can be performed by the network access control framework using local means in the form of a centralized authentication server. This is the case, for example, of a student connecting to the wireless network of her university. The other case consists of the roaming scenario. In this case, the client does not belong to the local access network and does not have authentication credentials verifiable using local means. In roaming scenarios, AAA protocols such as RADIUS [2] and Diameter [3] allow inter-domain collaboration for authenticating visiting users in foreign access networks. The authentication is "proxied" by the local access network and the visiting user is authenticated against an authentication server in the user's home network.

Motivations

Since authentication of visiting users involve inter-domain exchanges, the performance of this operation tightly depend on the performance of the network linking the two domains. If the Internet is used to carry the inter-domain authentication of roaming users, the authentication process may suffer delays depending on the status of the Internet links between the two domains.

The authentication of users for network access is a process that is carried out each time the client attempts to connect to an access node. For a roaming user in a foreign access network, the authentication process that involves the inter-domain exchanges occurs during the hand-off, introducing delays that may augment the overall hand-off delay. This may have a negative effect on real time applications that requires near seamless hand-offs. For this reason, it is important for an operator to evaluate its inter-domain authentication delays in order to estimate the quality of services that it can provide to roaming clients from different remote domains.

Contributions

In this paper, we examine the performance in terms of authentication delays measured as the time required to perform an authentication of a roaming user over the Internet. We consider one of the most popular EAP authentication methods called EAP-PEAPv0 [4]. Moreover, in an effort to understand the performance of Inter-domain authentication over the Internet, we model the authentication time using mathematical concepts. We discuss the different parameters of the model and investigate approaches for estimating them. The ultimate goal of the parameter estimation is to be able to estimate EAP authentication delays using the mathematical model.

Paper Layout

The remaining of this paper is organized as follows, in Section.2 , we introduce general concepts on network access control and EAP authentication. We then describe our experiment design in Section.3. Then, we discuss the experimental results in Section.4. In Section.5, we describe a mathematical model for inter-domain EAP authentication delays. Then in Section.6 we analyze the parameters of the model and explore possible approaches for estimating these parameters. Finally we conclude and discuss future work items in Section.7.

2   Network Access Control for Wireless Networks

Network access control architectures allow an operator to control the access to its network resources by means of authentication and policy enforcement points. The IETF as well as the IEEE has contributed to the standard framework for network access control that we will briefly explain in the following section.

The IEEE 802.11i [5] specification describes how access control is performed in 802.11 networks. A typical network access control infrastructure based on the 802.11i specification employs several other specifications such as the *Extensible Authentication Protocol(EAP)* [1], 802.1X [6] and RADIUS [2]. Within this framework, a wireless station (STA) wishing to access a certain network, would first start by a scanning phase to determine candidate access points (AP). Once an access point is selected, the STA attempts to associate with it. The association process involves authentication of the STA to the AP using the EAP protocol.

As shown in Figure.1, EAP messages between the STA and the AP are carried in 802.1X frames. In the first steps of the EAP conversation, the AP issues an *EAP Identity Request* message to which the STA replies with an *EAP Identity Response* message. The Response message from the STA is relayed to a back-end EAP server that is generally a part of a central AAA server. The EAP messages between the AP and the EAP server are carried over a AAA protocol such as RADIUS [2] or Diameter [3]. When the back-end EAP server receives the EAP Identity Response message, it decides how to authenticate the client. If the client is registered in the local domain, then the EAP server will attempt to authenticate the client using its own resources (LDAP database, Unix password file, etc..). If the client does not belong to the local domain (a roaming client), then the local EAP server will forward the EAP Identity Response message to the EAP server of the client's home domain. The EAP messages between the visited and the home EAP server are carried over AAA protocol such as RADIUS or Diameter. In the remaining of this paper, we only consider the roaming scenario involving inter-domain message exchange between the EAP servers of the visited and the home domain.

When the EAP server in the home domain receives the EAP Identity response message, it chooses which authentication method to use. Then issues an EAP message that encapsulates the first message of the selected authentication method. This EAP message from the home EAP server is relayed by the local EAP server and the AP to the STA. The EAP protocol is thus used to carry authentication methods between the STA (also referred to as EAP peer in this context) and the home EAP server. The STA and the EAP server will exchange several EAP Request and Response messages to execute a certain authentication

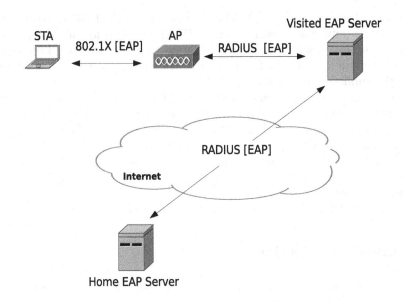

Fig. 1. Network access control in roaming scenarios

protocol. All the EAP messages are relayed by the local access network using the 802.1X (EAP over LAN) protocol at link layer between the STA and the AP on one side, and using a AAA protocol on the other parts of the framework.

After a certain number of EAP messages[1] exchanged between the STA and the home EAP server, the EAP server issues an *EAP Success* message. The EAP Success message indicates successful authentication of the roaming user. The EAP server derives a key called *Master Session Key(MSK)* and send it to the local EAP server. The MSK is secured using a shared key between the home EAP server and the local EAP server. The MSK is then delivered by the local EAP server to the AP over AAA, secured using a shared secret between the AP and the local EAP server. When the AP receives the EAP-Success message and the MSK, the last stage of the 802.11i protocol takes place. The four-way-hand shake phase, allows the STA and the AP to establish a security association based on the MSK. The resulting keying materials are then used to secure the communication at link layer between the two entities.

2.1   The EAP-PEAPv0 Authentication Method

In the experiments that we carried out, we used the EAP-PEAPv0 [4] method with tunneled EAP-MSCHAPv2 [7] authentication. This method uses TLS to secure a password based authentication. In a first step, a TLS security association (SA) is established, the SA is maintained between the client and the EAP server

---

[1] The number of round-trips between the STA and the home EAP server depends on the authentication method in use.

of the visited access network. The client authenticates the EAP server using the EAP server's public key certificate. EAP-PEAPv0 uses a feature of TLS called session resumption, which allows the client to re-use an existing TLS security association with the same EAP server without re-authenticating the EAP server using the public key certificate.

At each hand-off, the client resumes the TLS session with the EAP server, then authenticates using an MSCHAPv2 login and password. Messages between the client and the visited EAP server are protected using the TLS security association while the EAP messages between the EAP server of the visited network and the EAP server of the home network are protected using a shared secret.

The EAP-PEAPv0 method with inner EAP-MSCHAPv2 takes 14 messages at each hand-over, these messages include the TLS session resumption and the EAP-MSCHAPv2 authentication with the home EAP server.

3   Experiment Design

The goal of these experiments is to evaluate the authentication time that takes place between the STA and the home EAP server when the authentication takes place over Internet links. This is the case when the STA is in roaming situation requesting network access in a foreign network topologically distant from the home network. Or when the STA is requesting network access in the home domain but the EAP server is located in remote location that belongs to the home domain.

For this purpose, we used a software emulator to mimic different Internet conditions. We generate the traffic for authenticating a STA to an AP (This traffic corresponds to an EAP conversation carried over the RADIUS protocol) and we place the EAP server on the other side of the emulated Internet.

The traffic generated by the experiment corresponds thus to an EAP authentication where the network characteristics between the access point and the home EAP server are controllable. The experiment allows us to investigate the behavior of the EAP and RADIUS authentication protocols when communication over the Internet is involved for authenticating a client.

Since we are concerned with EAP authentication over the Internet and the communication latency within the local area network is generally negligible compared to the Internet latency, we did not implement a local AAA server or proxy and the access point communicates directly with the home AAA server. The scenario is thus simplified to a STA authenticating through an access point with the home AAA server in a remote location, which is equivalent to a roaming scenario.

The test-bed is composed of three machines, the first machine generates EAP traffic using an open source 802.1X supplicant software called "wpa_supplicant" [8]. This machine emulates the station and the access point in the same time.

We modified the RADIUS library of wpa_supplicant to support granularity in terms of milliseconds rather than seconds for computing re-transmission timers. The first machine is connected to a second machine that emulates the Internet,

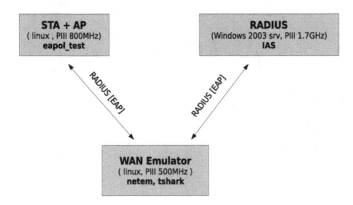

Fig. 2. Design of the experiment test-bed

for that we used netem [9] to emulate packet loss and latency. The third machine acts as the home EAP server, it runs Internet Authentication Server (IAS) on a Microsoft Windows machine. This machine is connected to the emulation box from which it receives RADIUS messages encapsulating the EAP packets.

The emulator machine connects the two machines and acts as an IP router. Each machine is directly connected to one of the emulator's interfaces and the capture is taken at the first machine (the machine that generates the emulated traffic).

The packet loss and latency are applied in equal proportions at the up-link and down-link. In other words, if we setup the emulator for using 10 percent packet loss and 150 milliseconds latency. Practically, this will result in 5 percent packet loss and 75 milliseconds latency in the incoming traffic from each machine to the emulator.

We ran the experiment while using different configurations of packet loss rates and network latency. The packet loss is completely random meaning that the size of loss bursts (number of consecutively lost packets) and the time separating two consecutive bursts are random uniform distributions.

The network latency is fixed before each experiment and has negligible variance during the experiment. When packets are dropped by the emulator, the machine that generates the EAP traffic detects the packet loss and re-sends the packet after a timeout. The re-transmission algorithm is the exponential back-off algorithm. The initial wait time is set manually each time we use different network latency. It is calculated as 150% of the emulated network latency.

4   Experiment Results

We have proceeded with a series of runs. At each run we modified the Internet conditions by changing packet loss rate and latency. In the following, we plot the data that we collected from these runs whilst highlighting some of the observations that we could gather.

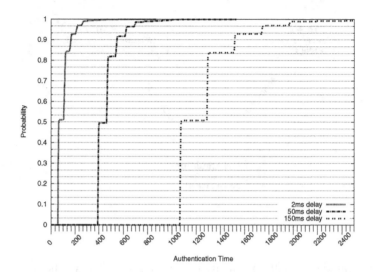

Fig. 3. CDF of Authentication time for EAP-PEAPv0 (10 % packet loss with different network latencies)

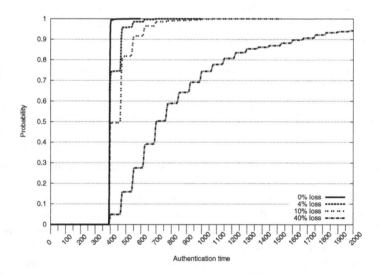

Fig. 4. CDF of Authentication time for EAP-PEAPv0 (50ms RTT, different loss rates)

Each Cumulative Distribution Functions (CDF) in Figure.3 is derived from a capture files where 2000 authentications are logged. The packet loss rate is fixed to 10% while the network latency is changed for each experiment. Figure.3 shows that the authentication time can be considered as a discrete probability distribution. We can observe steps, at different levels (probability = 0.5, 0,83,

0,93, 0.96, 1). We can observe that each CDF is constant at intervals of the same length. The number of intervals is the same amongst all the CDFs. However, each CDF has different interval length.

The stability of network latency and the complete randomness of packet loss in our test-bed contributed to the shape of these CDFs. We could have used different network latency distributions with more variance, this would result in more linear curves. However, in this study we focus on the theoretical under-standing of the EAP authentication time, and for simplicity reasons, we used a stable network latency and a random packet loss.

5   Mathematical Model for the EAP Authentication Time

In the following, we analyze the CDF of EAP-PEAPv0 authentication time and model it as a *step function*. A step function, informally speaking, is a piecewise constant function having only a finite number of pieces. This function can be used to well represent the shape of the CDFs shown in Figure.3. In the remaining of this paper, we take as an example the CDF of the authentication time with 10% packet loss and 150ms latency.

Let "x" be the discrete random variable representing the authentication time and "F(x)" the CDF of the discrete random variable x. F(x) according to Figure.3 is approximatively defined as follows:

$$
\begin{aligned}
0 < x \leq 1075 \quad &, F(x) = 0 \\
1075 < x \leq 1300 &, F(x) = 0.5 \\
1300 < x \leq 1525 &, F(x) = 0.83 \\
1525 < x \leq 1750 &, F(x) = 0.93 \\
1750 < x \leq 1975 &, F(x) = 0.96 \\
1975 < x \quad &, F(x) = 1
\end{aligned}
\tag{1}
$$

We can observe that the CDF is constant in intervals of fixed length of about 225 ms. Let this constant length be "S". Also, we define "A" as the minimum authentication time. According to the CDF we are considering, this corresponds to 1075 ms. Finally, we define "n" as the number or intervals seen in the CDF, in the CDF we are considering, n equals to 6.

We can define a set of interval margins x_i as follows:

$$
\begin{aligned}
&\{x_1 < \ldots < x_n\} \subset \mathbb{R} \\
&Such \quad that: \\
&x_1 = A, \quad x_{i+1} = x_i + S, \forall n \in \mathbb{N} \setminus \{0, 1\},
\end{aligned}
\tag{2}
$$

We can then define a set of intervals Ai as follows:

$$
\begin{aligned}
A_0 &= [0, x_1] \\
A_i &= [x_i, x_{i+1} for (i = 1, \cdots, n-2) \\
A_n &= [x_{n-1}, \infty], \quad Where \quad n = 5
\end{aligned}
\tag{3}
$$

From 1 we define a sequence of coefficients α_i that corresponds to the values of the CDF $F(x)$ in the intervals A_i.

$$
\begin{aligned}
\alpha_1 &= 0 \\
\alpha_2 &= 0.5 \\
\alpha_3 &= 0.83 \\
\alpha_4 &= 0.93 \\
\alpha_5 &= 0.96 \\
\alpha_6 &= 1
\end{aligned}
\tag{4}
$$

Given the notations above, the step function F(x) that represents the CDF is defined as follows:

$$
F(x) = \sum_{i=0}^{n} \alpha_i \cdot 1_{A_i}(x), \quad \forall x \in \mathbb{R}
\tag{5}
$$

Where 1_A, is the *Indicator Function* of the interval A, defined as follows:

$$
1_A(x) = \begin{cases} 1, \text{ if } x \in A \\ 0, \text{ otherwise.} \end{cases}
\tag{6}
$$

6   Prediction and Parameter Estimation

As we have shown in the previous section, given a certain packet loss rate *Loss* and network latency *Lat*, the CDF of the EAP authentication time over RADIUS can be modeled as a step function. The CDF is completely defined by the following parameters:

- The minimal authentication time: "A"
- Interval length: "S"
- The number of intervals "n"
- The sequence of coefficients α_i that corresponds to the value taken by the CDF at the intervals A_i.

In the following, we analyze these parameters one by one and explore possible approaches for estimating their values.

Minimal authentication time

According to Figure.3, the minimal authentication time varies according to the network latency. Theoretically, the minimal authentication time corresponds to the time consumed by an authentication where no packet were lost. This parameter thus does not depend on the packet loss rate. For the EAP-PEAPv0 authentication method, and for a given network latency "Lat"[2], the minimal authentication time "A_{Lat}" is calculated as follows:

---

[2] Network latency in this paper corresponds to round trip time of a packet between the visited and home EAP servers.

$$A_{Lat} = Nbmsg * Lat/2 + PrTime \qquad (7)$$

Where "Nbmsg" is the number of messages exchanged in one authentication. In the case of EAP-PEAPv0, Nbmsg equals 14. The parameter "PrTime" represents the processing time consumed by the communicating parties. In our test-bed, where we used hardware with average performance characteristics, this value is approximatively about 25ms. We can verify, this as follows:

$A_{150} = 14 * 75 + 25 = 1075$ ms
$A_{50} = 14 * 25 + 25 = 375$ ms
$A_{2} = 14 * 1 + 25 = 39$ ms

Interval length
The measured interval length in Figure.3 varies with the network latency. We can observe that the interval length is about 150% of the network latency. This value in fact corresponds to the re-transmission timer (In our experiment, we set the re-transmission timer to 150% of the network latency). Possible values of authentication time take discrete number of values. These values depend on the number of packets lost during the authentication and the burst of packet loss. Each time a packet is lost, the authentication time is augmented with the value of the re-transmission timer. This explains the relation between the interval length and the re-transmission timer. Figure.5 shows for example, that authentications with 0 packet loss and authentications with 1 packet loss are separated with 225ms (which corresponds to 150% of 150ms). When two packets are lost, if the same packet is lost twice (2), the authentication time is equal to an authentication time in the case where three distinct packets were lost (1,1,1).

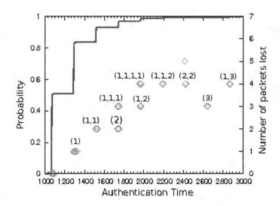

Fig. 5. CDF of authentication time and number of packets lost Vs authentication time for EAP-PEAPv0 (10% packet loss, 150ms latency)

Number of Intervals
In Figure.3 the observable number of intervals is equal to 6 for different latencies. Thus, we can infer that the number of intervals does not depend on the

latency. We could also observe that the number of intervals "6" corresponds to the maximum number of packets lost per authentication, which is equal to "5" as seen in Figure.6, plus 1. Note that the maximum number of lost packets depends on the packet loss rate and is theoretically unbounded. However, as shown in Figure.6, in the specific experiment (10% packet loss rate), the probability of having more that 5 packets lost per authentication is very small (less than 1 in a 1000). This correlation has a large chance of being correct since we can verify it for packet loss of 4%. According to Figure.4, the number of intervals in the CDF (4% packet loss) is 5. Which corresponds to the maximum number of packet loss per authentication with 4% packet loss rate (4 according to Figure.6) incremented by 1. In this paper, we don't demonstrate this correlation, we only point out to observations that can be good starting points for investigating an estimation method of number of intervals in the CDF we want to predict.

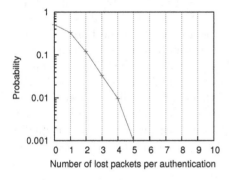

Fig. 6. PDF of number of packets lost per authentication (10% packet loss)

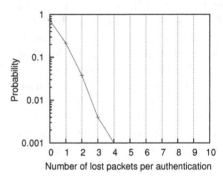

Fig. 7. PDF of number of packets lost per authentication (4% packet loss)

Sequence of probabilities α_i

We can notice from Figure.3 that the set of probabilities α_i is the same for all three CDFs, using different network latencies. We can infer that these parameters depend only on packet loss rates. We can see in Figure.4 that for different packet loss rates, we have different sequences of probabilities α_i.

Moreover, Figure.5 shows that there is a relationship between the number of packets lost and the probabilities α_i. The first element of the sequence, α_0, corresponds to the probability of having an authentication which takes less than the minimum authentication time. In other terms, α_0 is the probability of having less than 0 packets loss, this value is thus always equal to 0. α_1 corresponds to the probability of having an authentication with only one packet loss (1). α_2 corresponds to the probability of having two distinct packets lost during an authentication (1,1). α_3 corresponds to the probability of having three distinct packets lost (1,1,1) or a packet lost twice (2) during an authentication. α_4 corresponds to the probability of having four distinct packets lost (1,1,1,1) or three packets loss where one packet is lost twice (1,2). α_5 corresponds to the probability of having four distinct packets lost (1,1,1,1) or three packets loss where one packet is lost twice (1,2).

A possible approach for estimating the sequence of probabilities α_i would be to first calculate the authentication time for all possible combinations of packet losses. The authentication time is computed by adding round trip times, processing times and re-transmission timers accordingly. Then group combinations of packet losses that resulted in similar authentication time together. For example, combinations (1,1,1) and (2) of packet losses (meaning loosing three distinct packets and loosing the same packet twice) both result in the same authentication time of about 1730ms. These two combinations should be grouped together as a subset. Finally, we calculate the probability of each subset. The resulting probabilities when sorted, should correspond to the sequence α_i.

7   Conclusion

Network access control involves authentication of the client to the access network. The authentication of roaming users require communications between the authentication server of the visited access network and the client's home network. This inter-domain operation that takes place during the hand-off may introduce delays that can impact the quality of service of real time applications.

In this paper, we performed an experimental study of the EAP authentication time when the EAP exchange is carried over Internet links. We used an emulator to mimic the Internet. In this study we focused on one of legacy EAP authentication methods called EAP-PEAPv0. We examined the CDF of the authentication time in different configurations of network loss rate and latency. Finally, we proposed a model of EAP authentication time using a step function. Moreover, we analyzed the different parameters of the model and investigated possible approaches of estimating and calculating these parameters. Through this paper, we elaborated a framework not only for understanding the EAP authentication time over the Internet, but also for building a model and a method for predicting EAP authentication delays.

Some hypothesis made in this paper, are based on observations and common sense reasoning. We estimate that these hypothesis should be verified through more experimental results and comprehensive proofs, before being used as basis of further research.

In our future work, we intend to confirm initial results and observations stated in this paper. For that purpose, we will need to run more experiments that would help to formally express the correlations presented in this paper. Another item of our future work is to investigate solutions for enhancing inter-domain EAP authentication in order to reduce hand-off delays for roaming users.

References

1. Aboba, B., Blunk, L., Vollbrecht, J., Carlson, J., Levkowetz, H.: Extensible Authentication Protocol (EAP). RFC 3748 (Proposed Standard) (June 2004)
2. Rigney, C., Willens, S., Rubens, A., Simpson, W.: Remote Authentication Dia In User Service (RADIUS). RFC 2865 (Draft Standard) Updated by RFCs 2868, 3575 (June 2000)
3. Calhoun, P., Loughney, J., Guttman, E., Zorn, G., Arkko, J.: Diameter Base Protocol. RFC 3588 (Proposed Standard) (September 2003)
4. Kamath, V., Wodrich, M.: Microsoft's peap version 0. Internet draft, IETF (October 2002)
5. 802.11i: Amendment to IEEE std 802.11. part 11: Wireless lan medium access control (mac) and physical layer (phy) specifications–amendment 6: Medium access control (mac) security enhancements. IEEE Standards (2004)
6. 802.1X: IEEE standard for local and metropolitan networks — port-based network access control. IEEE Standards, Revision of 802.1X-2001 (2004)
7. Kamath, V., Palekar, A.: Microsoft eap chap extensions. Internet draft, IETF (September 2002)
8. Malinen, J.: Linux WPA Supplicant. Web page (As of July 2007), http://hostap.epitest.fi
9. Hemminger, S.: Network emulation with netem. Technical report, Open Source Development Lab (April 2005)

Unidirectional Lightweight Encapsulation with Header Compression for IP Based Satellite Communication over DVB-S

Chee-Hong Teh[1], Tat-Chee Wan[2], Rahmat Budiarto[3], and Way-Chuang Ang[4]

Network Research Group, School of Computer Sciences, Universiti Sains Malaysia,
11800, Minden, Penang, Malaysia
{chteh@,tcwan,rahmat,wcang}nav6.org

Abstract. The Multi-Protocol Encapsulation (MPE) is a standard method for encapsulating IP packets into MPEG-2 TS frames. However MPE has some disadvantages in simplicity and efficiency to support next generation network. The Unidirectional Lightweight Encapsulation (ULE) is a new solution to overcome limitations of MPE. In ULE, packets are layered directly into the payload field of MPEG-2 TS frames. This is a new encapsulation method for the transport of IPv4 and other network protocol packets directly over MPEG-2 TS. In this paper, we describe the principles and the benefits of ULE and we also proposed Robust Header Compression Scheme to work with ULE in order to enhance the performance of existing ULE. This paper also provides a simulation analysis to show that the new proposed method can offer a better performance in delay, throughput and overhead especially when the packet size is small.

1 Introduction

ULE [1] is a recently published standard. A ULE packet is layered directly into the payload field of MPEG-2 TS frame. This is a new encapsulation method to transport IPv4 and IPv6 datagrams and other network protocol packets directly over ISO MPEG-2 TS [2] as TS Private Data. ULE also supports DVB architecture [3], the Advanced Television Systems Committee (ATSC) system and other similar MPEG-2 based transmission systems.

ULE can encapsulate various PDUs [1], such as IP packets, Ethernet frames or packets from other network protocol as Subnetwork Data Units (SNDU) by adding a SNDU header to the given PDU. The resulting SNDU will then be sent as the payload part of a MPEG-2 TS packet.

However, the efficiency of ULE still can be improved. It is because the Internet packets still contribute significant overhead for small packet. It is possible to compress those headers and thus save the bandwidth and use the expensive resource efficiently. Header compression is a technique that compresses excess header before transmitting them on a link and uncompressing them to their original state by de-compressor at the receiver.

S. Fdida and K. Sugiura (Eds.): AINTEC 2007, LNCS 4866, pp. 99–113, 2007.
© Springer-Verlag Berlin Heidelberg 2007

2   The Concept of Header Compression

Before a packet is transmitted over a network, each protocol layer appends its own control information into a packet in form of a header. The concept of header compression is to reduce the header sizes of a packet that transmit over the network. The header of the packet can be reduced because there is significant redundancy in the packet header [5,6]. The redundancy is due to the fact that the fields in subsequent packets are duplicated for a particular packet stream.

The reduction in header sizes will help to increase the packets transmission efficiency. Efficiency is important when the cost of transmission is high. Examples include satellite links where the cost of the satellite bandwidth is high. Low transmission efficiency will affect other services that are unable to get required network capacity. In addition, reducing packet overheads can also reduce the transit delay of packets across the link.

Compression and decompression can be performed at the presentation layer to improve the data throughput. However in order to improve the transmission efficiency, the compression and decompression must be performed at the link layer. When a packet is transmitted over a network, static header information for the packet is sent only at the initial stage, while for dynamic fields are updated only when necessary. The trade off is in term of the computational cost, because an algorithm is needed to perform the packet header compression and decompression. In addition, it also requires additional processor hardware and may introduce extra delay. In some scenarios, this cost is acceptable compared to the cost of the bandwidth and the improvement in transmission efficiency.

3   RObust Header Compression (ROHC) Scheme

The ROHC scheme is the new header compression scheme. It was standardized and developed by the ROHC Working Group of the Internet Engineering Task Force (IETF). This compression schemes is developed for error-prone environments by utilizing feedback mechanisms. The feedback mechanisms consist of error detection and a correction mechanism, making ROHC robust against bit errors for IP data based streams.

The ROHC is a scheme that is able to compress many type of header, such as IP, UDP, RTP and TCP headers. ROHC is more robust on links with high BER and long round trip time (RTT). It can achieve higher compression ratio on the packet header and thus is more efficient than other header compression schemes. Even though ROHC is more complex than other header compression schemes like IP header compression and Van Jacobson compression, it is suitable for satellite networks where radio spectrum is a very expensive resource; in comparison, processing power is very cheap. Implementation or computational simplicity of a header compression scheme is therefore of less importance than its compression ratio and robustness.

The proposed approach to enhance the current ULE encapsulation mechanism is to establish a compressor and decompressor at the sender and receiver side.

Figure 1 below is to show the protocol stack for ULE with ROHC. With ROHC, the number of the SNDU can fit into MPEG-2 TS packet will be significantly increased. The size of the SNDU will be smaller because the IP packet header is replaced by a shorter ROHC header before ULE encapsulate the IP packet into SNDU. In this paper, we only focus on the compression and decompression for IPv4 packets.

As shown at Figure 1, the ROHC is located in the standard protocol stack between the IP-based network layer and link layer, just before the ULE encapsulator. The need for saving bandwidth is limited to the satellite link from the ground station terminal to the satellite. In the simplest configuration, the ground station terminal from each side, sender and receiver will have the compressor and the decompressor. The compression and decompression must only work between these two terminals and for the rest of the Internet, this operation remains invisible.

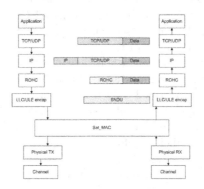

Fig. 1. Protocol Stack for ULE with ROHC

The word Robust in ROHC does not mean that the compressed traffic will be more robust than uncompressed traffic. But in fact, the compressed packet will normally offer a smaller target for bit errors. In order to achieve this goal, the ROHC compressor and decompressor need to communicate between themselves. However, the ROHC does not always work at the peak of its compression capacity. It is because sometimes the compressor needs to sacrify compression gain in order to keep the decompressor synchronized when error occurs on the link [10]. So in order to keep the tight interaction between compressor and decompressor on different level of compression and decompression, a state machine is established to increase the confident about the correctness of the initialization of the static header field and dynamic header field.

4   Use of ROHC with ULE over Uni-directional Links

In this section, the focus is on the performance of ROHC, U-mode. There are some compression parameters which need to be set in order to analyse the performance of the proposed solution-ULE with ROHC. However, the optimal values of these compression parameters were not specified in [5]. In order to analyse the parameters and how they affect the performance of ULE with ROHC, a set of simulations to simulate ULE with ROHC U-mode were performed. The compression parameters used in the simulations were varied to determine the best results. Through these simulations, some possible optimal values or best key parameters that determine the efficiency and robustness of ULE with ROHC could be defined. Henceforth, the ROHC compressor will be denoted by COMP whereas the decompressor will be denoted by DECOMP.

It should be noted that there are three compression and decompression states in ROHC which makes ROHC compression very robust and efficient. In U-mode, due to the lack of the feedback from the DECOMP, the transition between COMP states are performed based on parameters configured in COMP itself. As explained in Chapter 2 section 2.7.4, the three compression states at COMP are IR, FO and SO. During IR state, COMP will send all the static and non-static fields of the packet header to establish the DECOMP CONTEXT. While during FO state, partially compressed packet which contains information about the non-static or dynamic fields of the packet header will be sent. Finally, the full compressed packet will be sent when the COMP reach SO state.

In ROHC, the compression must start in U-mode [5], the transition between compression states are performed only on account of periodic refreshes as depicted in Figure 2. In [5], it was mentioned that the compressor will not transit to a higher compression state unless the compressor is fairly confident that the DECOMP has received sufficient information, and able to decompress the packets correctly. According to Figure 2, a transition between states happen when the COMP has consecutively sends out N packets at the corresponding states, but in [5], it does not specify or define the values for N and Refresh Rate.

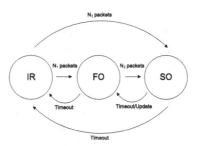

Fig. 2. State Machine of U-mode Compressor

To optimize the performance of ULE with ROHC for UDP traffic in MPEG-2 TS networks, two types of performance metrics were used as the benchmark for comparison, average lengths of the compressed headers and packet loss rate. First, the average length of compressed header for ULE in ROHC was investigated using different sets of parameters. The values of N were tested first. N is number of packets that have been decompressed correctly by DECOMP before transition between states happen. The best value of N was determined by running a series of simulations. The error conditions and long round trip time in satellite link were included in the simulation. According to [5], it is possible to start the transition after at least one packet has been correctly decompressed by DECOMP. Hence it is possible to configure the value $N_1 = N_2 = N_3 = 1$, but it is too optimistic if N =1 is used in normal satellite link where errors usually occur. Thus, a series of simulations were run to investigate the possible optimal values of N. In the simulations, the N_3 was omitted from the experiment because the fast operation mode (transitions from the IR state to the SO state directly, bypassing the FO state) could only be used in an error free satellite links. For this research project, the focus is on normal satellite links, where the BER of the satellite links is taken into account.

The result of different values of N on Average Compressed Header Length in ideal error free satellite link is shown in Figure 3. The result shows that the smaller the value of N, the smaller average compressed header length can be achieved. However, when the Refresh Rate was increasing, the average compressed header length for each different values of N become insignificant and nearly become constant after Refresh Rate exceeds 200 packets. From Figure 3, the N parameter contributes only a little to the average compressed header length when the Refresh Rate increase. It shows that parameter N only slightly affected the packet header length when the Refresh Rate was increasing. The rest of the following simulation, the value of N will be considered as a constant value of 3. This is because by using a higher value of N, it can increase the robustness of ULE with ROHC without contributed significant header length to the packet especially when the Refresh Rate is beyond 200 packets.

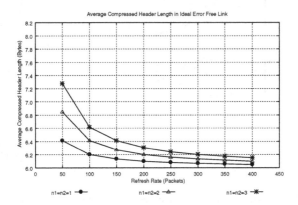

Fig. 3. Average Compressed Header Length in Ideal Error Free Link

The BER of satellite links can produce errors in compressed header. These errors in compressed header might generate a single packet loss or consecutive packets loss. A consecutive packets loss might also causing loss of packets that carry update information, and all of these errors will trigger another serious problem which is loss of CONTEXT synchronization. These errors can lead to the bad performance of the ULE with ROHC. Thus, a set of optimized parameters of ULE with ROHC needs to be defined to confront with these errors through simulation experiments. In the coming section, types of errors that will be tested in the simulation are:

1. Single Packet Drop
2. Consecutive packets drop
3. Propagation Error (Context damage)

4.1 Single and Consecutive Packet Loss with No Error Propagation

The ULE with ROHC U-mode over MPEG-2 TS networks will be studied under the condition where errors occur to the satellite link. In order to study the impact of errors in satellite link for U-mode, different error rate (BERs) will be applied in the simulation. The error model applied in the simulator generated errors affecting the header and the payload of the packets, causing packet corruption at the physical layer during the transmission in satellite link. Such packets received by the receiver will be dropped by the upper layers. Figure 4 depicts the Average Header Length of packet header over different error rate links.

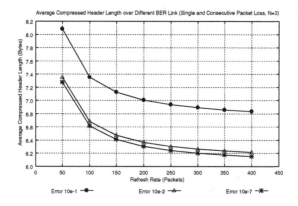

Fig. 4. Average Compressed Header Length in Different BER Link for N=3

In Figure 4, it shows that with a constant value of N=3, all the 3 different error rate show that the Average Compressed Header Length became shorter when the Refresh Rate value was increasing. From Figure 4, it also shows that when errors are applied on the link, the overall Average Compressed Header Length was slightly higher than the ideal error free link shown in Figure 3. This was because some burst errors occurred and caused a few packets loss occurred. The packets loss caused the DECOMP was unable to decompress the received packets correctly. Fortunately with the W-LSB encoding method, for a condition where only a few packets loss occurred, the DECOMP was assumed still able to decompress the newly received compressed packet correctly. This explains why the Average Compressed Header Length in Figure 3 is shorter than the Figure 4, but the difference was not so significant except for the error rate 1×10^{-1}. Thus, by assuming that a massive consecutive packets loss didnt occur during the transmission and the link errors didnt damage the CONTEXT packet while refreshing the DECOMP, ULE with ROHC would still be able to achieve a lower header length when the Refresh Rate was increasing.

4.2 Consecutive Packet Loss with Error Propagation

Although ULE with ROHC scheme is robust against errors, ULE with ROHC itself also has a drawback. For a DECOMP to decompress the compressed packet correctly, the CONTEXT in the DECOMP should contains the correct information for decompression. If the first loss events with a CONTEXT caused the decompression information in DECOMP to become unsynchronized with COMP, the decompression of the subsequent packets would be dropped or discarded at upper layer due to checksum error. This effect can be referred as Error Propagation. The effect of the Error Propagation in ULE with ROHC is depicted in Figure 5. The solution for Error Propagation in uni-directional link is to retransmit the uncompressed packet at regular intervals. The periodically retransmitted uncompressed packet to DECOMP was able to reduce the effect of Error Propagation, but this approach has a trade-off between compression efficiency and robustness. It is undeniable that higher Refresh Rate will reduce error propagation, but a too frequent transmission of uncompressed packet to restore the DECOMP CONTEXT will also reduce the compression efficiency. Although Error Propagation can severely degrade the compression efficiency, this can be countered by the proper choice of Refresh Rate. To study how to set these parameters, the ULE with ROHC was examined under different error conditions and Refresh Rates. The Average Compressed Header Length and Packet Drop Rate were defined as the metrics for comparison in this experiment. The results of the simulation were presented in Figure 5 and Figure 6.

Average Compressed Header Length. From Figure 5, it shows that when the link BER is too high, and Error Propagation occurred, the Average Compressed Header Length will increase rapidly when the Refresh Rate value was getting larger. This is because the ratio of incorrectly decompressed by DECOMP is high due to the Error Propagation. This shows that when CONTEXT corrupted due to the Error Propagation, the smaller the Refresh Rate is, the more robust it can be. For BER value of 1×10^{-7} (the average error rate of the common satellite link), the Average Compressed Header Length was decreasing slightly when Refresh Rate is increasing. In contrast, the result of BER of 1×10^{-1} shows the opposite behaviour.

From this experiment, it was shown that with different BER levels, Refresh Rate has contributed different compression efficiency to ULE with ROHC

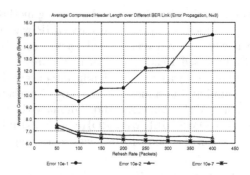

Fig. 5. Effect of Error Propagation on Average Compressed Header Length for N=3

U-mode. For the case of satellite link where the common error rate is 1 x 10^{-7}, the Average Compressed Header Length remains almost the same at the higher Refresh Rate such as 200, 250,...,400. Since the Average Compressed Header Length remains the same at higher Refresh Rate, it is recommended to use higher Refresh Rate. Based on the result in Figure 5, the Refresh Rate = 200 is advisable. The highest Refresh Rate was not selected because the compression efficiency and robustness must be balanced for ULE with ROHC. The robustness of the ULE with ROHC should not be scarified when selecting the optimized value for compression efficiency. This will be explained in more details in the next section.

Packet Drop Rate. Refresh Rate is one of the most important parameter contributing to Packet Drop Rate. It is because when consecutive packets loss occurred, and additionally if there are no other recovery mechanisms to prevent the Error Propagation, re-synchronized the CONTEXT between COMP and DECOMP can prevent the value of Packet Drop Rate getting increased. In Packet Drop Rate experiments, consecutive packets loss and Propagation Error is enabled when a different Refresh Rate in error links were used. The result of Packet Drop Rate of ULE with ROHC was presented in Figure 6.

According to Figure 6, note that for BER is 1 x 10^{-1} the Packet Drop Rate increased dramatically when the Refresh Rate was increasing. This shows that, when the CONTEXT was damaged, large number of packets were lost if a large Refresh Rate value was chosen. For the BER is 1 x 10^{-7}, the Packet Loss Rate achieved was almost 0. This was because at the low BER value, the probability of CONTEXT damage on the link was also very low.

The BER of satellite link varies over the time due to the satellite movement and multi-path fading. In the worse case, the BER in satellite link might be very high and Propagation Error might also happen. In such a case, if a large Refresh Rate value is chosen, it can cause a large number of packets drop. This problem diminished when a smaller value of Refresh Rate which is Refresh Rate =200 was selected. The Refresh Rate = 200 is sufficiently large, and able to prevent

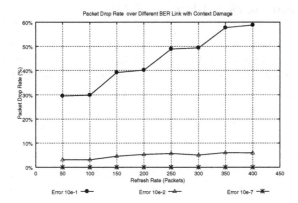

Fig. 6. Packet Drop Rate over Different BER Link with Context Damage

the consecutive undamaged packets drop too seriously. This explained why the highest Refresh Rate has not been selected in the previous section.

Conclusion of ULE with ROHC Parameters Evaluation. Compression efficiency clearly decreases when a smaller Refresh Rate is chosen. In the experiments, it shows that there were many parameters can affect the performance of ULE with ROHC. The bandwidth efficiency could be improved when more compressed header packets are sent especially in SO state, but it will also suffer from consecutive undamaged packets drop due to the occasional CONTEXT damage. Thus, to guarantee robustness, uncompressed packet in IR and FO state should be sent periodically.

As conclusion, one can see is different compression parameters can affect the performance of ULE with ROHC, when a short Refresh Rate is chosen, it resulted in a high robust performance, but unfortunately, it also degraded the bandwidth efficiency. Thus, in term of the robustness of ULE with ROHC, the efficient use of bandwidth should be taken into account. Therefore, based on the results of the experiments, a suitable values of N=3 is defined. In addition, the balance point for the values of ULE with ROHC parameters should be chosen based on the condition of the links. For the case of satellite links, Refresh Rate = 200 packets is proposed. This set of optimized compression parameters are expected to improve the ULE with ROHC performance in terms of compression efficiency and robustness for GEO satellite links.

The raw BER experienced in a GEO satellite links were in the order of 1 x 106−2 for 4.5 meters satellite dish of C-band Earth Station operated by the USM Network Research Group. However, all satellite data transmission is protected using suitable coding schemes such as Forward Error Correction (FEC), Reed Solomon (RS), and turbo codes. For USM link, it was protected using FEC $^3/_4$ and RS with 8PSK modulation, the resultant BER was 1 x 10^{-7} to 1 x 10^{-12} which is comparable to terrestrial network link.

5   Improvement of ULE with ROHC

The discussion in the previous section provides fruitful information on how to set compression parameters of ULE with ROHC to accommodate the ULE with ROHC in GEO satellite link. In this section, we will present the result from the simulation of the ULE with ROHC using the simulation configuration. This research project is analyzed using *ns2* [11] simulation tool. The existing satellite network model in *ns2* was selected as a simulation model for this research. There is an IP traffic source located behind the satellite terminal and traffic is transmitted to another satellite terminal via satellite. The simulation model that been used for study is shown in Figure 7 and it is a simple satellite access network. The fixed point to point satellite simulation model was chosen because it is a more simple approach and cut down on simulation time or complexity of the simulation, but it is sufficient for our research purpose. The traffic considered in this research is UDP traffic and it could be a voice over IP services in upper application.

In the simulation, the CBR traffic was chosen as voice traffic. The simulations were run with a different number of CBR traffic sources and CBR packet size in order to simulate various traffic loads.

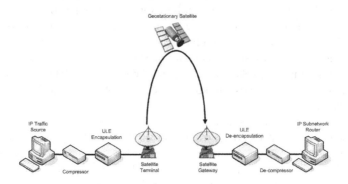

Fig. 7. Simulation Model

The results of the simulation are presented in Figure 8 to Figure 11 and discussions of the results of ULE with ROHC U-Modes are presented along with the simulation in the latter section. As can be seen from the Figure 8, ULE with ROHC has shown a better Average One Way Delay. Network delay can be affected by several different factors, such as congestion of network, transmission delay, queuing delay and others. From Figure 8(a), Average One Way Delay for ULE and ULE with ROHC is slightly reduced when the CBR transmission rate was increasing. As expected, when the traffic generation rate was increasing, the time for router to forward the packet is faster; thus, the bandwidth of the link was much greater than packet generation rate, it will show a reduction on the Average One Way Delay. However, when the CBR traffic generation rate was increasing and approaching the link capacity, the Average One Way Delay of the packets were substantially increased. This explained why the Average One Way Delay for ULE and ULE with ROHC reduced at the early stage and increased tremendously at the end.

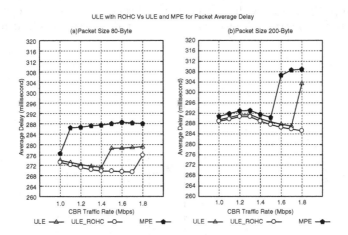

Fig. 8. Average Delay for UDP Packet with Different Encapsulation Mechanism, Traffic Generation Rate and Traffic Source

The ULE with ROHC had achieved a lower Average One Way Delay especially when packet sizes are small. Clearly, this is because after the compression of the packet headers, the packets are smaller than the original packets size. As a result, it will reduce the delay of packets transmission due to more SNDU packets can be inserted to MPEG-2 TS payload. Moreover, when the traffic generation rate was increasing, the Average One Way Delay for ULE with ROHC still performed better than ULE and MPE. This is because at the same rate of traffic generation, the packet size with header compression is relatively smaller than others without header compression.

However, the difference of the Average One Way Delay between ULE, ULE with ROHC and MPE are not significant when the packets size were increasing. This is expected because of the small ratio of packet header to the size of payload. When the packet payload size was increasing, the impact of the packet overhead is small and the transmission time for large packets is almost the same using different encapsulation mechanism. Hence the Average One Way Delay for these packets is almost similar.

The effect of the encapsulation mechanism on packet loss is another important parameter that is examined. The results in Figure 9 show that ULE with ROHC offer a better performance than ULE and MPE in heavy traffic load network environment. The results from the simulation also show that network congestion is the primary factor of the packet drop. The simulation results show that when the CBR rate was increasing, the number of packet drop also increased, especially for the small size packets. This is due to the fact that the UDP is not like TCP, the UDP doesnt has a network congestion control mechanism that can throttle the sender when the network become excessively congested. As a result, UDP traffic will still keep generating traffic at a constant rate without taking the network condition into consideration. MPE and ULE experience an earlier packet drops than ULE with ROHC. This is because with header compression, packets can be compressed into smaller size; it reduced the bandwidth required on the network.

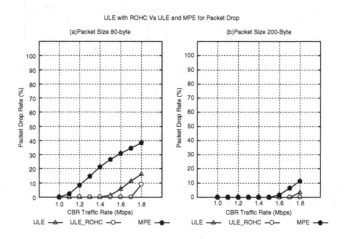

Fig. 9. Number of Packet Drop for UDP Packet with Different Encapsulation Mechanism, Traffic Generation Rate and Traffic Source

In addition, ULE with ROHC achieved lower packet drop compare to ULE and MPE (Figure 9). There are few processes before a UDP packet can be transmitted over the satellite link. Before the UDP packets are sent to the next layer for encapsulation, these packets are placed in the queue on particular node. The encapsulator will take the packet from the queue, encapsulate it and insert the encapsulated packet into MPEG-2 TS payload. When the packet generation rate of CBR was increasing, a large number of UDP packets arrived at the node, making the queue fulled. The number of encapsulated packets that can be inserted into MPEG-2 TS payload is limited due to the size of the MPEG-2 TS packet payload is constant at 184-byte. The encapsulator needs to wait for next new MPEG-2 TS packet to transmit the next UDP packets. This explained why the packets were seriously dropped when network congestion occurred.

Next, the comparison of Average Throughput for ULE, MPE and ULE with ROHC will be shown in Figure 10. The results of the simulation demonstrated that the ULE with ROHC has produced significant improvement of Average Throughput compared to ULE and MPE. The Average Throughput of ULE with ROHC was evaluated in both Single and Triple Simultaneous UDP Streams Traffic. Simulation results showed that ULE with ROHC has achieved 33% higher

Average Throughput than ULE and MPE for both Single and Triple Simultaneous UDP Streams Traffic when packet size is 80-byte. ULE with ROHC has achieved higher Average Throughput because by using ROHC, it can compress the packet header into smaller size, and therefore increased the amount of packet that can be sent through a single MPEG-2 TS in a given time period.

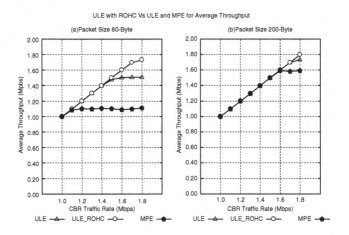

Fig. 10. Average Throughput for UDP Packet with Different Encapsulation Mechanism, Traffic Generation Rate and Traffic Source

The behaviour of the Average Throughput for Single UDP Stream Traffic with various packet sizes and packet generation rates were first evaluated. Figure 10 shows the measured Average Throughput as a function of the packet generation rate for UDP stream. According to Figure 10(a), it can be seen that both ULE and ULE with ROHC had achieved good Average Throughput when packet size is 80-byte. As shown in Figure 10, when the packet generation rate was increasing, the Average Throughput of the ULE, MPE and ULE with ROHC was increased at a linear rate but then they reach their highest Average Throughput at certain point. Then the Average Throughput for ULE, MPE and ULE with ROHC had remained at a constant level.

The UDP traffic was injected to the network at constant and fixed rate, as long as the bandwidth still able to accommodate the UDP traffic, the Average Throughput increased in linear pattern. Among the three encapsulation mechanisms, MPE achieved the lowest throughput especially for small packet size. Though the bandwidth of satellite link is 2Mbps, MPE for packet size 80-byte (Figure 10(a)) remained constant at 1.2 Mbps. The MPEs Average Throughput cant go up further is due to the early packet drop at the encapsulator queue. However, when the packet size was increasing, the difference of Average Throughput among these three encapsulation mechanism is not significant, but in generally for Average Throughput performance, the ULE with ROHC still achieved higher Average Throughput than other encapsulation mechanisms.

We next investigated the comparison of overhead percentage for ULE, MPE and ULE with ROHC. The comparison results will be shown in Figure 11. It can be seen that the ULE with ROHC had achieved a better Overhead performance when the packet size was small. However this Overhead performance was not significant when the packet size was increasing.

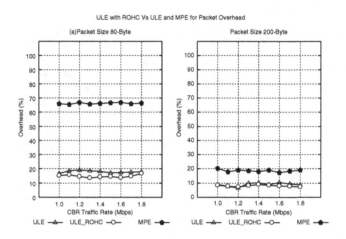

Fig. 11. Overhead for UDP Packet with Different Encapsulation Mechanism, Traffic Generation Rate and Traffic Source. Packet Size.

In Figure 10(a), we can observe that the ULE with ROHC is achieving a better overhead when the packet is relatively small in size. In comparison, ULE, MPE and ULE with ROHC achieve a similar overhead when CBR packet size is 200 bytes which is shown in Figure 10(b). This indicates that impact of the header compression on a large size packet has a little improvement on overhead and it also indicates that the packet size after the header compression is similar to the original size. Header compression only provides largest gain when the ratio of payload size to packet header size is small, thus ULE with ROHC provides significant benefits with small packets.

6   Conclusion and Future Work

We first present some improvements of the ULE encapsulation mechanism. We have presented our solutions on IP datagrams transmission over DVB-S networks that combine ULE encapsulation mechanism and ROHC header compression scheme. We have proposed to compress the packet before encapsulated by ULE in order to reduce the overhead of the packet, at the same time to increase the efficiency of the ULE encapsulation mechanism. We have introduced ROHC to reduce the header sizes of a packet that transmit over the network because there is a significant redundancy fields in the packet header before ULE encapsulate the IP packet to become SNDU. In other words, we are sending the header-compressed unicast packet over DVB-S using ULE. The overhead of headers, especially UDP packet over DVB-S using ULE is a main focus. With ROHC, the number of the SNDU packet can fit into MPEG-2 TS packet will significant increase, and it will help to increase the efficiency of the packets transmission.

In the next generation internet, the current IPv4 will soon replace by IPv6. The main difference between IPv6 packet and IPv4 packet is their length of network addresses. IPv6 addresses are 128 bits long, whereas IPv4 addresses are 32 bits long. Solution like header compression need to be implemented in order to reduce this expanded header. IPv6 datagram over MPEG2-TS in DVB-S network using ULE with ROHC can be a good future work of this research.

References

1. Fairhurst, G., et al.: Unidirectional Lightweight Encapsulation (ULE) for Transmission of IP Datagrams over an MPEG-2 Transport Stream (TS) [Online]. RFC 4326. IETF (2005) [Accessed 23th Feb 2006]. Available from World Wide Web: http://www.ietf.org/rfc/rfc4326.txt?number=4326
2. ISO/IEC, 13818-1: 2005. Information Technology - Generic Coding of Moving Pictures and Associated Audio Information. Part 1: Systems. Switzerland: International Organization for Standardization and International Electrotechnical Commission (1994)
3. EBU & ETSI: EN 300 421 v1.1.2.: Digital Video Broadcasting (DVB): Framing structure, channel coding and modulation for 11/12 GHz satellite services. France: European Broadcasting Union & European Telecommunication Standards Institutes (1997)
4. Deering, S.: Internet Protocol, Version 6 (IPv6) Specification, [Online]. RFC 2460. IETF (1998) [Accessed 12th October 2006]. Available from World Wide Web: http://www.ietf.org/rfc/rfc0768.txt?number=2460
5. Bormann, C., et al.: RObust Header Compression (ROHC): Framework and four profiles: RTP, UDP, ESP, and uncompressed [Online]. RFC 3095. IETF (2001) [Accessed 1st March 2006]. Available from World Wide Web: http://www.ietf.org/rfc/rfc3095.txt?number=3095
6. Matyasovszki, I., et al.: Packet Level Symbiosis. In: IEEE INFOCOM 2005. Poster/Demo Session (2005)
7. Packet Size Distributions (2004) [Online]. [Accessed 3rd March 2006]. Available from World Wide Web:
   http://ipmon.sprint.com/packstat/viewresult.php?0:pktsz:sj-20.0-040206
8. Fraleigh, C., et al.: Packet-Level Traffic Measurements from the Sprint IP Backbone. IEEE Network 17(6), 6–16 (2003)
9. Thompson, K., et al.: Wide-Area Internet Traffic Patterns and Characteristics. IEEE Network 11(6), 10–23 (1997)
10. Fitzek, F., et al.: Header Compression Schemes for Wireless Internet Access. In: Wireless Internet: Technologies and Applications, pp. 10.1–10.24. CRC Press, Florida (2004)
11. Fall, K., Varadhan, K.: The ns Manual [Online]. [Accessed 22th July 2005] (2006) Available from World Wide Web:
    http://www.isi.edu/nsnam/ns/ns-documentation.html

Analysis of FEC Function for Real-Time DV Streaming

Kazuhisa Matsuzono, Hitoshi Asaeda, Kazunori Sugiura,
Osamu Nakamura, and Jun Murai

Graduate School of Media and Governance
Keio University, 252-8520 Kanagawa, Japan
{kazuhisa,asaeda,uhyo,osamu,jun}@sfc.wide.ad.jp

Abstract. Due to the dissemination of high speed DSL and FTTH, real-time streaming applications transmitting high quality audio and video data have been commonly used on the Internet. These applications usually have strict requirements on delay and packet loss. However, it is difficult to fully satisfy the requirements in general, since the end users cannot guarantee the streaming quality on the best-effort Internet. In this paper, we investigate an FEC (Forward Error Correction) function on DV streaming. We study the relation between network bandwidth and FEC recovery rate upon data transmission, and the receiver's play quality and FEC calculation cost. Our experimental results given on top of our testbed network show that the FEC function can provide the best possible streaming quality, without leading the further disruption of video and audio irrespective of the available network bandwidth.

Keywords: DVTS, real-time streaming, FEC (Forward Error Correction), streaming quality.

1 Introduction

Recently, real-time streaming applications have been commonly used in the Internet. Due to the widespread dissemination of high speed DSL and FTTH, the demands of transmitting high quality audio and video data have been also increased. The real-time applications require stable data tramsissions to keep the streaming quality. However, it is impossible to preclude the possibility of data transmission delay and packet loss on the best-effort Internet.

As a high quality real-time streaming applications, we consider Digital Video Transport System (DVTS) [1,2] used in various research comunities. DVTS contributes to end users to play with the DV transmision over IP, because it simply uses general consumer products which support a DV format, and does not require any professional equipment. However, DVTS consumes 30Mbps for its transmission and requires high speed networks for the DV transmission. Since the current Internet is heterogeneous and does not guarantee the Quality of Service (QoS), end users must take into account network congestion that causes the disruption of video and audio upon its use.

S. Fdida and K. Sugiura (Eds.): AINTEC 2007, LNCS 4866, pp. 114–122, 2007.
© Springer-Verlag Berlin Heidelberg 2007

As the possible approach, for keeping a stable streaming quality, a sender must dynamically adjust the transport method according to the network condition. Yet, deciding the appropriate transmission method like a reduction of consumption bandwidth, Automatic Repeat reQuest (ARQ), and Forward Error Correction (FEC), is a real challenge for a real-time streaming.

Real-time streaming is usually transmitted over RTP [3] carried on top of UDP and IP, and RTCP [3] sent with RTP supports "Rate Control" as one of the fundamental functions to adjust the transmission rate based on the capacity of the available bandwidth or to adapt to network congestion. ARQ is used to recover packet loss by retransmitting the lost packet. In real-time streaming, however, low transmission delay is very important, and a sender and a receiver cannot use a large amount of buffer. Therefore, real-time streaming cannot often apply ARQ. There is another technology, by which a sender adds redundant data to its steam and a receiver detects and corrects errors being happened during transmission without the need to ask the sender for additional data. As its typical approach, a "Forward Error Correction (FEC)" algorithm [4,5] has been notably used in various applications.

Our motivation is to make an adaptive rate control mechanism for smooth DV streaming in an end-to-end communication model. By the ideal mechanism, according to the network condition, a sender adjusts both frame rate and FEC encoding rate to provide a stable quality for end users and utilize network resources.

In this paper, as the first step for our motivation, we investigate FEC function on DV streaming that keeps a stable quality. We then study the relation between the network bandwidth and FEC recovery rate upon data transmission in a congested network, and the relation between the receiver's play quality and FEC calculation cost. Our experimental results on top of our testbed network shows that FEC function can provide the best possible streaming quality, without leading the further disruption of video and audio irrespective of the available network bandwidth.

2   Digital Video Streaming

2.1   Transport Method

In an end-to-end communication model, real-time streaming generally tries to keep a stable quality irrespective of the change of network condition. When network congestion occurs and causes packet loss, a sender must execute a supportive packet loss avoidance and quality adaptation mechanism, such as Frame Rate Control and FEC. If a sender can not adjust transport method, packet loss severely effects on streaming quality.

Rate Control such as Frame rate control is used to reduce the consumed bandwidth by discarding Video data. A sender can quickly execute this method, which means that the delay does not become very long. Therefore, Rate Control is the most important method for congestion control. Changing the rate of compression is not suitable for real-time streaming, because it takes more time to execute.

As its typical approach, FEC scheme is so suitable for real-time streaming that many streaming applications have applied it. Because, a sender decide the appropriate FEC encoding rate, by which a receiver can quickly recover packet loss to maintain streaming quality without receiver reporting action.

As a way of another technology, there is network resource management technology. One of its major protocols is "Resource Reservation Protocol (RSVP)" [6], which reserves network bandwidth between a sender and a receiver for data transmission. "Class-Based Queuing (CBQ)" [7] is a resource sharing mechanism that shares the bandwidth on a link in packet networks. Both require resource management mechanisms at the network equipment level, where requiring a gateway to accommodate an essential component is hard to assume and lacks the flexibility of communication. It is difficult to adopt these techniques for every common streaming architecture used over the wide-spread Internet.

2.2 Requirements

To keep stable streaming quality and effectively utilize network resources in an end-to-end communication model, it is necessary for a sender to adapt both frame rate and FEC encoding rate.

A congestion control mechanism would be indispensable to avoid packet loss, and rate control is often used as the congestion control mechanism. It solves the disruption of video and audio by reducing the consumed bandwidth and sending data within the network bandwidth. However, simply reducing the transmission rate is ineffective for the use of network resource, and does not provide the best possible streaming quality. One of the notable and possible approaches is "TCP friendly rate control" [8,9]; it behaves fairly with respect to coexistent TCP flows in order to provide a promising mechanism for avoiding severe fluctuations in the transmission rate. While it ensures fairness with competing TCP flows, the throughput of non-TCP flows does not exceed the throughput of a conformant TCP connection under the same conditions, where this condition is not reasonable for DV streaming that consumes high bandwidth.

FEC is effective especially for streaming applications because it adds redundant information to packets in order to allow a receiver to correct missing packets without retransmission requests. This redundancy level is defined as FEC encoding rate, which is decided by a Bit Error Rate (BER) of the receiving side and the previously used encoding rate. The FEC rate control is used to change the redundancy of data. Its higher value increases the possibility of recovering the stream but increases the amount of traffic. Therefore, additional network congestion and disturbing other communication may be occurred if no intellectual decision is given in this mechanism. According to the analysis in [10] that relates to packet loss recovery, an FEC mechanism is effective for a streaming application especially when lost packets pattern is "pulse" through the stream of packets, or when network condition is unstable or changed at frequent intervals. This analysis inspires us to monitor the FEC recovery rate in the stream to expect the network condition, because the packet loss is recovered only when it is lower than the FEC encoding rate. For instance, if FEC does not completely recover the lost packets during streaming for a certain period, it implies that the network congestion may not be converged and more rate control would be needed.

To keep stable streaming quality and effectively utilize network resource in end-to-end model, it is necessary but very difficult for a sender to adapt the best combination between Frame rate and FEC encoding rate.

2.3 Related Work

A proposal [11] verified adjusting FEC with quality scaling for MPEG streaming. It defines a quality adjusted FEC (QAFEC) mechanism. QAFC tries to adapt MPEG scaling level and FEC encoding rate according to the distortion of streaming quality. The problem of this proposed mechanism is that it can detect the best combination of FEC and scaling level under a certain capacity such as maximum transmission rate adjusted by a TCP-friendly method. TCP-friendly approach is not suitable for high bandwidth DV streaming. Because, DV streaming generally requires more network bandwidth and needs more protection of the packet loss than TCP flow. Moreover, although their approach highly depends on the FEC encoding scheme, they estimated the data transmission cost but did not take care of the additional FEC calculation cost which leads to increasing delay.

3   Design and Implementation of FEC Function for DVTS

To investigate FEC effectiveness for making an adaptive system using frame rate control and FEC rate control, we implemented static FEC using Reed-Solomon Code with DVTS. The characteristic of Reed-Solomon Code is that processing speed is fast, and consumed bandwidth is large. In a real-time streaming, low delay is so important that we chose Reed-Solomon Code.

To utilize FEC function, a sender adds redundant packets with FEC encode module, while a receiver recovers loss packets with FEC decode module by using redundant packets according to need.

Using Reed-Solomon Code, both DV/RTP and FEC packet size must be the same. Therefore, DV/RTP packet must be padded according to need. Moreover, recovering packet loss with FEC, a receiver must recognize both the group which a redundant packet belongs to, and redundant packet ID which indicate the created number within the group. Then, we have extended RTP header format. A sender execute FEC encode every one DV Frame.

Fig.1 shows receiver FEC decoding. When a receiver gets the all DV/RTP packets which belong to the same group, redundant packets are thrown and DV/RTP packets are stocked with play buffer. A receiver recovers the packet if packet loss is observed and redundant packet is encoded. If it is impossible to recover loss packet due to exceeding packet loss, a receiver throws redundant packets and stock DV/RTP packets with play buffer.

Using static FEC DVTS, a user can decide FEC encoding rate and monitor FEC recovery rate. If the encoding rate is appropriate, loss packets on the pass can be recovered fully.

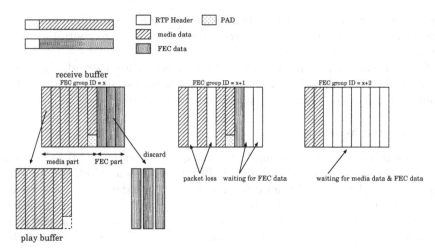

Fig. 1. FEC decode management

4   Analysis of FEC Function

We carried out experimental analysis in the testbed network(2) in order to create the algorithm that provides stable streaming quality with FEC. Table 1 shows the hardware spec and OS of a DV sender, receiver and dummmynet. Network emulation is made by dummynet [13].

Table 1. Hardware in our experiment

	sender and receiver	*dummynet*
CPU	Intel Pentium M 1GHz	Intel Xeon 3.60GHz
Memory	512 MB	3 GB
OS	Linux Kernel 2.6.17	FreeBSD 5.4 Release
NIC	RealTech 100Base-TX	Intel 1000Base-T

4.1   Processing Cost of FEC

Table 2 shows the processing costs of encoding and decoding FEC redundancy. The first line shows the sender-side and receiver-side processing speed of the normal DVTS (without the FEC function). It is inevitable that increasing FEC redundancy requires additional cost. In the 90% FEC encoding rate, a receiver requires 62.9msec for FEC decoding. Therefore, using the large amount of FEC packets, buffer overrun could occur at receiver side according to receiver processing situation. Because buffer overrun leads to the disruption of video and audio, we have to implement flow management module to keep stable streaming quality. Moreover, we found that buffer overrun could occur at sender side in the transmission of DV full rate with about more than 30% FEC encoding rate.

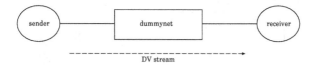

Fig. 2. Testbed network for analysis of FEC

Table 2. Costs of encoding and decoding FEC redundancy

FEC rate	encoding	decoding	total
0%	1.0 msec.	10.2 msec.	11.2 msec.
30%	11.8 msec.	21.9 msec.	33.7 msec.
60%	27.1 msec.	61.4 msec.	88.5 msec.
90%	39.7 msec.	62.9 msec.	102.6 msec.

We must also take account of the maximum FEC encoding rate in according to the hardware spec and buffer size at sender side.

4.2 Experimental Analysis

The sender and the receiver are directly connected to the dummynet. Using Dummynet, network bandwidth is configured to proportionally narrow the available bandwidth at 50 Mbps to 25 Mbps within 125 seconds.

We analyzed the FEC effectiveness according to the DV frame rate 100% and 50%. The reason why we choose only two types of DV frame rate is that frequently changing frame rate is not highly effective or rather decreases DV streaming quality [12]. In addition, a little change of frame rate can not effectively decrease packet loss rate due to the current Linux driver that sends DV/RTP packets at a burst.

In the first experiment, the sender sent full frame rate, which consumes about 30Mbps, to the receiver. The sender then statically added FEC redundancy in the streaming data. The FEC encoding rate was changed from 0% to 10%, 20% and 30% by configuration, in order to understand the relation with FEC rate and non-recovery rate in full rate DV stream. The reason why the sender adopt more than 40% FEC encoding rate is that the buffer overflow occurs at sender side by the lack of sender PC ability. Fig.3 shows the measurement results. In the regular DV transmission, the packet loss was observed from 50 seconds (at 40 Mbps bandwidth). In the DV transmission with 10% FEC redundancy, the packets were lost 65 sec. after (37 Mbps b/w). With 20% FEC redundancy, non-recovered data was observed in 75 sec. (35 Mbps b/w). With 30% FEC redundancy, non-recovered data was observed in 85 sec. (33 Mbps b/w). In 90 sec. from the transmission (32 Mbps b/w), the non-recovery rate was turned over by the transmission with higher FEC redundancy, because the total amount of traffic was gradually increased and hence additional packet loss was triggered. Therefore, in the case of increasing of FEC redundancy, a sender must carefully execute not to result in further disruption of the quality in the full frame rate transmission.

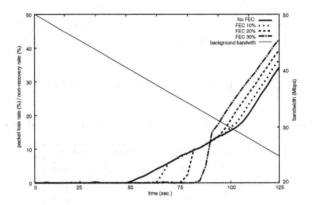

Fig. 3. Packet loss and non-recovery rate in full rate DVTS

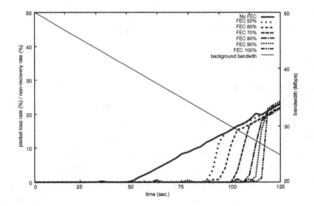

Fig. 4. Packet loss and non-recovery rate in half rate DVTS

In the second experiment, the sender sent half frame rate and changed FEC encoding rate from 50% up to 100%. According to the results shown in Fig4, when the sender sent half rate DV stream with no FEC redundancy, the packet loss was observed in nearly the same timing in the full rate transmission (i.e. in 50 seconds). However, in the half rate transmission with 50% FEC redundancy, non-recovery data was appeared in 85 sec. (33 Mbps b/w), and with 60% FEC redundancy, non-recovery data was observed in 95 sec. (31 Mbps b/w). When the FEC redundancy is 100%, DV packets would be able to be recovered if the available bandwidth is more than 26 Mbps.

According to the experimental results, when non-recovered data is observed in condition with 30% FEC redundancy in full rate, it is not highly effective to increase more FEC redundancy. Because the packet loss rate of the regular DV transmission could be less than DV transmission with FEC redundancy. In this case, it is effective for a sender to change from full rate to half rate with more than FEC 50%. After changing from full rate to half rate, it is necessary for a sender to decide the most appropriate FEC redundancy, which means that all of the lost packets on the pass could be fully recovered with the minimum FEC redundancy for saving the consumption bandwidth.

5   Conclusion and Future Work

In this paper, we analyze FEC function with DV streaming. According to the result, it is very effective to provide the best possible streaming quality by using the appropriate decided frame rate and FEC encoding rate. However, when a sender does not decide the proper FEC encoding rate and frame rate toward the current network bandwidth, the disruption of video and audio occurs due to increasing non-recovery data and buffer overflow at receiver side. We will have to take into account increasing FEC encoding rate which causes the increasing non-recovery rate and congestion collapse.

In our future work, we will verify and define the algorithm for adaptive rate control using FEC. A sender negotiates with receiver in order to get the network and receiver condition which means the packet loss rate, non-recovery rate and the amount of receiver buffer. Since frame rate control is used to reduce the consumed bandwidth by discarding DV frame, which leads to reducing the video quality, this method must be applied only when the network congestion is highly observed in which any FEC encoding rate in the current frame rate can not recover all loss packets. On the other hand, FEC will be used to recover packet loss and prove available bandwidth with packet error tolerance; when a sender recognizes the reduction of streaming quality, it increases the FEC encoding rate in the same frame rate to recover packet loss for maintaining play quality without changing the frame rate. By sending data with FEC packets and monitoring FEC recovery rate reported by the receiver, the sender recognizes the network condition and proves the available bandwidth in order to provide the best possible quality without a significant distortion of streaming quality. To quickly adopt the best combination between frame rate and FEC encoding rate, we will study the packet loss patterns within the defined interval which have a relation to the FEC recovery rate.

Then, according to our proposal scheme, a sender examine and adjust the frame rate and FEC encoding rate in order to provide the best possible streaming quality. We will evaluate our proposed mechanism on a heterogeneous communication environment in order to analyze the effectiveness of the adaptive DVTS.

References

1. Ogawa, A., Kobayashi, K., Sugiura, K., Nakamura, O., Murai, J.: Design and Implementation of DV based video over RTP. In: Proc. of Packet Video Workshop 2000 (May 2000)
2. Kobayashi, K., Ogawa, A., Casner, S., Bormann, C.: RTP Payload Format for DV (IEC 61834) Video, RFC 3189 (January 2002)

3. Schulzrinne, H., Casner, S., Frederick, R., Jacobson, V.: RTP: A Transport Protocol for Real-Time Applications, RFC 3550 (July 2003)
4. Bolot, J.C., Garcia, A.V.: Control Mechanisms for Packet Audio in the Internet. In: Proc. of IEEE INFOCOM (March 1996)
5. Perkins, C., Hodson, O.: Options for Repair of Streaming Media, RFC 2354 (June 1998)
6. Braden, R., Zhang, L., Berson, S., Herzog, S., Jamin, S. (eds.): Resource ReSerVation Protocol (RSVP) – Version 1 Functional Specification, RFC 2205 (September 1997)
7. Floyd, S., Jacobson, V.: Link-sharing and Resource Management Models for Packet Networks. IEEE/ACM Transactions on Networking 3(4), 365–386 (1995)
8. Floyd, S., Fall, K.: Promoting the Use of End-to-End Congestion Control in the Internet. IEEE/ACM Transactions on Networking 7(4), 458–472 (1999)
9. Handley, M., Floyd, S., Padhye, J., Widmer, J.: TCP Friendly Rate Control (TFRC): Protocol Specification, RFC 3448 (January 2003)
10. Bolot, J.C., Crépin, H., Vega-Garcia, A.: Analysis of Audio Packet Loss over Packet-Switched Networks. In: Proc. of ACM NOSSDAV 1995, New Hampshire, USA (April 1995)
11. Wu, H., Claypool, M., Kinicki, R.: Adjusting Forward Error Correction with Quality Scaling for Streaming MPEG. In: Proc. of ACM NOSSDAV 2005, Washington, USA (June 2005)
12. Ogawa, A.: Design and Implementation of DV Based Video Transportation with Congestion Control. Ph.D. Thesis, Graduate School of Media and Governance, Keio University (2003)
13. Rizzo, L.: dummynet, http://info.iet.unipi.it/~luigi/ip_dummynet/

Ubiquitous Devices, Mobility and Context Awareness

Jean-Marie Hullot[1,2]

[1] Former CTO Applications Division, Apple
[2] Distinguished Adjunct Researcher at Internet Education and Research Lab, AIT
Thailand

Abstract. We all have access today to many devices of all sort: computers, TVs, mobile phones, music players, cameras, video game consoles,
navigation systems,... Without some sort of connectivity between then,
most of these devices would be useless. What would you do with a music
player if you were not able to connect it to an external source of music?
One way or another, with or without wires, you must be able connect
it to a computer, local or remote, in order to transfer the music you are
interested in. The challenge here is to make this as transparent as possible since, from a user perspective, the only thing that counts is that you
like this music and you want to have access to it whenever and wherever you want, be it on your music player, on your computer or on your
home cinema. Once your music is on one of them, you would like it to
be available everywhere else where it makes sense.

Smart synchronization is thus the first piece of infrastructure that has
to be built. Synchronizing music between a computer and a music player
is one example, synchronizing personal information like contacts or cal-
endars between a computer and a mobile phone is another one. But it
should not be limited to local synchronization between a computer and
a device, synchronizing two computers over the internet is a technology
that is now a must have, computer at home, computer at work. Synchronizing a mobile phone over the air is also becoming a necessity. And all
this should happen transparently, mere mortals do not want to have to
think about "uploading" or "downloading", these are just geeks concepts
they should not even know about. Once your data becomes ubiquitous
through transparent synchronization, once it is omnipresent, everywhere
at the same time, you do not have anymore to administer your devices,
you can start using them. We shall go over some scenarios showing the
growing importance of ubiquitous data in the years to come.Early mobile devices have usually been designed with only one task in mind. A
mobile phone to give and receive calls, a music player, to listen to music,
a camera to take pictures... Then technology made it possible to compress everything in a single device, and now most mobile phones offer
also music player and camera capabilities among others. Unfortunately
it seems that for these devices where external connectivity is so important as we have shown above, internal connectivity or inter-application
communication within the device has been totally forgotten. You may
well have your address book inside the phone, a satellite navigation system with embedded maps, but no way to show a vicinity map for one of

S. Fdida and K. Sugiura (Eds.): AINTEC 2007, LNCS 4866, pp. 123–124, 2007.
© Springer-Verlag Berlin Heidelberg 2007

your contacts because these two applications cannot talk to each other. This is where we consider most "smart phones" fail to be smart, because they are just a juxtaposition of features, not an integrated set of features leveraging on each other. If the initial lack of true operating systems for phones has certainly be the cause of this situation, the brutal introduction of computers operating systems inside phones more recently has lead to a even worse situation: while before it was still possible to make a call in an easy way, you now have to go through an unbelievable computer-like menu system to perform any kind of operation. We shall analyze in details during this talk how Apple did a very clever job with the iPhone by introducing the power of a true operating system together with a user interface designed for a phone, not for a computer.

Another key feature for these new devices will be the capacity to adapt to the environment in which they find themselves: capacity to switch transparently to a different network using a different protocol, ability to discover another device around with which it can interact is around... We shall go over such examples during the presentation.

Improving the Load Balancing Performance of Reliable Server Pooling in Heterogeneous Capacity Environments[*]

Xing Zhou[1], Thomas Dreibholz[2], and Erwin P. Rathgeb[2]

[1] Hainan University
College of Information Science and Technology
Renmin Road 58, 570228 Haikou, Hainan, China
Tel.: +86 898 6625-0584; Fax: +86 898 6618-7056
xing.zhou@uni-due.de
[2] University of Duisburg-Essen
Institute for Experimental Mathematics
Ellernstrae 29, D-45326 Essen, Germany
Tel.: +49 201 183-7637; Fax: +49 201 183-7673
dreibh@iem.uni-due.de

Abstract. The IETF is currently standardizing a light-weight protocol framework for server redundancy and session failover: Reliable Server Pooling (RSerPool). It is the novel combination of ideas from different research areas into a single, resource-efficient and unified architecture. Server redundancy directly leads to the issues of load distribution and load balancing. Both are important and have to be considered for the performance of RSerPool systems. While there has already been some research on the server selection policies of RSerPool, an interesting question is still open: Is it possible to further improve the load balancing performance of the standard policies without modifying the policies – which are well-known and widely supported – themselves? Our approach places its focus on the session layer rather than the policies and simply lets servers reject inappropriately scheduled requests. But is this approach useful – in particular if the server capacities increase in terms of a heterogeneous capacity distribution? Applying failover handling mechanisms of RSerPool, in this case, could choose a more appropriate server instead.

In this paper, we first present a short outline of the RSerPool framework. Afterwards, we analyse and evaluate the performance of our new approach for different server capacity distributions. Especially, we are also going to analyse the impact of RSerPool protocol and system parameters on the performance of the server selection functionalities as well as on the overhead.

Keywords: Reliable Server Pooling, Redundancy, Load Balancing, Heterogeneous Pools, Performance Evaluation.

---

[*] Parts of this work have been funded by the German Research Foundation (Deutsche Forschungsgemeinschaft).

S. Fdida and K. Sugiura (Eds.): AINTEC 2007, LNCS 4866, pp. 125–140, 2007.

1   Introduction and Scope

Service availability is getting increasingly important in today's Internet. But – in contrast to the telecommunications world, where availability is ensured by redundant links and devices [1] – there had not been any generic, standardized approaches for the availability of Internet-based services. Each application had to realize its own solution and therefore to re-invent the wheel. This deficiency – once more arisen for the availability of SS7 (Signalling System No. 7 [2]) services over IP networks – had been the initial motivation for the IETF RSerPool WG to define the Reliable Server Pooling (RSerPool) framework. The basic ideas of RSerPool are not entirely new (see [3,4]), but their combination into one application-independent framework is.

The Reliable Server Pooling (RSerPool) architecture [5] currently under standardization by the IETF RSerPool WG is an overlay network framework to provide server replication [6] and session failover capabilities [7, 8] to its applications. Server redundancy leads to load distribution and load balancing [9], which are also covered by RSerPool [10, 11]. But in strong contrast to already available solutions in the area of GRID and high-performance computing [12], the fundamental property of RSerPool is to be "light-weight", i.e. it must be usable on devices providing only meagre memory and CPU resources (e.g. embedded systems like telecommunications equipment or routers). This property restricts the RSerPool architecture to the management of pools and sessions only, but on the other hand makes a very efficient realization possible [13]. A generic classification of load distribution algorithms can be found in [9]; the two most important classes – also supported by RSerPool – are non-adaptive and adaptive algorithms. Adaptive strategies base their assignment decisions on the current status of the processing elements and therefore require up-to-date information. On the other hand, non-adaptive algorithms do not require such status data. More details on such algorithms can be found in [14, 15].

There has already been some research on the performance of RSerPool usage for applications like SCTP-based endpoint mobility [16], VoIP with SIP [17], web server pools [18], IP Flow Information Export (IPFIX) [19], real-time distributed computing [6, 7] and battlefield networks [20]. A generic application model for RSerPool systems has been introduced by [10, 6], which includes performance metrics for the provider side (pool utilization) and user side (request handling speed). Based on this model, the load balancing quality of different pool policies has been evaluated [10,11,6].

2   "Reject and Retry" – Our Performance Improvement Approach

The question arisen from these results is whether it is possible to improve the load balancing performance of the standard policies by allowing servers to reject requests, especially in case of pool capacity changes. The merit of our approach is that the policies themselves are not modified: they are widely supported and their performance is well-known [10]. Furthermore, implementing only a very limited number of policies is quite easy [21, 13] (which is clearly beneficial for a "light-weight" system). That is, applying a specialised new policy to only improve a temporary capacity extension may be unsuitable ("Never change a running system!"). Therefore, we focus on the session layer instead: if a request gets rejected, the failover mechanisms provided by RSerPool could choose a possibly better server instead. For a pool of homogeneous servers, we have already shown in [22] that our approach works quite well. Even when the capacity distribution within the pool changes – while the overall pool capacity remains constant – it is useful to apply "reject and retry" (see our paper [23]). But what happens when the pool capacity temporarily increases, e.g. due to spare capacity on some servers? The goal of this paper is to evaluate the performance of our strategy in such situations, with respect to the resulting protocol overhead. We also identify critical configuration parameter ranges in order to provide a guideline for designing and configuring efficient RSerPool systems.

3   The RSerPool Protocol Framework

Figure 1 illustrates the RSerPool architecture [6]. It contains three classes of components: in RSerPool terminology, servers of a pool are called *pool elements* (PE), a client is denoted as *pool user* (PU). The *handlespace* – which is the set of all pools – is managed by redundant *pool registrars* (PR). Within the handlespace, each pool is identified by a unique *pool handle* (PH). PRs of an *operation scope* synchronize their view of the handlespace using the Endpoint haNdlespace Redundancy Protocol (ENRP [24]), transported via SCTP [25, 26]. An operation scope has a limited range, e.g. an organization or only a building. In particular, it is restricted to a single administrative domain – in contrast to GRID computing [12] – in order to keep the management complexity [13] reasonably low. Nevertheless, it is assumed that PEs can be distributed globally for their service to survive localized disasters [27].

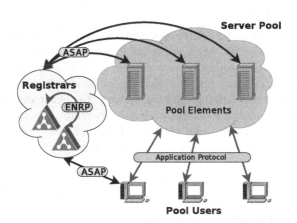

Fig. 1. The RSerPool Architecture

PEs choose an arbitrary PR of the operation scope to register into a pool by using the Aggregate Server Access Protocol (ASAP [28]), again transported via SCTP. Upon registration at a PR, the chosen PR becomes the Home-PR (PR-H) of the newly registered PE. A PR-H is responsible for monitoring its PEs' availability by keep-alive messages (to be acknowledged by the PE within a given timeout) and propagates the information about its PEs to the other PRs of the operation scope via ENRP updates.

In order to access the service of a pool given by its PH, a PU requests a PE selection from an arbitrary PR of the operation scope, again using ASAP [28] transported via SCTP. The PR selects the requested list of PE identities by applying a pool-specific selection rule, called *pool policy*. Adaptive and non-adaptive pool policies are defined in [29], relevant to this paper are the non-adaptive policies Round Robin (RR) and Random (RAND) as well as the adaptive policy Least Used (LU). LU selects the least-used PE, according to up-to-date load information; the actual definition of *load* is application-specific. Round robin selection is applied among multiple least-loaded PEs [13]. Detailed discussions of pool policies can be found in [10, 6].

The PU writes the list of PE identities selected by the PR into its local cache (denoted as *PU-side cache*). From the cache, the PU selects – again using the pool's policy – one element to contact for the desired service. The PU-side cache constitutes a local, temporary and partial copy of the handlespace. Its contents expire after a certain timeout, denoted as *stale cache value*. In many cases, the stale cache value is simply 0s, i.e. the cache is used for a single handle resolution only [10].

4   Quantifying a RSerPool System

In order to evaluate the behaviour of a RSerPool system, it is necessary to quantify RSerPool systems. The system parameters relevant to this paper can be divided into two groups: RSerPool system parameters and server capacity distributions.

4.1   System Parameters

The service provider side of a RSerPool system consists of a pool of PEs. Each PE has a request handling *capacity*, which we define in the abstract unit of calculations per second[1]. Each request consumes a certain number of calculations; we call this number *request size*. A PE can handle multiple requests simultaneously, in a processor sharing mode as provided by multitasking operating systems. The maximum number of simultaneously handled requests is limited by the parameter MinCapPerReq. This parameter defines the minimum capacity share which should be available to handle a new request. That is, a PE providing the capacity (peCapacity) only allows at most

$$\text{MaxRequests} = \text{round}(\frac{\text{peCapacity}}{\text{MinCapPerReq}}) \qquad (1)$$

simultaneously handled requests. Note, that the limit is rounded to the nearest integer, in order to support arbitrary capacities. If a PE's requests limit is reached, a new request gets rejected. For example, if the PE capacity is 10^6 calculations/s and MinCapPerReq=$2.5*10^5$, there is only room for $\text{MaxRequests} = \text{round}(\frac{10^6}{2.5*10^5}) = 4$ simultaneously processed requests. After the time ReqRetryDelay, it is tried to find

---

[1] An application-specific view of capacity may be mapped to this definition, e.g. CPU cycles or memory usage.

another PE for a rejected request (such a delay is necessary to avoid request-rejection floods [30]).

On the service user side, there is a set of PUs. The number of PUs can be given by the ratio between PUs and PEs (*PU:PE ratio*), which defines the parallelism of the request handling. Each PU generates a new request in an interval denoted as *request interval*. The requests are queued and sequentially assigned to PEs.

The total delay for handling a request d_{Handling} is defined as the sum of queuing delay d_{Queuing}, startup delay d_{Startup} (dequeuing until reception of acceptance acknowledgement) and processing time $d_{\text{Processing}}$ (acceptance until finish):

$$d_{\text{Handling}} = d_{\text{Queuing}} + d_{\text{Startup}} + d_{\text{Processing}}. \tag{2}$$

That is, d_{Handling} not only incorporates the time required for processing the request, but also the latencies of queuing, server selection and protocol message transport. The *handling speed* is defined as: $\text{handlingSpeed} = \frac{\text{requestSize}}{d_{\text{handling}}}$. For convenience reasons, the handling speed (in calculations/s) can also be represented in % of the average PE capacity. Clearly, the user-side performance metric is the handling speed – which should be as fast as possible.

Using the definitions above, it is possible to delineate the average system utilization (for a pool of NumPEs servers and a total pool capacity of PoolCapacity) as:

$$\text{systemUtilization} = \text{NumPEs} * \text{puToPERatio} * \frac{\frac{\text{requestSize}}{\text{requestInterval}}}{\text{PoolCapacity}}. \tag{3}$$

Obviously, the provider-side performance metric is the system utilization, since only utilized servers gain revenue. In practise, a well-designed client/server system is dimensioned for a certain *target system utilization*, e.g. 80%. That is, by setting any two of the parameters (PU:PE ratio, request interval and request size), the value of the third one can be calculated using equation 3. See also [6, 10] for more details on this subject.

4.2 Heterogeneous Server Capacity Distributions

In order to present the effects introduced by heterogeneous servers, we have considered three different and realistic capacity distributions (based on [6]) for increasing the pool capacity: a single powerful server, multiple powerful servers and a linear capacity distribution. Clearly, the goal of our "reject and retry" approach (see section 2) is to make best use of the additional capacity for increasing the request handling speed.

A Single Powerful Server. A dedicated powerful server is realistic if there is only one powerful server to perform the main work and some other older (and slower) ones to provide redundancy. To quantify such a scenario, the variable φ (denoted as *capacity scale factor*) is defined as the capacity ratio between the new (PoolCapacity$_{\text{New}}$) and the original capacity (PoolCapacity$_{\text{Original}}$) of the pool:

$$\varphi = \frac{\text{PoolCapacity}_{\text{New}}}{\text{PoolCapacity}_{\text{Original}}}. \tag{4}$$

A value of $\varphi=1$ denotes no capacity change, while $\varphi=3$ stands for a tripled capacity. In case of a single powerful server, the variation of φ results in changing the capacity of the designated PE only. That is, the capacity increment $\Delta_{\text{Pool}}(\varphi)$ of the whole pool can be calculated as follows:

$$\Delta_{\text{Pool}}(\varphi) = \underbrace{(\varphi * \text{PoolCapacity}_{\text{Original}})}_{\text{PoolCapacity}_{\text{New}}} - \text{PoolCapacity}_{\text{Original}}. \qquad (5)$$

Then, the capacity of the i-th PE can be deduced using equation 5 by the following formula (where NumPEs denotes the number of PEs):

$$\text{Capacity}_i(\varphi) = \begin{cases} \frac{\text{PoolCapacity}_{\text{Original}}}{\text{NumPEs}} + \Delta_{\text{Pool}}(\varphi) & (i = 1) \\ \frac{\text{PoolCapacity}_{\text{Original}}}{\text{NumPEs}} & (i > 1) \end{cases}.$$

That is, $\text{Capacity}_1(\varphi)$ stands for the capacity of the powerful server.

Multiple Powerful Servers. If using multiple powerful servers ($\text{NumPEs}_{\text{Fast}}$) instead of only one at one time, the capacity of the i-th PE can be calculated as follows (according to equation 5):

$$\Delta_{\text{FastPE}}(\varphi) = \frac{\Delta_{\text{Pool}}(\varphi)}{\text{NumPEs}_{\text{Fast}}},$$

$$\text{Capacity}_i(\varphi) = \begin{cases} \frac{\text{PoolCapacity}_{\text{Orig}}}{\text{NumPEs}} + \Delta_{\text{FastPE}}(\varphi) & (i \leq \text{NumPEs}_{\text{Fast}}) \\ \frac{\text{PoolCapacity}_{\text{Orig}}}{\text{NumPEs}} & (i > \text{NumPEs}_{\text{Fast}}) \end{cases}$$

A Linear Capacity Distribution. In real life, a linear capacity distribution is likely if there are different generations of servers. For example, a company could buy a state-of-the-art server every half year and add it to the existing pool. In this case, the PE capacities are distributed linearly. That is, the capacity of the first PE remains constant, the capacities of the following PEs are increased with a linear gradient, so that the pool reaches its desired capacity $\text{PoolCapacity}_{\text{New}}$. Therefore, the capacity of the i-th PE can be obtained using the following equations (again, using $\Delta_{\text{Pool}}(\varphi)$ as defined in equation 5):

$$\Delta_{\text{FastestPE}}(\varphi) = \frac{2 * \Delta_{\text{Pool}}(\varphi)}{\text{NumPEs}},$$

$$\text{Capacity}_i(\varphi) = \underbrace{\underbrace{\frac{\Delta_{\text{FastestPE}}(\varphi)}{\text{NumPEs} - 1}}_{\text{Capacity Gradient}} * (i - 1)}_{\text{Additional Capacity for PE } i} + \frac{\text{PoolCapacity}_{\text{Original}}}{\text{NumPEs}}.$$

5   Setup Simulation Model

For the performance analysis, the RSerPool simulation model RSPSIM [6, 10] has been used. This model is based on the OMNET++ [31] simulation environment and contains

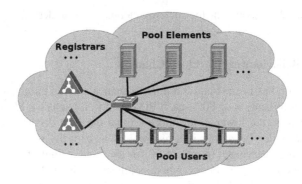

Fig. 2. The Simulation Setup

the protocols ASAP [28] and ENRP [24], a PR module as well as PE and PU modules for the request handling scenario defined in section 4. Network latency is introduced by link delays only. Therefore, only the network delay is significant. The latency of the pool management by PRs is negligible [13].

Unless otherwise specified, the basic simulation setup – which is also presented in figure 2 – uses the following parameter settings:

- The target system utilization is 80% for φ=1.
- Request size and request interval are randomized using a negative exponential distribution (in order to provide a generic and application-independent analysis).
- There are 10 PEs; in the basic setup, each one is providing a capacity of 10^6 calculations/s.
- The heterogeneity parameter φ is 3 (we analyse variations in subsection 6.2).
- A PU:PE ratio of 3 is used (this parameter is analysed in subsection 6.1).
- The default request size:PE capacity ratio is 5 (i.e. a size of $5 * 10^6$ calculations; subsection 6.1 contains an analysis of this parameter).
- ReqRetryDelay is uniformly randomized between 0ms and 200ms. That is, a rejected request is distributed again after an average time of 100ms. This timeout is recommended by [30] in order to avoid overloading the network with unsuccessful trials.
- We use a single PR only, since we do not examine failure scenarios here (see [10] for the impact of multiple PRs).
- No network latency is used (we will examine the impact of delay in subsection 6.4).
- The simulated real-time is 60m; each simulation run is repeated at least 25 times with a different seed in order to achieve statistical accuracy.

GNU R has been used for the statistical post-processing of the results. Each resulting plot shows the average values and their corresponding 95% confidence intervals.

6   Performance Analysis

[10] shows that an inappropriate load distribution of the RR and RAND policies leads to low performance in homogeneous capacity scenarios. Therefore, the first step is

to examine the behaviour in the heterogeneous case under different workload parameters.

6.1 General Behaviour on Workload Changes

The PU:PE ratio r has been found the most critical workload parameter [10]: e.g. at $r=1$ and a target utilization of 80%, each PU expects an exclusive PE during 80% of its runtime. That is, the lower r, the more critical the load distribution. In order to demonstrate the policy behaviour in a heterogeneous capacity scenario, a simulation has been performed varying r from 1 to 10 for $\varphi=3$ and a single fast server (we will examine distributions and settings of φ in detail in subsection 6.2). The handling speed result is shown on the left-hand side of figure 3 and clearly reflects the expectation from [10]: the lower r, the slower the request handling.

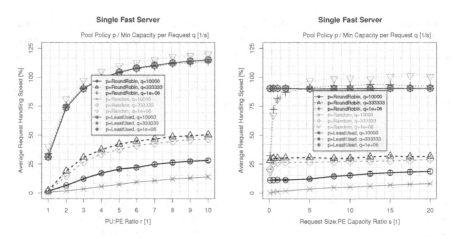

Fig. 3. Varying the Workload Parameters

Applying our idea of ensuring a minimum capacity MinCapPerReq q for each request in process by a PE, it is clearly shown that the performance of RR and RAND is significantly improved: for $q = 10^6$, it is even comparable to LU.

Varying the request size:PE capacity ratio s for a fixed setting of $r=3$ (the handling speed results are presented on the right-hand side of figure 3), the handling speed slightly sinks with a decreasing s: the smaller s, the higher the frequency of requests. That is, while the workload keeps constant, there are 100 times more requests in the system for $s=10^5$ compared with $s=10^7$. However, comparing the results for different settings of MinCapPerReq q in this critical parameter range, a significant impact can be observed: the handling speed for using a high setting of q significantly drops. The reason is that each rejection leads to an average penalty of 100ms (in order to avoid overloading the network with unsuccessful requests [30]). But for smaller s, the proportion of the startup delay gains an increasing importance in the overall request handling time of equation 2. For larger requests, the delay penalty fraction of the request handling time becomes negligible.

The results for varying the request interval can be derived from the previous results (see also equation 3) and have therefore been omitted. Note that also the utilization plots have been omitted, since the larger φ, the higher the pool capacity. Consequently, at φ=3, the utilization is already in a non-critical range.

In summary, it has been shown that our idea of using MinCapPerReq for rejecting inappropriately distributed requests can lead to a significant performance improvement. But what happens if the server capacity distribution and heterogeneity are changed?

6.2   Varying the Heterogeneity of the Pool

In order to show the effect of varying the heterogeneity of different server capacity distributions (φ; denoted as *phi* in the plots), simulations have been performed for the scenarios defined in subsection 4.2. The results are presented for a single fast server out of 10 (figure 4), 3 fast servers out of 10 (figure 5) and a linear capacity distribution (figure 6). For each figure, the left-hand side shows the handling speed, while the right-hand side presents the overhead in form of handle resolutions at the PR. We have omitted utilization plots, since they are obvious and would not provide any new insights.

In general, the LU policy already provides a good load balancing, leading to no significant room for improvement by our MinCapPerReq approach. However, a significant performance gain can be achieved for RR and RAND for all three capacity distributions: the higher MinCapPerReq q, the better the handling speed. Interestingly, the handling speed for RR and RAND at $q = 10^6$ calculations/s even slightly exceeds the speed of LU for $\varphi > 2$ in the case of the "fast servers" scenarios! The reason for this behaviour is that LU selects the least loaded PE rather than the fastest one. That is, if all faster PEs have a higher load than a slow one, the slow one is always chosen by definition. In contrast, the linear distribution is much less critical (except for the first PE, all other PEs are "faster" ones) and LU performs better here. Another interesting observation is that the performance of RAND becomes better than RR for large q (here: $q = 10^6$ calculations/s): RR deterministically selects the PEs in turn. In the worst case, if all 9 slow PEs are already loaded up to their limit, there will be 9 rejections until the fast one gets selected again. Clearly, selecting randomly will provide a better result here.

Comparing the results of the different capacity distributions, it is clear that the "single fast server" scenario (see also subsubsection 4.2) is the most critical one: for higher settings of φ, most of the pool's capacity is concentrated at a single PE. Therefore, this dedicated PE has to be selected in order to achieve a better handling speed. If three of the PEs are fast ones, the situation becomes better, leading to a significantly improved handling speed compared with the first scenario. Finally, the linear distribution is the least critical one: even if randomly selecting one of the slower PEs, the next handle resolution will probably return one of the faster PEs. For RR, this behaviour will even be deterministic and LU again improves it by PE load state knowledge.

In summary, it has been shown that our request rejection approach is working for RR and RAND in all three heterogeneous capacity distribution scenarios, while there is no significant benefit for LU. But what about its overhead? The handle resolutions overhead is significantly increased for a small setting of φ: here, the overall pool capacity is still small and the PEs are working at almost their target utilization. This means that the selection of an inappropriate PE becomes more probable and therefore the rejection

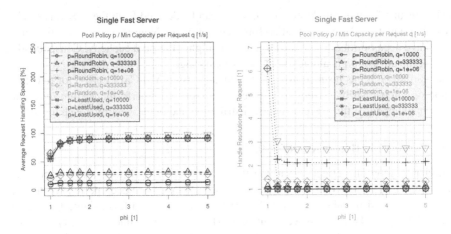

Fig. 4. The Impact of the Pool Heterogeneity for a Single Fast Server

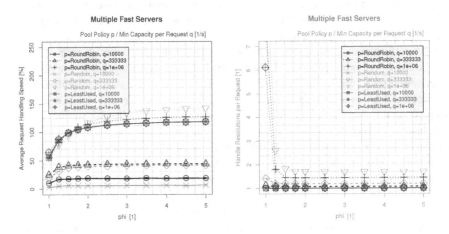

Fig. 5. The Impact of the Pool Heterogeneity for a Multiple Fast Servers

probability higher. Obviously, the probability of a rejection is highest for RAND and lowest for LU.

From the results above, it also can be observed that the overhead is highest for the "single fast server" setup and lowest for the linear distribution. Clearly, the more critical the distribution, the higher the chance to get an inappropriate PE. But interestingly, the overhead for RR and RAND at $\varphi > 2$ almost keeps constant for the two fast servers scenarios – while it decreases for the linear distribution as well as for using LU: the non-adaptive policies may try to use fully occupied PEs due to their lack of load state knowledge, which leads to rejections and therefore to increased overhead. However, even for the scenario of a single fast PE, this overhead keeps below 2.75 handle resolutions per request for $\varphi \geq 2$. But is it possible to reduce this overhead – without a significant penalty on the handling speed improvement?

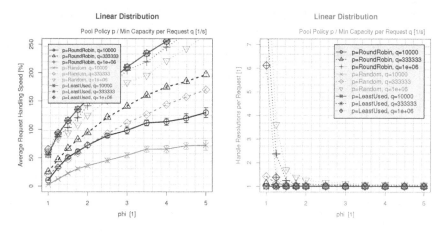

Fig. 6. The Impact of the Pool Heterogeneity for a Linear Capacity Distribution

6.3   Reducing the Network Overhead by Cache Usage

In order to present the impact of the PU-side cache on performance and overhead, we have performed simulations using a setting of $\varphi=3$ (i.e. a not too critical setting) and varying the stale cache value c (given as ratio between the actual stale cache value and the request size:PE capacity ratio) from 0.0 to 1.0. This cache value range has been chosen to allow for cache utilization in case of retries and to also support dynamic pools (PEs may register or deregister). Figure 7 presents the results for a single fast server (i.e. the most critical distribution) and figure 8 the plots for a linear distribution. We have omitted results for multiple fast servers for space reasons, since they would not provide any new insights.

Taking a look at the "fast server" results, it is clear that even a small setting of c results in a significantly reduced overhead while the handling speeds of RR and RAND are not negatively affected. Even better, the handling speed of RR slightly increases! The reason for this effect is that each cache constitutes an additional selection instance performing round robin choices independently of the PR and other PU-side caches. That is, while each instance performs its selections in turn, the global view of the selections in the system differs from the desired round robin strategy. Instead, it gets more and more random – but the local selection still avoids that a rejected request is mapped to the same PE again (which may happen for RAND). For LU, the load state information gets the more out of date the higher c. This leads to a decreasing handling speed if $\mathrm{MinCapPerReq}$ q is low (here: q=333,333 calculations/s) – using a larger setting, inappropriate choices are "corrected" by our "reject and retry" approach.

Having multiple fast servers or even a linear capacity distribution, the number of rejections and retries – and therefore the number of handle resolutions – is significantly smaller (see also subsection 6.2). Therefore, the impact of the cache gets less significant in comparison with the scenario of a single fast server. The most interesting observation here is the behaviour of the RR policy: for a linear distribution, the cache leads to a slightly reduced handling speed. The reason is the caches which perform round

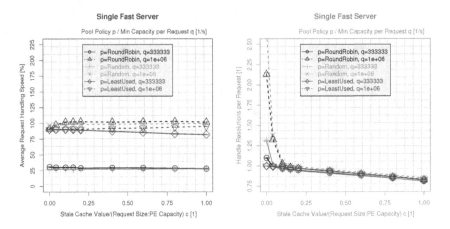

Fig. 7. The Impact of the Stale Cache Value for a Single Fast Server

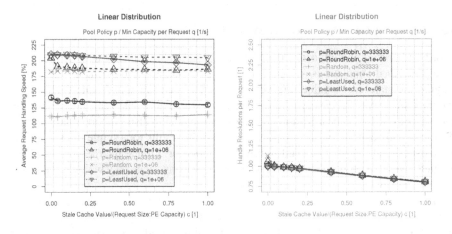

Fig. 8. The Impact of the Stale Cache Value for a Linear Capacity Distribution

robin selections independently. But here, the independent selections work counterproductively: almost all PEs can be considered to be fast ones (at least more powerful than the first one), so the selection order gets irrelevant – which is confirmed by the RR curve for MinCapPerReq $q = 10^6$ converging to the speed of RAND for increasing c.

In summary, the PU-side cache can achieve a significant overhead reduction for the RR and RAND policies, while the performance does not suffer. However, care has to be taken for RR effects. The speed of LU suffers for higher settings of c, at only a small achievable overhead reduction (LU already has a low rejection rate).

6.4   The Impact of Network Delay

Although the network latency for RSerPool systems is negligible in many cases (e.g. if all components are situated in the same building), there are some scenarios where

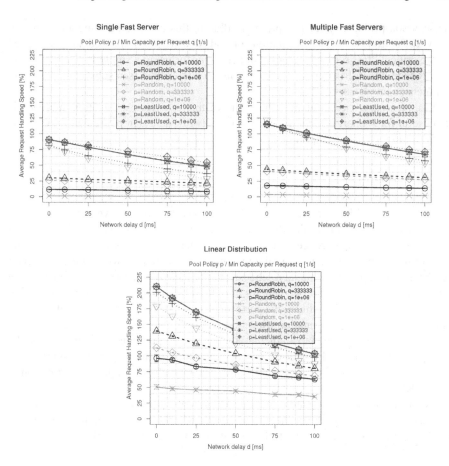

Fig. 9. The Impact of the Network Delay on the Handling Speed

components are distributed globally [27]. It is therefore also necessary to consider the impact of network delay on the system performance. Clearly, network latency only becomes significant for small request size:PE capacity ratios s. For that reason, figure 9 presents the performance results for varying the delay in the three capacity distribution scenarios at $\varphi=3$ (i.e. not too critical) for $s=1$.

As it can be expected, the handling speed sinks with rising network delay: in equation 2, the startup delay gains an increasing importance to the overall handling time due to the latency caused by querying a PR and contacting PEs.

Comparing the curves for the different settings of MinCapPerReq, the achieved gain by a higher minimum capacity shrinks with the delay: while the request rejection rate of the PE keeps almost constant, the costs of a rejection increase: now, there is not only the penalty of ReqRetryDelay but an additional latency for querying the PR and contacting another PE. This is particularly important for the LU policy: as adaptive policy, it relies on up-to-date load information. However, due to the latency, this information becomes more obsolete the higher the delay. That is, the latency increases the selection probability for inappropriate PEs. In this case, using a higher setting of MinCapPerReq (here: 10^6 calculations/s) leads to a slightly improved handling speed for the critical "fast servers" setups – in particular for using a single fast server. However, for the linear distribution – which is much less critical (see subsection 6.2) – no significant change can be observed.

As a summary, the simulations have shown that our request rejection approach is also useful for scenarios having a significant network delay. In particular, it even gets useful for the adaptive LU policy.

7   Conclusions

We have indicated by our evaluations that it is possible to improve the request handling performance of the basic RSerPool policies under varying workload parameters in different server capacity scenarios of varying heterogeneity – without modifying the policies themselves – by setting a minimum capacity per request to limit the maximum number of simultaneously handled requests. Our "reject and retry" approach leads to a significant performance improvement for the RR and RAND policies, while – in general – it does not provide a benefit for the performance of LU. However, in case of a significant network delay in combination with short requests, our approach also gets useful for LU. Request rejections lead to an increased overhead, in particular to additional handle resolutions. Usage of the PU-side cache can reduce this overhead while not significantly affecting the system performance – with care to be taken for the capacity distribution in case of RR.

As part of our future research, we are currently also validating our simulative performance results in real-life scenarios, using our RSerPool prototype implementation RSPLIB [6, 27] in the PLANETLAB; first results can be found in [27, 6].

References

1. Rathgeb, E.P.: The MainStreetXpress 36190: a scalable and highly reliable ATM core services switch. International Journal of Computer and Telecommunications Networking 31, 583–601 (1999)
2. ITU-T: Introduction to CCITT Signalling System No. 7. Technical Report Recommendation Q.700, International Telecommunication Union (March 1993)
3. Alvisi, L., Bressoud, T.C., El-Khashab, A., Marzullo, K., Zagorodnov, D.: Wrapping Server-Side TCP to Mask Connection Failures. In: Proceedings of the IEEE Infocom 2001, Anchorage, Alaska/U.S.A, vol. 1, pp. 329–337 (2001) ISBN 0-7803-7016-3
4. Sultan, F., Srinivasan, K., Iyer, D., Iftode, L.: Migratory TCP: Highly available Internet services using connection migration. In: Proceedings of the ICDCS, Vienna/Austria 17–26 (2002)
5. Lei, P., Ong, L., Tüxen, M., Dreibholz, T.: An Overview of Reliable Server Pooling Protocols. Internet-Draft Version 02, IETF, RSerPool Working Group, draft-ietf-rserpool-overview-02.txt, work in progress (2007)
6. Dreibholz, T.: Reliable Server Pooling – Evaluation, Optimization and Extension of a Novel IETF Architecture. PhD thesis, University of Duisburg-Essen, Faculty of Economics, Institute for Computer Science and Business Information Systems (2007)

7. Dreibholz, T., Rathgeb, E.P.: RSerPool – Providing Highly Available Services using Unreliable Servers. In: Proceedings of the 31st IEEE EuroMirco Conference on Software Engineering and Advanced Applications, Porto/Portugal, pp. 396–403 (2005) ISBN 0-7695-2431-1

8. Dreibholz, T.: An Efficient Approach for State Sharing in Server Pools. In: LCN 2002. Proceedings of the 27th IEEE Local Computer Networks Conference, Tampa, Florida/U.S.A, pp. 348–352 (2002) ISBN 0-7695-1591-6

9. Gupta, D., Bepari, P.: Load Sharing in Distributed Systems. In: Proceedings of the National Workshop on Distributed Computing (January 1999)

10. Dreibholz, T., Rathgeb, E.P.: On the Performance of Reliable Server Pooling Systems. In: Proceedings of the IEEE Conference on Local Computer Networks (LCN) 30th Anniversary, Sydney/Australia, pp. 200–208 (2005) ISBN 0-7695-2421-4

11. Dreibholz, T., Zhou, X., Rathgeb, E.P.: A Performance Evaluation of RSerPool Server Selection Policies in Varying Heterogeneous Capacity Scenarios. In: Proceedings of the 33rd IEEE EuroMirco Conference on Software Engineering and Advanced Applications, Lübeck/Germany, pp. 157–164 (2007) ISBN 0-7695-2977-1

12. Foster, I.: What is the Grid? A Three Point Checklist. GRID Today (2002)

13. Dreibholz, T., Rathgeb, E.P.: Implementing the Reliable Server Pooling Framework. In: ConTEL 2005. Proceedings of the 8th IEEE International Conference on Telecommunications, Zagreb/Croatia, vol. 1, pp. 21–28 (2005) ISBN 953-184-081-4

14. Kremien, O., Kramer, J.: Methodical Analysis of Adaptive Load Sharing Algorithms. IEEE Transactions on Parallel and Distributed Systems 3(6) (1992)

15. Dykes, S.G., Robbins, K.A., Jeffery, C.L.: An Empirical Evaluation of Client-Side Server Selection Algorithms. In: Proceedings of the IEEE Infocom 2000, Tel Aviv/Israel, vol. 3, pp. 1361–1370 (2000) ISBN 0-7803-5880-5

16. Dreibholz, T., Jungmaier, A., Tüxen, M.: A new Scheme for IP-based Internet Mobility. In: LCN 2003. Proceedings of the 28th IEEE Local Computer Networks Conference, Königswinter/Germany, pp. 99–108 (2003) ISBN 0-7695-2037-5

17. Conrad, P., Jungmaier, A., Ross, C., Sim, W.C., Tüxen, M.: Reliable IP Telephony Applications with SIP using RSerPool. In: Proceedings of the State Coverage Initiatives, Mobile/Wireless Computing and Communication Systems II, Orlando, Florida/U.S.A, vol. X (2002) ISBN 980-07-8150-1

18. Siddiqui, S.A.: Development, Implementation and Evaluation of Web-Server and Web-Proxy for RSerPool based Web-Server-Pool. Master's thesis, University of Duisburg-Essen, Institute for Experimental Mathematics (2006)

19. Dreibholz, T., Coene, L., Conrad, P.: Reliable Server Pooling Applicability for IP Flow Information Exchange. Internet-Draft Version 04, IETF, Individual Submission, draft-coene-rserpool-applic-ipfix-04.txt, work in progress (June 2007)

20. Uyar, Ü., Zheng, J., Fecko, M.A., Samtani, S., Conrad, P.: Evaluation of Architectures for Reliable Server Pooling in Wired and Wireless Environments. IEEE JSAC Special Issue on Recent Advances in Service Overlay Networks 22(1), 164–175 (2004)

21. Dreibholz, T., Rathgeb, E.P.: An Evalulation of the Pool Maintenance Overhead in Reliable Server Pooling Systems. In: FGCN 2007. Proceedings of the IEEE International Conference on Future Generation Communication and Networking, Jeju Island/South Korea (December 2007)

22. Zhou, X., Dreibholz, T., Rathgeb, E.P.: A New Approach of Performance Improvement for Server Selection in Reliable Server Pooling Systems. In: ADCOM 2007. Proceedings of the 15th IEEE International Conference on Advanced Computing and Communication, Guwahati/India (December 2007)

23. Zhou, X., Dreibholz, T., Rathgeb, E.P.: Evaluation of a Simple Load Balancing Improvement for Reliable Server Pooling with Heterogeneous Server Pools. In: FGCN 2007. Proceedings of the IEEE International Conference on Future Generation Communication and Networking, Jeju Island/South Korea (December 2007)
24. Xie, Q., Stewart, R., Stillman, M., Tüxen, M., Silverton, A.: Endpoint Handlespace Redundancy Protocol (ENRP). Internet-Draft Version 16, IETF, RSerPool Working Group, draft-ietf-rserpool-enrp-16.txt, work in progress (July 2007)
25. Stewart, R., Xie, Q., Morneault, K., Sharp, C., Schwarzbauer, H., Taylor, T., Rytina, I., Kalla, M., Zhang, L., Paxson, V.: Stream Control Transmission Protocol. Standards Track RFC 2960, IETF (October 2000)
26. Jungmaier, A., Rathgeb, E.P., Tüxen, M.: On the Use of SCTP in Failover-Scenarios. In: Proceedings of the State Coverage Initiatives, Mobile/Wireless Computing and Communication Systems II, Orlando, Florida/U.S.A, vol. X, pp. 980–987 (July 2002) ISBN 980-07-8150-1
27. Dreibholz, T., Rathgeb, E.P.: On Improving the Performance of Reliable Server Pooling Systems for Distance-Sensitive Distributed Applications. In: KiVS 2007. Proceedings of the 15. ITG/GI Fachtagung Kommunikation in Verteilten Systemen, Bern/Switzerland (Setember 2007)
28. Stewart, R., Xie, Q., Stillman, M., Tüxen, M.: Aggregate Server Access Protcol (ASAP). Internet-Draft Version 16, IETF, RSerPool Working Group, draft-ietf-rserpool-asap-16.txt, work in progress (July 2007)
29. Tüxen, M., Dreibholz, T.: Reliable Server Pooling Policies. Internet-Draft Version 05, IETF, RSerPool Working Group, draft-ietf-rserpool-policies-05.txt, work in progress (July 2007)
30. Zhang, Y.: Distributed Computing mit Reliable Server Pooling. Master's thesis, Universität Essen, Institut für Experimentelle Mathematik (April 2004)
31. Varga, A.: OMNeT++ Discrete Event Simulation System User Manual - Version 3.2, Technical University of Budapest/Hungary (March 2005)

WOD – Proxy-Based Web Object Delivery Service

Kai-Hsiang Yang and Jan-Ming Ho

Institute of Information Science, Academia Sinica
{khyang, hoho}@iis.sinica.edu.tw

Abstract. With the tremendous growth of World Wide Web (WWW), the door has been opened to a multitude of services and information for even the most casual of users. Today, many wireless and mobile devices are being produced to provide access to this information, and the capabilities of these devices can vary depending on characteristics such as physical memory, storage space, and network speed. In the future, it is expected to see a rich variety of devices that can browse the WWW, and any given user is likely to own more than one type. When a user browses the WWW by small handy devices, such as PDAs or mobile phones with low network bandwidth, the storage space limitation and long download time make a user unable to download large-size web objects such as software zip files. One possible solution is for the user to memorize the URL of the desired web object, and download it when he reaches his home or office computer, but this is extremely inconvenient, and in most cases highly impractical. In this paper, we propose that using a proxy-based web object delivery system is a much more convenient and efficient solution. The proposed system is actually an HTTP proxy server that automatically checks all the requested web objects according to user-defined rules. If one or more rules are found to match, and the web object needs to be delivered to the user's account, the proposed system does some translations for the web object depending on its Content Type, and then delivers it via the Simple Mail Transfer Protocol (SMTP) or File Transfer Protocol (FTP). Users need merely set up the rules, and the web objects can proceed to be sent to their email or ftp site. There it can be downloaded at the user's leisure in high speed network environments such as at home or at one's office. In addition, a scheduling mechanism has been designed in order to enhance performance and improve the quality of service (QoS) for the users. We have tested the proposed system on the Windows platform, and have also evaluated it by a Pocket PC emulator.

1 Introduction

The era of PC-dominated applications is coming to an end. Today, we see widespread use of mobile devices that have sufficient computing and networking capabilities to browse the Web. The network-enabled devices come in a variety of types, including cell phones, Personal Digital Assists (PDAs), Pocket PCs, hand-held PCs, car navigation systems, and notebook PCs. An average person may

S. Fdida and K. Sugiura (Eds.): AINTEC 2007, LNCS 4866, pp. 141–155, 2007.

already own several of such devices, and it is expected that in the near future, the number of such devices will far exceed the number of desktop PCs. These devices have different capabilities due to varying processors, physical memory, network protocols, screen sizes, input methods, software libraries, and more. And with this variety of devices, certain inconveniences arise for users who want to browse the web. This paper focuses on a problem users often encounter while on their wireless and mobile devices; the problem is described in the following section.

The current network-enabled devices are becoming more and more diverse. However wireless and mobile devices with small memory and lower network bandwidth are unsuitable for complicated computations and downloading large files. For example, a user may want to surf the net using a mobile phone while taking the mass transit system. Due to low connection speed and the fact that the user is mobile, interruptions may occur, causing the user to only be able to access simple web-based information. This would prevent him from retrieving more abundant information such as business achievement reports or zipped software files. Another challenge that users might face is the low speed of the public wireless connection or of the dial-up services through PHS- or GPRS-type mobile phones. Because these services charge based on the amount of information downloaded, users are less likely to want to retrieve information or files of larger size. These problems may result from the following situations: (1) Small storage - If the devices such as Palms of Pocket PCs can only contain a limited amount of information, large-sized files are impossible to download. (2) Differing web page protocols and file format support - Some devices, such as mobile phones, contain browsers different from general web page protocols and file format support. There are even some special embedded systems that only accept pure text files, and no other complicated file formats. (3) Low network bandwidth and user mobility - When users are moving or connection speed is low, it becomes extremely difficult to directly download files of large size. (4) Browsing a web site with slow network speed - When users surf web sites that have slow network speed, download time will be very long and the connection will likely time out. This kind of problem is called the "web object downloading problem".

Because of this problem, users need to find a better solution than directly downloading web objects in the current conditions. The simplest solution is to have users memorize or write down the URL of the web object, and have them download it when they arrive someplace where the network speed is fast and stable. However this solution has three obvious drawbacks: The first is that it is cumbersome to have users do such a thing, and there is always the possibility of misspelling or forgetting the URL, especially when the URL is long and contains many unmeaning symbols. The second drawback is that, the user cannot initiate the download until he reaches the place where network speed is faster. As a result, time is lost waiting for files of large size to finish downloading. Third, some web objects cannot be directly downloaded by a URL because of the security policy of web sites. Users have to repeat those serial of browsing actions to be able to download the objects.

In this paper, we propose a proxy-based web object delivery (WOD) system as the solution for this problem. This system is a personal proxy server that can be deployed for personal use or as a general network proxy server. When users use different wireless and mobile devices, by setting the WOD as the default proxy server, the WOD system automatically checks all the requested web objects against the user's rules. If there is one rule matched and the web object needs to be delivered to the user's account, the proposed system does some translations for the web object depending on its Content Type, and then delivers it via the Simple Mail Transfer Protocol (SMTP) or File Transfer Protocol (FTP). Users can browse the web object later by checking their email or connecting to their ftp site when they are in a high speed network environment.

In the proposed system, we have designed a rule model suitable for most situations, which focuses on the Content Type and Content Length of web objects. These rules can be set for one or more delivery methods, such as email, ftp, or for several methods simultaneously. Users can change the delivery rules any time, and the WOD system immediately follows the rules to work. Also, taking into consideration system performance, to improve quality of service (QoS) we have developed a delivery scheduling component to schedule all the delivery tasks according to their priorities. Delivery scheduling can prevent deadlock and allow the high priority tasks to be delivered more quickly. The proposed system is implemented under the Windows platform, and based on the proxy module of the Apache web server. We used a MySQL database to store each user's rules, web objects, and delivery status, etc. For the user profile management aspect of the system, we used PHP scripting language to implement a rule management page; this is for rule setup and for checking delivery task statuses.

This paper is organized as follows: Section 2 discusses related works. Section 3 presents an overview of the proposed web object delivery service. Section 4 describes the delivery rule model we used. In section 5 we present the delivery scheduling model. Section 6 describes the implementation details and related technologies. And section 7 is the conclusion.

2   Related Work

There are some commercial products [1, 2, 3] and research works [4, 5] for the problem of heterogeneous client devices. These products focus on providing quality of service and performing content transformation in proxy of a variety of client devices through a process called "transcoding." By maintaining separate caches for different categories of clients, such as PC, PDA, Mobile, etc., it is possible to translate large size objects to small size ones at the proxy servers. Besides, some works [6, 7, 8] focus on Web page layout modification techniques to fit the mobile devices. However, although the transcoding technique solves part of the problem, such as the issue of image translation, there are a couple of problems that can arise. First, there are objects that cannot be translated by transcoding, such as zip files. Next, there are problems that occur when clients download web objects that cannot be handled by their devices. But our proposed system can handle these problems. This system filters these web objects according to user-defined rules, and delivers the objects to the user's email account or ftp space; the web objects are not downloaded directly into the client device so users can access them later from the medium of choice.

Generally, current proxy systems applying conventional page-level caching cannot function effectively for those larger and dynamic web objects. These proxies can be configured to download web objects for users even if the request connection is closed in the middle of a transfer. The proxy systems will complete the transfer to the cache if it has already transferred more than a specified percentage. Generally a number between 60% and 90% is usually what's recommended. However, due to space consideration, general proxy systems will have a higher percentage setting. Another important setting in proxy is the max cache size. Web objects with size greater than the max cache size will not cached by the proxy. Even if the proxy caches some of such web objects, they will most likely be replaced by the cache replacement mechanism before the user has a chance to download them later. Several new caching strategies [9, 10, 11, 12] have been proposed, where a fragment-level caching strategy is applied, to solve the problems. A recent work [13] focuses on integrating a Web content adaptation algorithm and a caching mechanism to serve dynamic content in a mobile computing environment. However, one disadvantage of using existing proxy systems is that the user has to download these objects from the proxy that his device connected to. A user will probably want to use the device outside and then browse those web objects later in his office with high speed network; he will not want to remote connect to the proxy his device connected to. Our proposed system can solve this problem by delivering the web objects to user's email account or ftp space close to him. After the web objects are delivered, proxy can delete them immediately without affects on the space and performance.

3   Proposed System

This section will introduce the web object delivery (WOD) system, including its logical concepts, system architecture, rule model, scheduling, and delivery modules.

3.1   Logical Concepts

Figure 1 illustrates the logical concepts of the WOD system. The circle on the right is the network environment in the company or organization. Each user has his mail account and ftp site in the email server and ftp server. The circle on the left represents the locations such as a user's home, a coffee shop, or even a train station; places where users may use different devices to surf the Internet. If the Internet Service Provider (ISP) provides WOD for users, the web object-downloading problem will be easily solved. Users can initially define which web objects have to be delivered, and where they should be delivered. After the rule setup, users can start surfing the Internet via the WOD system. When the

WOD system receives a request, it tries to get the web object and its header information. According to the Content-Type and Content-Length in the header, the proposed system checks the user's rules to decide whether or not the web object should be delivered. If the web object has to be delivered, the system first does the proper translations, and then delivers it via email or ftp. This way, when users are mobile or in a slow network speed environment, they can deliver important files, software zip file, specification PDF files, or even mp3 files to their accounts the WOD system provided by the ISP. This solution will prevent users from having to write down URLs, and will also save users the download time by delivering to users' accounts.

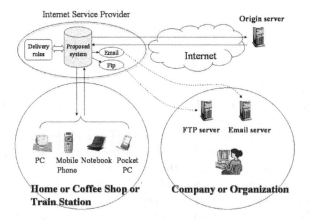

Fig. 1. Logical Concepts

3.2   System Architecture

This section details the system architecture of the WOD. Figure 2 illustrates all the elements in the WOD system. When receiving a request, the system tries to get the web object and its header information from the cache or origin server. After saving the web object into the cache, the system checks the user's rules to decide whether the web object has to be delivered. The six important elements in this system are described in the following sections.

Proxy authentication. To distinguish users, the authentication mechanism is necessary for the WOD system. The HTTP 1.0/1.1 protocols provide a simple challenge-response authentication mechanism which is used by the proxy to challenge a client request by requiring that the client provide authentication information. It uses an extensible, case-insensitive token to identify the authentication scheme. A 407 (Proxy Authentication Required) response message is used by a proxy to challenge the authorization of a client. The response includes a "Proxy-Authenticate" header field containing the information for the proxy authentication. This proxy authentication mechanism is supported by almost every existent browser. Hence, the WOD system applies this standard mechanism to authenticate users.

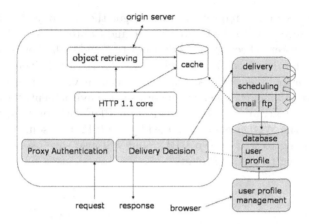

Fig. 2. System Overview

Delivery decision element. The Delivery Decision (DD) element is used to decide whether the requested web object has to be delivered, and guarantees the robustness of the proposed system by determining if each step has been successfully completed or not. This element only takes care of the decision-making, but does not play a part in the action of making a delivery. To increase download speed help make the network connections reliable, the general proxy server returns all receiving packets to users immediately after it receives parts of requested web objects. This method will help to prevent connections timeouts when users attempt to download large-size files. Therefore, the DD element must make decision in a short amount of time. If the requested web objects need to be delivered, the DD element returns the delivery messages to users. Otherwise the DD element has to work as the conventional proxy server. If the web objects need to be delivered, the DD element first stores necessary information into the database, then immediately closes the client connections. But the connections to origin servers are still preserved so it can continue to receive the web objects. After the web objects have been completely delivered, the DD element updates the status of web objects, including the cache file paths and the delivery accounts.

Delivery element. The delivery element ensures that each delivery file is complete and ready to be sent to the 'Scheduling' element. It is revoked every several minutes, checks whether all web objects are complete, and then checks that their Content Types and Content Lengths are also correct. Also, for the web objects that expire at the delivery time, the element will mark those filenames with the notation "[expired]". Most importantly, only the tasks with complete files will be processed. This way, a preceding large-file download task will not affect later small-file download tasks. Before sending tasks to the Scheduling element, the delivery element has to compute the priority of each task. We define 10 different user levels from 1 to 10, and each user level has 10 units of priority. Also, users can set each delivery rule different priority from -5 to +5. For example, one user is the user level 3, and sets the first delivery rule with the priority '+4', and the second delivery rule to the priority '-2'. According to the above settings, the delivery tasks that satisfy the first delivery rule have the priority 34 (3 * 10 + 4 = 34), and those that satisfy the second delivery rule have the priority 28 (3 * 10 - 2 = 28).

Scheduling element. The scheduling element focuses on delivering tasks according to their priorities from highest to lowest. The element also updates the priority of the tasks that have been delivered failed, in order to prevent the deadlock situation. All the details are described in section 5.

Database. All the information about the delivery tasks is stored in the database. By using the database, the proposed system can easily manage the data and provides users with the status of their delivery tasks.

User Profile Management. This management element provides users an interface to customize their preferences. Through the element, users can set their rules, delivery accounts, methods, and also view the historical logs and status of delivery tasks. Aside from the convenience, users can setup different rule groups for different device properties, in order to quickly open or close some specific rules. Each rule group also can be configured to automatically open according to the user's IP.

4   Rule Model

4.1   Field Selection

In order to define one rule model which is suitable for all situations, the rule model should contain the information in the header of web object. However there are many fields in the HTTP header, how to choose the proper fields is very important. We choose the fields by the following policies: 1. The field should be in most header of web object. 2. The field is suitable for most situations. 3. Fewer fields are better. According to these policies, we choose the Content-Type and Content-Length for our rule model. Content-Type is a critical attribute of web objects for many applications. Some types of documents are probably not supported by the client device, and users can set up rules to deliver web objects with those specific Content-Types. Content-Length is another important attribute. At high network bandwidth environment, hundreds of mega bytes are allowed to download. However when client devices connect to Internet by the dial-up services through PHS- or GPRS-type mobile phones, only web objects with few Kbytes are allowed to download. Moreover, to download the large-size web objects, the stable connection is necessary otherwise the download process may be going to fail. However in the wireless network, the connection usually is not stable.

4.2   Positive List of Rules

According to the above consideration, a positive list of rules is used in the proposed system for the following two advantages.

1. Low complexity
   The system cannot spend much time on each task for deciding the delivery method. There may be some advanced methods which could make better decision, but they are usually complex. A positive list of rules can make the decision quickly even with a large number of requests.
2. Clear definition
   Another benefit of the positive list of rules is the definite result. It is essential and brings better performance. Basically, it is not expected if there are too many rules to be triggered. Therefore, only the first matched rule is triggered once. There are two advantages of this design. (1) Simplify the rules: each rule can be made shorter, and several rules are grouped to achieve one goal. The speed of checking rules doesn't decrease because not all of them are checked. Actually the checking time is less than the time for checking a long rule. (2) Avoid contradiction: if some rules are matched with the contradiction, it certainly makes troubles. Our design can prevent the situation by only trigger one rule. Figure 3 shows the rule checking flow. Each rule contains four fields, including an owner ID, a Content-Type, a Content-Length, and an Action, where the action has two values, 'D' refers to deliver the web objects and 'R' refers to return the web objects to clients. Assume there is one web object W, and rules R_j, where j is from 1 to n. If (W's Content-Type matches R_j's) and (W's Content-Length is greater than R_j's) then the rule will be applied.

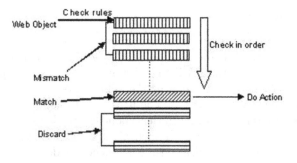

Fig. 3. Rule Checking Flow

4.3   Example

Assume that client connects to the Internet by the dial-up services, and the slow speed just accepts browsing the normal web page. The size of web page usually is smaller than 1MB; therefore the following rules are set for this situation.

{Owner,Type,Length,Action}={"Jacky","*",1000000,"D"}

Any web objects with Content-Length larger than 1MB will be delivered. This also shortens the download time and saves the network bandwidth.

5   Scheduling

In this section, we will discuss the scheduling element. Generally speaking, the delivery tasks are produced in a fast speed. To prevent from affecting the system performance and provide the quality of service (QoS), it is necessary to develop one scheduling mechanism to schedule these delivery tasks.

5.1   Purpose

There are several purposes for implementing the scheduling element. (1) Without reducing the system performance: the system performance must be considered foremost during our design. The delivery process may be very fast or very slow, so the delivery time is always unexpected and the system can't deliver the tasks on line. (2) Priority support: the proposed system wants to provide the quality of service for different users. Therefore each task has its own priority and is scheduled by the scheduling element.

5.2   Scheduling Mechanism

The concept of scheduling mechanism is shown in Figure 4. The scheduling mechanism contains a dispatcher, multiple priority queues, a selector, and a module interface.

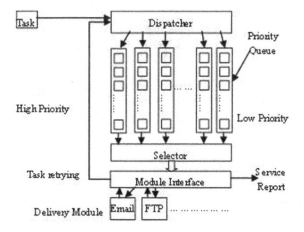

Fig. 4. Scheduling Model Diagram

When a task comes in, it is dispatched by the dispatcher element to the corresponding priority queue according to its priority. The left priority queues have higher priority than the right ones. The selector element chooses the tasks from the priority queue and sends them to the specific delivery modules. All delivery modules are external and are managed by one module interface. The external modules communicate with the interface to get the delivery web objects and return the status of delivery tasks. Some special issues are described as follows.

5.2.1 Batch Processing
In order to make the system resources perform more efficiently and do not reduce the proxy performance, the scheduling element is revoked every several minutes, and all the tasks will be batch-processed.

5.2.2 First-In-First-Out
In each priority queue, the delivery order is FIFO to ensure that all tasks in the same priority queue are processed by order. The FIFO design and again mechanism can prevent the deadlock situation.

5.2.3 Aging Mechanism
The aging mechanism is used to deal with some exceptions. When the task gets in trouble during delivering, the scheduling element has to recompute its priority. If one task is delivered with errors, we believe that it cannot be delivered in a short time to prevent encountering the same errors. Therefore, the priority of the task will be decreased as shown in Figure 5. If the task is delivered with error many times, the system will drop it and reports to users. If one task is waiting for a long time, the priority of it will be increased. The aging mechanism is to guarantee the system robustness by checking each task with error or not.

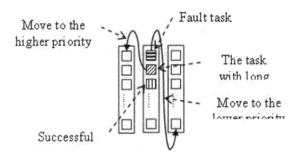

Fig. 5. Aging Mechanism

5.2.4 Module Interface
The module interface aims to integrate different delivery modules, control these modules' behavior and immediately report the current status of delivery tasks.

6   Implementation and Experimental Results

In this section, we describe the implementation details and present the experimental results of testing on the Pocket PC emulator in the Microsoft embedded visual tools. We start in section 6.1 by describing the system environment that the proposed system is implemented. In section 6.2 we discuss the implementation issues of each component. Finally, we present the experimental results in section 6.3.

6.1   System Environment

Our implementation is on the Windows platform, and is based on the proxy module in the Apache web server. For the considerations about system scalability and security, the MySQL database locates on another computer under the RedHat Linux platform. This design can improve the system reliability, and is easy to extend to a cluster architecture. We used the Visual C++ to develop the whole proxy system, and used the PHP language to develop the user profile management system.

6.2   Implementation Issues

The implementation issues of each component are described as follows:

1. **Proxy Authentication.** The Proxy Authentication component is designed to follow the HTTP 1.0/1.1 standard. When one request comes in, the WOD system checks its username and password pairs with the valid user data in the MySQL database. If they do not match, an error message is sent to client. After the authentication, the username is saved in the connection structures for the future use.

2. **Delivery Decision element.** This element is called by the proxy core, and is responsible for checking in a very short period of time whether the request web objects should be returned to users. A proxy probably has many threads corresponding to requests at the same time, and each thread must decide every decision as soon as possible. If the web objects should be returned to users, the DD element returns small packets immediately when it has been received, without waiting for the file to complete being sent.

3. **Delivery element.** This element is also called by the proxy core. It has to confirm the integrity of web objects. After the web objects are complete, it assigns a priority to these tasks according to the user's settings, and then sends the tasks to scheduling element.

4. **Scheduling element.** In our system, the priority queues are divided into 10 different queues. The first queue, Q1, contains the tasks with priorities between 1 and 10, and Q2 contains the task with priorities between 11 and 20, etc. We also assign each user a priority from 10 to 100.

5. **Database.** We choose the MySQL database as our storage element. When a large number of requests come, the proxy server creates many threads for handling these requests at the same time. Each thread has to connect to the MySQL database for checking the rules and storing the web objects for delivery. In order to avoid opening large number of connections simultaneously, we develop all threads using one connection, and create a critical section between the beginning of each query and the ending of storing the results.

6. **User profile manager.** We use the PHP to develop the user profile management, and for the convenience, users can input the system IP address like "http://proxy-ip/" to setup their rules.

6.3 Experimental Results

In this section we present the experimental results by showing the user management and the physical situations tested by the Pocket PC emulator software. After user authentication, valid users can see the following management page like Figure 6. Users can configure their own rules and accounts, switch each rule on and off, and group some rules as one rule group. All these operations are very easy for users.

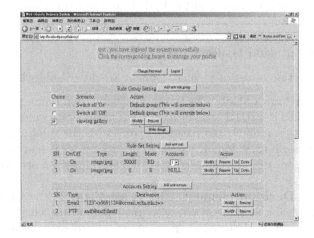

Fig. 6. User Profile Management System

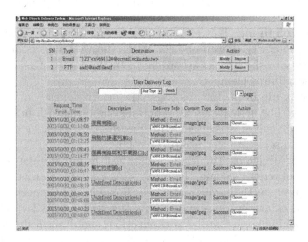

Fig. 7. Delivery histories

Fig. 8. Proxy authentication mechanism and user profile management pages

Fig. 9. Situations before and after using the WOD system

Besides, users can see the delivery histories, access time, delivery time, and other related information in this page. Figure 7 shows the delivery histories. For each delivery record, users even can write the comments for it to explain what it is. One simple search engine is implemented to help users finding the records by searching the comments.

We then used a Pocket PC emulator to test the WOD system. After setting the wireless connections and assigning the WOD system as default proxy server, a proxy authentication page is shown up (the left picture in Figure 8). When users pass the authentication, they can browse the Web as usual. Figure 8 also shows the user profile management page in Pocket PC.

After users set up a rule to deliver all images large than 50 Kbytes, the WOD system immediately works. Figure 9 shows a page before and after setting the

rule. In the right picture of figure 9, a large picture is replaced by a small picture
"D" to notify users that the picture is delivered by the system.

7 Conclusion

In this paper, we have presented a proxy-based system that automatically delivers web objects for the assortment of devices a client may own. It is the
middleware between the client and original server, and the client does not need
to install any software. We have also designed a simple rule model which is sufficient for all situations. By following the users' rules, the proposed system filters
and delivers web objects via email or ftp protocols, and users can download them
later at other working environments. The system also provides a user management system for users to set up and change their delivery rules, and it keeps a
delivery log for users to manage and search their rules. Lastly, in consideration of
the performance of the proposed system, a delivery scheduling scheme has been
designed to optimize the delivery process. The delivery scheduling can prevent
the deadlock and it improves on quality of service.

As well as developing a Web object delivery system, which we are now doing, there are several promising directions for future research. The file distribution has been an intensively studied research topic in the past few years. One
of those established technologies is the Content Distribution Network (CDN),
where a number of servers are deployed at the edge of the Internet, and clients
request file download service from their closest servers. More recently, peer-to-
peer (P2P) based file distribution techniques have quickly gained popularity, we
plan to study how to make proxy systems into a structured or a unstructured
P2P network, and combine our previous techniques on structured [14] and unstructured [15] P2P networks to enhance the system performance and scalability.

References

1. Maheshwari, A.S., Ramamritham, K., Shenoy, P.: TranSquid: Transcoding and
   caching proxy for heterogeneous ecommerce environments. In: RIDE 2002. Proc.
   of 12th IEEE Workshop on Research Issues in Data Engineering (February 2002)
2. IBM Web Intermediaries (WBI), WebSphere Transcoding Publisher,
   http://www.almaden.ibm.com/cs/wbi/
3. Bharadvaj, H., Joshi, A., Auephanwiriyakul, S.: An active transcoding proxy to
   support mobile web access. In: Proceedings of IEEE Symposium on Reliable Distributed Systems (1998)
4. Lara, E.D., Wallach, D.S., Zwaenepoel, W.: Puppeteer: Component-Based Adaptation for Mobile Computing. In: Proceedings of Third Usenix Symposium of Internet
   Technologies and Systems (March 2001)
5. Cardellini, V., Yu, P.S., Huang, Y.W.: Collaborative Proxy System for Distributed
   Web Content Transcoding. In: Proceedings of ACM CIKM, pp. 520–527 (2000)
6. Stuary, G., Rag, T., Sreedhar, K.: ATTENUATOR: Towards Preserving Originally
   Appearance of Large Documents when Rendered on Small Screen. In: Proceedings
   of International Conferences of Multimedia Expo 2003 (July 2003)

7. Hori, M., Kondoh, G., Ono, K., Hirose, S., Singhal, S.: Annotation-Based Web Content Transcoding. In: Proceedings of 9th Would Wide Web Conference (May 2000)
8. Chen, Y., Ma, W.Y., Zhang, H.J.: Detecting Web Page Structure for Adaptive Viewing on Small Form Factor Devices. In: Proceedings of 12th Would Wide Web Conference (May 2003)
9. Li, W.S., Hsuing, W.P., Kalashnikov, D.V., Sion, R., Po, O., Agrawal, D., Candan, K.S.: Issues and Evaluations of Caching Solutions for Web Application Acceleration. In: Bressan, S., Chaudhri, A.B., Lee, M.L., Yu, J.X., Lacroix, Z. (eds.) CAiSE 2002 and VLDB 2002. LNCS, vol. 2590, Springer, Heidelberg (2003)
10. Yagoub, K., Florescu, D., Valduriez, P., Issarny, V.: Caching Strategies for Data-Intensive Web Sites. In: VLDB 2000. Proceedings of 26th International Conference of Very Large Data Bases (September 2000)
11. Yuan, C., Chen, Y., Zhang, Z.: Evaluation of Edge Caching/Offloading for Dynamic Content Delivery. In: Proceedings of 12th Would Wide Web Conference (May 2003)
12. Zeng, D., Wang, F.Y., Liu, M.: Efficient Web Content Delivery Using Proxy Caching Techniques. IEEE Transactions on Systems, Man, and Cybernetics 34(3) (August 2004)
13. Hua, Z., Xie, X., Liu, H., Lu, H., Ma, W.Y.: Design and Performance Studies of an Adaptive Scheme for Serving Dynamic Web Content in a Mobile Computing Environment. IEEE Transactions on Mobile computing 5(12) (December 2006)
14. Yang, K.-H., Ho, J.-M.: Proof: A Novel DHT-based Peer-to-Peer Search Engine. IEICE Transactions on Communications E90-B(4), 817–825 (2007)
15. Yang, K.-H., Wu, C.-J., Ho, J.-M.: AntSearch: An Ant Search Algorithm in Unstructured Peer-to-Peer Networks. IEICE Transactions on Communications E89-B(9), 2300–2308 (2006)

Implementation Issues of Early Application Identification

Laurent Bernaille and Renata Teixeira

Centre National de la Recherche Scientifique (CNRS) and
Université Pierre et Marie Curie - Paris 6
Paris, France

Abstract. The automatic identification of applications associated with network traffic is an essential step to apply quality-of-service policies and profile network usage. Our prior work proposes EARLY APPLICATION IDENTIFICATION, a method that accurately identifies the application after the first four packets of a TCP connection. However, an online implementation of this method faces two challenges: it needs to run at high speed and with limited memory. This paper addresses these issues. We propose an algorithm that implements EARLY APPLICATION IDENTIFICATION plus a number of computation and memory optimizations. An evaluation using traffic traces collected at our university network shows that this implementation can classify traffic at up to 6 Gbit/s. This speed is more than enough to classify traffic at current edge networks.

1   Introduction

Administrators of enterprise or campus networks often want to apply different quality of service policies depending on the applications (to prioritize Voice over IP connections over data transfers, for instance). Besides, network administrators need to know what applications traverse their network to enforce institutional policies (such as no peer-to-peer traffic) and plan for traffic evolution. This requirement leaves network administrators with the daunting task of (1) identifying the application associated with a traffic flow as early as possible, and (2) applying network policies when needed. Therefore, there is a need for the development of tools that can identify applications associated with network traffic *accurately and early*. In this paper, we discuss the implementation of an online application classifier.

The simplest approach to traffic classification is to examine TCP port numbers. Port-based methods are simple because many well-known applications use standard port numbers (for instance, HTTP traffic uses port 80 and FTP port 21). However, the research community now recognizes that port-based classification is inadequate [1,2,3,4], mainly because many applications use dynamic port-negotiation mechanisms to hide from firewalls and network security tools. An alternative approach is to use content-based mechanisms, which search the content of packets for well-known application signatures [5,6,7]. Although very effective and accurate, content-based mechanisms are easy to evade by using encryption. In addition, there is a high storage and computational cost to study every packet that traverses a link (in particular at very high-speed links).

S. Fdida and K. Sugiura (Eds.): AINTEC 2007, LNCS 4866, pp. 156–166, 2007.

There have been several proposals [2,8,9,3,4] to address the limitations of port-based and content-based classification. Most of the proposed mechanisms perform traffic classification using flow statistics such as duration, number of packets, mean packet size, or inter-arrival time. Unfortunately, these techniques are not appropriate for early application identification as they only classify a flow after it is finished.

Our earlier work [10], which we refer to as EARLY APPLICATION IDENTIFICATION, proposes a behavior-based method to classify connections that relies only on information from the first four application packets of a TCP connection. Although EARLY APPLICATION IDENTIFICATION presents the methodology to build a classifier that acts on the beginning of a TCP connection, it does not addresses the issues to implement a classifier that runs online, in particular:

- **The links that connect large edge networks to the Internet are usually high speed.** Many universities use 1Gbits/s Ethernet connections. Some larger networks already use OC-48 links (2.5Gbits/s), and we can expect the bandwidth of edge links to continue to increase. An online classifier has strict performance requirements to analyze all packets at line rate on these high speed links.
- **Memory is a major bottleneck for tools that analyze TCP connections** [11], because they need to keep information about all active connections. On high speed links, the number of active connections can exceed one million [?], which involves a large amount of memory. Besides, the traffic analyzers need to perform numerous lookups in the list of connections, which requires fast memory.

This paper presents an algorithm that addresses these issues. We start by summarizing the EARLY APPLICATION IDENTIFICATION method [10] in Sec. 2. Sec. 3 presents the online classification algorithm and some optimizations to reduce memory consumption and computation cycles. We discuss the complexity of this algorithm in Sec. 4 and evaluate the implementation using traces collected in our university network in Sec. 5.

2   Overview of EARLY APPLICATION IDENTIFICATION

EARLY APPLICATION IDENTIFICATION uses the observation that the *size and direction* of the first few data packets of a TCP connection are expressive enough to distinguish among different applications. Intuitively, the size of the payload of the first few packets captures the application's negotiation phase, which is usually a pre-defined sequence of messages different between applications. We define the *behavior* of an application as the size and direction of the first P packets it exchanges over a TCP connection, where P is an integer value.

We design a classifier to run at the *edge* of a network (i.e., where the network connects to the Internet). Thus, the classifier can access all packets associated with a TCP connection in both directions (from sender to receiver and vice-versa). The classifier contains a set of rules to map each TCP connection (represented by its first P packets) into an application. EARLY APPLICATION IDENTIFICATION works in two distinct phases: an offline training phase and an online classification phase. Figure 1 presents an overview of this method. The left side represents the steps of the training phase and right side the components of the classifier. These two phases run at separate locations and time-frames. The training phase runs offline at a management site, whereas the classifier runs online at a management host that has online access to packet headers or in a network processor at the monitored router. Sec. 3 presents the implementation of the steps of the online classifier. Table 1 presents a summary of the notation used in the rest of this paper.

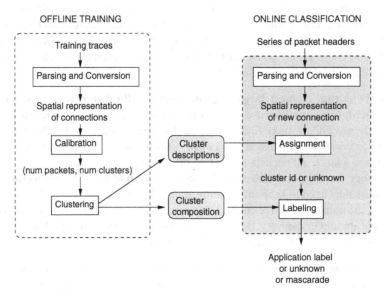

Fig. 1. Overview of EARLY APPLICATION IDENTIFICATION

Table 1. Notation

P	Number of packets considered
K	Number of clusters
c_i	center of cluster i
Σ_i	covariance matrix of cluster i
α	Assignment function
λ	Labeling function
T	Threshold to detect unknown connections
$\mathcal{A}(i)$	Set of applications present in cluster i
$\pi(i, a)$	% of connections associated to cluster i from app. a
$\mathcal{S}$	Set of standard ports
$std(p)$	Application associated with standard port p

2.1 Training Phase

The training phase runs offline and consists in detecting common behaviors in a set of connections. It applies clustering techniques to a set of training data to group TCP connections with similar behavior. The training traces contain examples of TCP connections pre-labeled with the application name. We proposed two methods to represent connections spatially and evaluated different clustering methods and showed that Gaussian Mixture Models (GMM) represents the best trade-off between accuracy and complexity to identify application behaviors [10]. Therefore, the implementation presented here is based on GMM, which models each cluster by one gaussian (represented by its center and covariance matrix). We assume diagonal covariance matrices, because they model well our dataset and the clustering algorithm is simpler in this case. This assumption also speeds up our classifier, as explained in Sec. 4.

The GMM algorithm relies on two important parameters: K, the number of clusters, and P, the number of packets. We selected these parameters by spanning the parameter space and selecting the solution that maximizes clustering quality. We found that $P = 4$ and $K = 30$ led to the best cluster quality for our training traces. Hence, we use these values in the rest of this paper.

The training phase outputs two sets: one with the description of each cluster i (or the center of the cluster center, c_i, and the covariance matrix, Σ_i) and $\mathcal{A}(i)$, which represents the set of applications in cluster i. We use both these sets to classify connections online.

2.2 Classification Phase

The classification phase uses the clusters found in the training phase to configure the online classifier. An *assignment heuristic* determines whether a new TCP connection belongs to a pre-defined cluster. Connections that do not belong to any cluster are labeled as "unknown". This approach allows the classifier to detect new applications or new modes of operation of known applications. A *labeling heuristic* selects the application label for the connection among the applications in a cluster. This heuristic can use any information from the first packets of the connection to improve classification accuracy. In particular, we use port numbers when meaningful. We now detail the assignment and labeling heuristics [10] that we adopt in the implementation presented in Sec. 3.

Assignment heuristics. Using the Gaussian Mixture Model, we can compute the a posteriori probability (i.e. the probability that a connection x belongs to a Gaussian mixture element i with center, c_i, and covariance matrix, Σ_i):

$$\mathbb{P}(i, x) = \frac{\mathcal{N}_P(c_i, \Sigma_i)(x)}{\sum_{i=1}^{K} \mathcal{N}_P(c_i, \Sigma_i)(x)}.$$

Based on these probabilities, we define the **GMM Proba** heuristic, which associates x with a Gaussian element using a maximum likelihood criterion. We define the following assignment function (we evaluate the logarithm of the probability to simplify the online computation):

$$\alpha_p(x) = \underset{i \in 1..K}{\operatorname{argmax}} \ln \mathcal{N}_P(c_i, \Sigma_i)(x).$$

This simple heuristic cannot detect unknown traffic (it will assign all connections to a cluster, even if the probability of the connection to belong to a cluster is very small). To tackle this limitation, we use a probability threshold T, and define the **GMM Thresh** heuristic as:

```
Function αₜ(x)
```
$$\text{Function } \alpha_t(x)$$
$$\quad \text{If } \not\exists i \in 1..K \text{ such that } \mathbb{P}(i,x) > T$$
$$\quad\quad \alpha_t(x) = \text{unknown}$$
$$\quad \text{else } \alpha_t(x) = \text{argmax}_{i \in 1..K} \ln \mathcal{N}_P(c_i, \Sigma_i)(x)$$

Labeling heuristics. When the cluster assignment heuristic finds the best cluster for a connection, the next step is to label it with an application. EARLY APPLICATION IDENTIFICATION has two different labeling heuristics: *predominant*, which labels connections with the predominant application in their assigned cluster, and *cluster+port*, which also uses the destination port number. Our online implementation uses the more sophisticated cluster+port heuristic.

Let $port(x)$ be the server port used by connection x, $\mathcal{S}$ the set of ports corresponding to standard client-server applications (for the applications we study, $\mathcal{S} =\{21, 22, 25, 80, 110, 119, 443, 995\}$), and std the function that associates a standard port with an application label (for this study $std(\mathcal{S}) =\{$FTP, SSH, SMTP, HTTP, POP3, NNTP, HTTPS, POP3S$\}$). We define the Cluster+Port labeling function as:

$$\text{Function } \lambda(x)$$
$$\text{If } \alpha(x) = \text{unknown}$$
$$\quad \lambda(x) = \text{unknown}$$
$$\text{Else If } port(x) \in \mathcal{S}$$
$$\quad \text{If } std(port(x)) \in \mathcal{A}(\alpha(x))$$
$$\quad\quad \lambda(x) = std(port(x))$$
$$\quad \text{Else } \lambda(x) = masquerade$$
$$\text{Else}$$
$$\quad \text{If } |\mathcal{A}(\alpha(x)) \setminus \mathcal{A}(\mathcal{S})| = 0$$
$$\quad\quad \lambda(x) = masquerade$$
$$\quad \text{Else } \lambda(x) = \text{argmax}_a(\pi(\alpha(x), a), a \in \mathcal{A}(\alpha(x)) \setminus \mathcal{A}(\mathcal{S})$$

If x is using a standard port, and if the application associated to this port is part of the cluster, the connection is labeled with this application. Otherwise, the connection uses a standard port, but does not behave accordingly. We choose to flag such connections as *masquerade*, because they can be dangerous connections using ports associated to "safe" applications to bypass firewall rules.

If the port is not standard, the connection is labeled with the predominant application among those that do not use standard ports. If the cluster consists of standard services only, we flag the connection as *masquerade* because it is probably a standard service using a non-standard port.

3   Online Application Identification

This section presents the algorithm to implement EARLY APPLICATION IDENTIFICATION with cluster descriptions obtained from GMM. We use the assignment heuristic with threshold, $\alpha_t(x)$, and the cluster+port labeling heuristic, $\lambda_c(x)$ (both these heuristics are presented in Sec. 2.2). After presenting a general algorithm to classify connections online, we describe some optimizations to this algorithm.

3.1   Algorithm

Our goal is to present a basic function to label connections with applications, and not to restrict how network operators will use this functionality. The online classifier is described in Algorithm 1. We envision that this algorithm will be integrated in a larger management system that could, for instance, apply policies online based on application labels.

Algorithm 1 takes as input descriptors of the packets entering and leaving the network. Upon capturing the header of a new packet, the classifier first maps the packet to a connection x and verifies whether x is a known connection (lines 2 and 3 of Algorithm 1). All known connections are stored in a hash table, $\mathcal{C}$. We identify each connection using a four-tuple (IPsrc, IPdst, Port src, Port dst) of the first data packet in the connection. Follow-up packets identified as either (IPsrc, IPdst, Port src, Port dst) or (IPdst, IPsrc, Port dst, Port src) belong to the same connection. When a packet does not belong to any known connection and the SYN flag is set (which indicates a new connection), we create a new entry for this connection (lines 25 to 29). If the packet flags do not correspond to a new connection, then we cannot classify the connection because we have missed the first packets of the connection. We label such connections as "unclassifiable" (line 23). Lines 4 and 5 ignore all connections that have already been labeled. If the packet contains application data, then we store the payload size in the connection descriptor (lines 7 to 15). Otherwise, we ignore the packet. Upon the reception of the P-th packet, we can label the connection using our labeling function (lines 16 to 18).

This algorithm defines the data structures *packet* and *connection*. *Packet* is a structure describing an incoming packet with attributes payloadSize (size of TCP payload), dport (destination port, to decide whether the packet was sent by the client or the server of the TCP connection), flags (TCP flags) and IPsrc, IPdst, Port src, Port dst (4-tuple of the packet). Each *connection* is described by the attributes label (application associated with the connection), pkts (number of packets with application data of the connection that have already traversed the link), sizes (vector with the sizes of the first P payloads) and the 4-tuple of the connection.

3.2   Optimizations

Running our classifier online on fast links is challenging because the classifier has little time to process each packet, and it must use as little memory as possible because fast memories (such as SRAM) are expensive and limited in size. To improve the efficiency of our implementation we explored several techniques:

1. **Compute the logarithm of the probability** to belong to each cluster, to avoid the evaluation of exponentials, as explained in Sec. 2.2.
2. **Limit lookups to packets that contain application data.** Looking up the connection associated with a packet in the list of connections based on a 4-tuple takes time. We reduce the number of accesses to the list of connections by only performing the lookup for packets that contain application data. Besides, we only create entries

```
 1: procedure CLASSIFIER(packet)
 2:     x ← connection(packet)
 3:     if x ∈ C then
 4:         if x.label != "None" then
 5:             Connection already labeled, ignore packet
 6:         else
 7:             if packet.payloadSize = 0 then
 8:                 No application data, ignore packet
 9:             else
10:                 x.pkts ← x.pkts + 1
11:                 if packet.dport = x.serverPort then
12:                     x.sizes[x.pkts] ← packet.payloadSize
13:                 else
14:                     x.sizes[x.pkts] ← −packet.payloadSize
15:                 end if
16:                 if x.pkts = P then
17:                     x.label ← λ(x)
18:                 end if
19:             end if
20:         end if
21:     else
22:         if packet.flags! = SY N then
23:             x.label ← "Unclassifiable"
24:         end if
25:         x.label ← "None"
26:         x.pkts ← 0
27:         x.serverPort ← packet.dport
28:         x.sizes[1..P] ← 0
29:         C ← C ∪ c
30:     end if
31: end procedure
```

Algorithm 1. Online Classifier

for connections with a SYN packet. This represents a small reduction of the list of active connections, but greatly reduces the number of lookups.

3. **Storage optimization:** When we label a connection, we update statistics and remove the connection from the list. This optimization can greatly reduce the amount of memory used by our algorithm. However, the applicability of this optimization will depend on how network administrators use the classification algorithm. Some usages can require the application label of a connection anytime during the connection life time.

4. **Garbage collection:** We regularly parse the list of known connections to remove connections that have expired (i.e., for which there has been no packet for one minute). We also remove connections from the list when we see a flag indicating the end of the connection (RST or FIN).

4   Complexity of Online Classification

This section compares the complexity of our classifier to port-based and content-based classifiers. At running time, any of these classifiers needs to analyze the header of all incoming packets to assign the packet to a connection. Subsequent steps depend on the classifier. Table 2 summarizes the complexity of each type of classifier.

Port-based classification only requires an additional look up of the port number in a list of pre-defined ports with the associated applications (one basic operation).

Content-based classification needs to inspect the payload of packets (which is not be possible in the case of encryption). These classifiers use substring matching algorithms. In the best case, these algorithms are known to have a running time of the order of n/m, where n is the length of the searched text and m the length of the searched string [13][1]. A content-based classifier needs to search for the signature of each target application in all packets until the connection is classified. Let $\mathcal{A}$ be the set of target applications, and $\bar{p}$ the average of the ids of the first packet that contains the signature for the set $\mathcal{A}$. Content-based classifiers requires $\frac{n}{m} \times |\mathcal{A}| \times \bar{p}$ basic operations to label a connection. For traffic classification, the searched text is the TCP payload and the search string is an application signature. In traces collected in our universtiy network, we found that the average payload size of data packets is 600 bytes, which is consistent with findings from a large network [?]. Say that the average application signature has four characters (for instance, HTTP). Then, content-based tools need in average $600/4 = 150$ comparisons to find a signature in a TCP payload. We also use our university traces to estimate the value of $\bar{p}$. We found that for most applications, the signature that allows labeling the connection is in the third or fourth packet. Putting all these values together, we get the result presented in Table 2. In addition to the number of comparisons required to identify applications, content-based classification requires a considerable amount of memory to store packets while they are processed.

Our classifier needs to store the sizes of the first P packets of the connection and the TCP port. This requires little storage (a few bytes for each connection). After P packets, our classifier assigns the connection to a cluster and labels it. The cluster+port labeling heuristic requires a small number of comparisons. The assignment heuristic, $\alpha_t(x)$, is more complex because it has to compute the probability to belong to every clusters. The probability that a connection, x, with packet sizes, $x_1, ..., x_P$, belongs to a cluster with center, $c = [c_1, ..., c_P]$, and diagonal covariance matrix, $\Sigma = [\sigma_1, ..., \sigma_P]$ is:

$$f_x = \frac{1}{(2\pi)^{P/2}|\Sigma|^{1/2}} e^{-\frac{1}{2}(x-c)^T \Sigma^{-1}(x-c)} = \frac{1}{(2\pi)^{P/2}(\prod_{i=1}^{P} \sigma_i^2)^{1/2}} e^{-\frac{1}{2}\sum_{i=1}^{P}(\frac{x_i - c_i}{\sigma_i})^2}.$$

We simplify the the computation of this probability by using a diagonal covariance matrix and computing $2 \times \ln f_x$ as follows.

---

[1] This analysis focuses on simple patterns and does not apply to regular expressions involving wildcard characters such as "*", which are necessary to identify some protocols. This means that content-based classifiers are most likely more computationally intensive than our analysis indicates.

$$2 \times ln(f_x) = cst - \sum_{i=1}^{P}(x_i - c_i)^2 \times \frac{1}{\sigma_i^2},$$

where cst is a constant defined as $cst = -P \times ln(2\pi) - \sum_{i=1}^{P} ln(\sigma_i^2)$. Overall, our classifier requires $3 \times P$ multiplications to evaluate the probability that a connection belong to a cluster (we compute $(x_i - c_i)^2 \times \frac{1}{\sigma_i^2}$ for $i \in 1..P$), and $3 \times P \times K$ multiplications to evaluate this probability for all clusters. As shown in Table 2 our classifier is at least an order of magnitude faster than signature-matching algorithms.

Table 2. Comparison of the running times for each type of classifier

	Port-based	Content-based	EARLY APPLICATION IDENTIFICATION
Basic operations to label a connection	1	$\frac{n}{m} \times \|\mathcal{A}\| \times \tilde{p}$	$3 \times K \times P$
Example with $n/m = 150, \|\mathcal{A}\| = 10$ $\tilde{p} = 3, K = 30 , P = 4$	1	4500	360

5 Evaluation

To evaluate our algorithm, we implemented it in C using the optimizations described in Sec. 3.2. We did our evaluations with a 2.4GHz opteron using a one-hour trace from our university network described in Table 3.

Table 3. Description of the traffic trace collected at the border of the Universit Pierre et Marie Curie

Duration	3600 s
Size	35.5 GB
Packets	60 236 915
Non TCP/IP packets	3 123 504
Connections	659 178
Connections with SYN	634 314
New Connections/sec	180

Table 4 compares different versions of our algorithm according to the number of entries in the connection table, $\mathcal{C}$; the number of lookups; the total CPU time; and the maximum memory (obtained using valgrind [14], a well-known memory profiler). Without any optimization our algorithm classifies the trace in 53 CPU seconds (the total time is longer due to delays in disk accesses). The maximum number of active connections stored in memory reaches 659,000 (i.e., all connections are stored) for a total storage of 55MB. Our algorithm does 86 millions lookups. The minimization of lookups reduces the classification time to 50 seconds and reduces the number of lookups to 60 millions.

Storage optimization reduces the maximum number of connections stored to 313,000 (for a total storage of 24MB), but increases a little the number of lookups (removing a connection from the list adds lookups). Finally, we evaluate garbage collection. We remove expired connections (i.e., without any packet for more than 60s) with two time intervals: 300s and 60s. Garbage collection greatly reduces the use of memory (less than 2MB) and even decreases the classification time because it speeds up lookups.

Table 4. Evaluation

Optimization	Max Entries	Lookups	Time	Max Memory
None	659k	86M	53s	55MB
Lookups	634k	60M	50s	50MB
Storage	313k	72M	50s	24MB
Garbage (300s)	20k	74M	46s	2MB
Garbage (60s)	12k	74M	47s	1.2MB

Table 4 shows that we are able to classify 35.5 GB of traffic in 46s, which corresponds to 6Gbits/s. This is very fast compared to implementations based on pattern-matching methods. Recent studies [15,16] analyze two well-known classifiers: bro [5] and l7-filter [17], and show that they classify traffic at rates lower than 500Mbits/s on machines similar to the one we used. In addition, our implementation is fast enough for most edge networks because their connections are usually 1Gbit/s (Ethernet) or 2.5Gbits/s (OC-48).

To understand where our classifier spends most of the time, we profiled it using gprof [18]. Table 5 presents the proportion of time spent handling active connections (lookups, additions, deletions), parsing packets (finding TCP payload, creating new connections, storing packet sizes) and assigning and labeling connections. We see that managing active connections and parsing packets (which all classification methods must perform) account for 90% of the processing. Cluster assignment and labeling only account for 10% of the processing. Parsing packets and managing connections are simple tasks, which could be performed much faster on dedicated hardware such as network processors. Therefore, with such hardware our classifier could probably run on even faster links.

Table 5. Time spent

Handling connection list	55%
Parsing packets	35%
Assignment and labeling	10%

6   Conclusion

This paper presented the implementation of a classifier based on the EARLY APPLICATION IDENTIFICATION method and proposed optimizations to speed-up the classification and limit memory usage. We showed that our implementation can classify traffic at rates up to 6Gbits/s, which is enough for edge networks. In addition, we profiled our program and showed that our classification method can be added to any tool that gathers per-connection statistics at a small cost.

The Matlab library used to create models and the code of our classifier are available for download at: http://rp.lip6.fr/~bernaill/earlyclassif.html. The implementation from this library can also identify applications in connections encrypted with SSL [19].

Acknowledgements

This study was supported by the RNRT through the project OSCAR and by the ACI "Sécurité Informatique" through the project METROSEC.

References

1. Karagiannis, T., Broido, A., Brownlee, N., Claffy, K., Faloutsos, M.: Is P2P dying or just hiding? In: IEEE Globecom (2004)
2. Roughan, M., Sen, S., Spatscheck, O., Duffield, N.: Class-of-service mapping for QoS: A statistical signature-based approach to ip traffic classification. In: Proceedings of ACM Internet Measurement Conference (2004)
3. Moore, A., Zuev, D.: Internet traffic classification using bayesian analysis. In: Proceedings of ACM SIGMETRICS (2005)
4. Karagiannis, T., Papagiannaki, D., Faloutsos, M.: Blinc: Multilevel traffic classification in the dark. In: Proceedings of ACM SIGCOMM (2005)
5. Paxson, V.: Bro: a system for detecting network intruders in real-time. In: Computer Networks, Amsterdam, Netherlands, 31, 2435–2463 (1999)
6. Snort: http://www.snort.org
7. Levchenko, Ma., Kreibich, Savage, Voelker: Unexpected means of protocol inference. In: Proceedings of ACM Internet Measurement Confererence (2006)
8. McGregor, A., Hall, M., Lorier, P., Brunskill, J.: Flow clustering using machine learning techniques. Passive and Active Measurement (2004)
9. Zuev, D., Moore, A.: Traffic classification using a statistical approach. Passive and Active Measurement (2005)
10. Bernaille, L., Teixeira, R., Salamatian, K.: Early application identification. In: CoNext 2006. Conference on Future Networking Technologies (2006)
11. Estan, C., Keys, K., Moore, D., Varghese, G.: Building a better netflow. In: Proceedings of ACM SIGCOMM, pp. 245–256. ACM Press, New York (2004)
12. IPMON: http://ipmon.sprintlabs.com
13. Boyer, R., Moore, J.: A fast string searching algorithm. Communications of the ACM (1977)
14. Valgrind: http://valgrind.org/
15. Yu, F., Chen, Z., Diao, Y., Lakshman, T.V., Katz, R.H.: Fast and memory-efficient regular expression matching for deep packet inspection. In: Proceedings of the ACM/IEEE Symposium on Architecture for networking and communications systems, pp. 93–102. ACM Press, New York (2006)
16. Dreger, H., Mai, M., Feldmann, A., Paxson, V., Sommer, R.: Dynamic application-layer protocol analysis for network intrusion detection. In: Usenix Security Symposium (2006)
17. l7filter: http://l7-filter.sourceforge.net/
18. gprof: http://www.gnu.org/software/binutils/manual/gprof-2.9.1/
19. Bernaille, L., Teixeira, R.: Early recognition of encrypted applications. Passive and Active Measurement (2007)

Securing Internet Coordinate Systems

Dali Kaafar[1], Laurent Mathy[2], Kavé Salamatian[3], Chadi Barakat[1],
Thierry Turletti[1], and Walid Dabbous[1]

[1] INRIA Sophia-Antipolis, France
[2] Lancaster University, UK
[3] LiP6, France

Abstract. Internet coordinate systems (e.g. [1,?]) have been proposed
to allow for distance (Round-Trip Time, shortly RTT) estimation between nodes, in order to reduce the measurement overhead of many applications and overlay networks. Indeed, by embedding the Internet delay
space into a metric space – an operation that only requires each node in
the system to measure delays to a small set of other nodes (its neighbors),
nodes are attributed coordinates that can then be used to estimate the
RTT between any two nodes, without further measurements, simply by
applying the distance function associated with the chosen metric space
to the nodes' coordinates.

Recently, these coordinates-based systems have been shown to be accurate, with very low distance prediction error. However, most, if not
all, of current proposals for coordinate systems assume that the nodes
partaking in the system cooperate fully and honestly with each other –
that is that the information reported by probed nodes is correct – this
could also make them quite vulnerable to malicious attacks. In particular, insider attacks executed by (potentially colluding) legitimate users
or nodes infiltrating the system could prove very effective.

As the use of overlays and applications relying on coordinates increases, one could imagine the release of worms and other malware, ex-
ploiting such cooperation, which could seriously disrupt the operations of
these systems and therefore the virtual networks and applications relying
on them for distance measurements.

In this talk, we first identify such attacks, and through a simulation
study, we observed their impact on two recently proposed positioning
systems [3], namely Vivaldi and NPS. We experimented with attack
strategies, carried out by malicious nodes that provide biased coordinates information and delay measurement probes, and that aim to (i)
introduce disorder in the system, (ii) fool honest nodes to move far away
from their correct positions and (iii) isolate particular target nodes in
the system through collusion. Our findings confirm the susceptibility of
the coordinate systems to such attacks.

Our major contribution is therefore a model for malicious behavior
detection during coordinates embedding [4]. We first show that the dy-
namics of a node, in a coordinate system without abnormal or malicious
behavior, can be modeled by a Linear State Space model and tracked by
a Kalman filter. Then we show, that the obtained model can be gener-
alized in the sense that the parameters of a filter calibrated at a node

S. Fdida and K. Sugiura (Eds.): AINTEC 2007, LNCS 4866, pp. 167–168, 2007.

can be used effectively to model and predict the dynamic behavior at another node, as long as the two nodes are not too far apart in the network. This leads to the proposal of a Surveyor infrastructure: Surveyor nodes are trusted, honest nodes that use each other exclusively to position themselves in the coordinate space, and are therefore immune to malicious behavior in the system. During their own coordinate embedding, other nodes can then use the filter parameters of a nearby Surveyor as a representation of normal, clean system behavior to detect and filter out abnormal or malicious activity. A combination of simulations and PlanetLab experiments are used to demonstrate the validity, generality, and effectiveness of the proposed approach for both Vivaldi and NPS.

Finally, we address the issue of asserting the accuracy of Internet coordinates advertised by nodes of Internet coordinate systems during distance estimations. Indeed, some nodes may even lie deliberately about their coordinates to mount various attacks against applications and overlays.

Our proposed method consists in two steps: 1) establish the correctness of a node's claimed coordinate by using the Surveyor infrastructure and malicious embedding neighbor detection; and 2) issue a time limited validity certificate for each verified coordinate. Validity periods are computed based on an analysis of coordinate inter-shift times observed by Surveyors. By doing this, each surveyor can estimate the time until the next shift and thus, can limit the validity of the certificate it issues to regular nodes for their calculated coordinates. Our method is illustrated using a trace collected from a Vivaldi system deployed on PlanetLab, where inter-shift times are shown to follow long-tail distribution (lognormal distribution in most cases, or Weibull distribution otherwise). We show the effectiveness of our method by measuring the impact of a variety of attacks, experimented on PlanetLab, on distance estimates.

References

1. Ng, T.E., Zhang, H.: A Network Positioning System for the Internet. In: Proceedings of the USENIX annual technical conference, Boston (June 2004)
2. Dabek, F., Cox, R., Kaashoek, F., Morris, R.: Vivaldi: A decentralized network coordinate system. In: Proceedings of the ACM SIGCOMM, Portland, Oregon (August 2004)
3. Kaafar, M.A., Mathy, L., Turletti, T., Dabbous, W.: Virtual Networks under Attack: Disrupting Internet Coordinate Systems. In: Proceedings of CoNext 2006, Lisboa (December 2006)
4. Kaafar, M.A., Mathy, L., Barakat, C., Salamatian, K., Turletti, T., Dabbous, W.: Securing Internet Coordinates Embedding Systems. In: SIGCOMM 2007 (2007)

A Real-Time Performance-Monitoring Tool for Emergency Networks

Shuprabha Shakya, Mohamad Abdul Awal, Dwijendra K. Das,
Yasuo Tsuchimoto, and Kanchana Kanchanasut

Internet Education and Research Laboratory intERLab,
Asian Institute of Technology, Bangkok, Thailand
{shupa643, aawal}@gmail.com, {dwijendra, yasuo, kanchana}@ait.ac.th
http://www.interlab.ait.ac.th

Abstract. Emergency networks normally operate under highly unpredictable wireless environment and hence real time performance information holds a great significance that cannot be reflected by the conventional post evaluation approach. In this paper, we propose a performance monitoring tool to display the network performance in real-time for mobile ad hoc network using OLSR protocol, deployed under emergency conditions. Moreover, simplified GUI with real time visualization, network performance summarization along with run time triggering of sudden change in the network has been introduced to provide user with easier, user-friendly and comprehensible perception on the run time network performance.

1 Introduction

The rising dominance of computing devices ubiquitously has acknowledged Mobile Ad-hoc network (MANET) as a promising approach for next generation wireless network. Such networks are highly useful for collaborative computing, emergency network and disaster relief operation; a proof of concept has been demonstrated successfully in the DUMBOnet in 2006[5] with a MANET using OLSR[1] protocol. From a series of experiments conducted on the test-bed, it was observed that in emergency situation; the network environment is extremely unpredictable, the network equipment in use tends to have different transmission signal levels and they also tend to be fragile due to limited power supply. To ensure the endurance of emergency multimedia communication in such difficult conditions, we need an ability to assess the network performances in real-time and adjust the routing parameters or the network topology. In other words, fine-tuning by adjusting the protocol parameters or the network topology, at each participating node has to be done in real-time for the survival of the network in an extremely ad hoc scenario of emergency networks.

Common approach for performance measurement involves post evaluation procedures based on the preliminary offline traces. The general trend involves capturing of the packets using various sniffing tools followed by the prolonged

S. Fdida and K. Sugiura (Eds.): AINTEC 2007, LNCS 4866, pp. 169–183, 2007.
© Springer-Verlag Berlin Heidelberg 2007

post parsing and calculation for analysis purpose. The measures seem to be complicated and time consuming for a non-programmer analyst under time critical circumstances. Besides, the necessity to maintain the huge traces proves to be challenging for conducting test for a long term, especially under consideration of small handheld devices with limited memory capacity.

We present a real-time performance-monitoring tool, RTPMt, capable of detecting and monitoring traffic flows in emergency mobile ad hoc network. The system provides information on packet and message loss, link failure and the control packets statistics. It provides a simplified GUI with real time visualization and network performance summary with automatic warning mechanisms for the users upon significant events. It is user-friendly with comprehensible perception on the run time network performance. Such tool though intended for emergency network, it can be advantageous for normal mobile ad hoc networks where a novice operator can examine the performance at a glance. The tool has a huge benefit that opens up a wide possible future dimensions for further development of the protocol.

In this paper, we describe the design and implementation of RTPMt with the experimental tests. We first review existing performance monitoring tools that could be deployed for MANET and then describe DUMBOnet emergency network test bed in section 2 and 3. In section 4, the design and implementation of RTPMt is depicted along with its evaluation in section 5.

2   Related Work

Performance measurement tools found so far involve post evaluation procedures based on the preliminary offline traces. The common method undergoes capturing of data packets using various sniffing tools; most commonly used being ethereal[3], tcpdump[11] and dsniff[2] that prove to be tedious in account of post parsing and analysis phase. Under time critical circumstances, the approach seems to be time consuming and complicated for a non-programmer analyst. These methods requires to maintain the huge traces of traffic records that could be hindrance while conducting long term test when we are under limited resource scenario.

Different real-time monitoring framework have been developed for fixed networks such as the traditional MRTG[9] that monitors traffic, logs the traffic data, and represents them and many others as listed in [8]. These real-time monitoring tools are mainly developed for existing Internet hence are not suitable for MANET environment. An attempt was made to study the protocol performance through laboratory test-beds like mLAB that uses mDog to sniff the packets with additional visualization utilities to observe the signal strength[6]. However, this is an emulation approach, illustrated with one of the proactive MANET protocols, developed to reflect the real world scenario. In another paper[7], the author discuss about a traffic monitoring system that is used for detecting mobile IPv6 traffic flows. These approaches are not capable of handling the real time performance monitoring of routing protocols in mobile ad-hoc network in real life environment.

3   DUMBOnet Emergency Network

DUMBOnet is an experimental setup of several geographically isolated disaster sites interconnected by a satellite network[5] using MANET over OLSR, as shown in Figure 1. The long delay satellite links are considered as a link within the same MANET in DUMBOnet. Nodes within the net communicate with each other in a multi-hop ad-hoc network with IP packets routed by OLSR routing protocol. OLSR protocol is a table driven; proactive routing protocol that inherits the stability of link state routing algorithm. It periodically constructs and maintains the neighbor information using Multi-Points Relay (MPR) nodes[1].

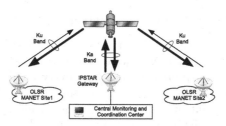

Fig. 1. Architecture of DUMBOnet

Within the network, nodes communicate using a unified OLSR packet format, embedded in UDP datagram for transmission over the network. The packets are transmitted to neighbor nodes by increasing the packet sequence number, each time a packet is created. Each packet can encapsulate one or more messages that share a common header format. The message sequence number of every newly generated message is also incremented. Thus generated message can be flooded onto the entire network through multiple intermediate nodes, or flooding can be limited to nodes within a diameter from the originator of the message.

4   RTPMt

From our experiments on DUMBOnet in 2006[5], the performance monitoring tools for an emergency network should be able to perform automated calculation based on the captured packet flows in the network, provide graphical performance monitoring tool for detecting the network performance in real time. It should be able to distinguish between different packet flows and should be able to extract information specific to the protocol in use. It should provide with the detailed traffic analysis along with summarized output in real time, detect changes in certain performance metrics at runtime and trigger the user of any sudden changes in the network whenever some monitored values exceed the threshold values. It should be designed for mobile units with optimized memory utilization and minimum processor overhead while being able to maintain the calculated trace logs which can be further utilized for post analysis purpose.

With above requirements, RTPMt was designed and developed to observe and analyze the runtime performance of MANET with OLSR protocol to be used for our future DUMBOnet experiments. From the architectural point of view, the system is devised to work with ad-hoc network topologies and is independent of the wireless technologies in use. The system has been designed as a plug-in and is integrated over the routing protocol. It is capable of accessing various functionalities, variables and repositories like neighbor tables maintained by the protocol necessary for performing real time calculation of protocol specific parameters. The plug-in architecture makes the implementation isolated and hence flexible for the future extension.

4.1   Real-Time Performance Parameters

The tool is designed for each individual node to do its own evaluation of the network condition and its environment in a distributed system. In MANET, node mobility is random and unpredictable where every node would have to come across multiple paths in the network, thus an average performance observed by a node at any instant over the network is particularly useful for real-time performance tuning. Different parameters measured by the tool are described below:

Packet Loss/Packet Loss Rate/Packet Delivery Ratio: The packet loss observed by a node i over the link between node i to node j at any instant is given by the difference of P_{ji}, packet generated by node j to node i and P_{ij}, packet received by node i from node j at that instant. The average packet loss $\overline{P_{L_i}}$ observed by a node i at any instant is determined by

$$\overline{P_{L_i}} = \frac{1}{N} \sum_{j=1}^{N} P_{ji} - P_{ij}$$

Similarly, the average packet loss rate $\overline{P_{LR_i}}$ is determined as average ratio of loss packets to the total packets transmitted.

$$\overline{P_{LR_i}} = \frac{Packet\_Loss}{Total\_Packets} = \frac{1}{N} \sum_{j=1}^{N} \frac{P_{ji} - P_{ij}}{P_{ji}}$$

For the packet delivery ratio over a link, the received packets can be determined as the difference between the packets transmitted and packets loss. Thus, the average Packet delivery ratio observed by node i is determined as:

$$\overline{P_{pdr}} = \frac{1}{N} \sum_{j=1}^{N} \frac{P_{ji} - (P_{ji} - P_{ij})}{P_{ji}}$$

Message Loss/Message Loss Rate: In a network, a node can receive messages originated from different nodes that may come directly or relayed through intermediate nodes. If a node i receives messages originated from nodes $j = 1, 2, 3 \cdots N$, where M_{ji} represents the message originated from originator j to node i and M_{ij} be the messages received by node i from originator j, then the average message loss observed by node i at any instant is observed as:

$$\overline{M_{L_i}} = \frac{1}{N} \sum_{j=1}^{N} M_{ji} - M_{ij}$$

Similarly, the average message loss rate observed by the node i at any instant is given by

$$\overline{M_{L_i}} = \frac{Message\_Loss}{Total\_Messages} = \frac{1}{N} \sum_{j=1}^{N} \frac{M_{ji} - M_{ij}}{M_{ji}}$$

Control Overhead: In OLSR, nodes generated four types of messages, the HELLO, TC, MID and HNA as control messages, to perform the routing operation. The overhead is considered as the sum of the total number of control messages generated from the originator at any instant. Depending upon the algorithm, flooding mechanism and network changes, control overhead generated in the network might vary. This gives the notion of the traffic level in the network at any instant. The control overhead observed by a node i at any instant is obtained by taking average of the overhead generated by each originator node j.

$$\overline{M_{overhead_i}} = \frac{1}{N} \sum_{j=1}^{N} (HELLO_{ji} + TC_{ji} + MID_{ji} + HNA_{ji})$$

Link Failure/Link Failure Frequency: In the real network, the link failure occurs due to multiple reasons like node mobility; environmental factors like obstacles, surroundings, human presence; node failure; fading and collision in wireless environment etc. In RTPMt, a link failure is defined as the number of times a neighbor node on the link disappears from the neighbor list. If $n(i, j)$ represents the number of link failures across the links between node i and node j and N be the number of links, the average link failures observed by node i at any instant is given by

$$\overline{L_{fi}} = \frac{1}{N} \sum_{j=1}^{N} \overline{L_{fij}} = \frac{1}{N} \sum_{j=1}^{N} n(i, j)$$

If t_s is the test time duration at that instant, then the average link failure frequency observed by the node i at that instant is given by

$$\overline{L_{ffi}} = \frac{1}{t_s} \sum_{j=1}^{N} \frac{n(i, j)}{N}$$

4.2   RTPMt Implementation and Output Display

The system has been implemented on Linux platform. Currently, the OLSR daemon used for the study is Unik olsrd implementation (olsrd-0.4.10 Released Version)[12]. The system has been developed in GNU C using GTK[4] and relevant packages. The detail description of RTPMt implementation and evaluation is given in the report[10]. In RTPMt, the required OLSR packets information are extracted, processed and then provided to the real-time processing unit to update the runtime repositories. Information of each packet as parsed by the system is shown in Figure 2 below where the display starts as soon as the system starts capturing the network traffic.

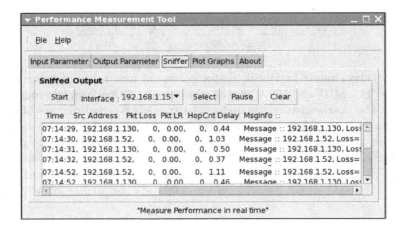

Fig. 2. Sniffer —displays detail information of the received packets

The information displayed per packet includes the *time duration* of the packet received, *source ip address* of the node-generating packet, *average accumulated packet loss* observed at the moment, *average packet loss rate*, and *message information* encapsulated within the OLSR packet. Sniffer, thus, provides a broad picture that would be useful for a user in an emergency network to observe the ongoing network traffic in the network and also useful for subsequent analysis to study the network performance using per packet information.

OLSR control and topology related parameters like *HELLO interval, TC interval*, and other parameters like *hysteresis threshold limits, hysteresis Scaling, willingness, MPR coverage, debug level* can be entered by the users, otherwise the default setting are used. This is useful for users to fine-tune the values of these parameters at runtime to see the impact of tuning on OLSR performance.

RTPMt has a real time processing unit which maintains three run-time repositories comprising of *Link Failure Repository, Run Time Packet Repository* and *Run Time Message Repository*. Within this unit, there is a validation controller that updates the information in the repositories and removes some obsolete information during some specified validation period for each entity under observation in order to optimize the run-time memory usage of the system. These repositories are processed dynamically to refresh the information on arrival of the new packets. Whenever any relevant packet is received in the network interface as determined by the system filter, it automatically triggers the real time processor. The run-time packet repository utilizes the packet information and determines the parameters like packet loss, packet loss rate, and packet delivery ratio at run time. The packet loss is determined by considering packet sequence number in the packet header of the OLSR packet. Packet loss at any instant is given by the number of missing sequence numbers from the corresponding neighbor. The received packet sequence numbers are tracked so as to determine the total packets received and loss packets. It is further used to calculate the performance parameters according to the respective definition discussed earlier. Similarly, the run time message repositories determine the parameters like message loss, message loss rate and control overhead received dynamically. Here, the message sequence number from each originator is taken into consideration where number of missing numbers accounts for the loss at any instant. The packet and message repositories retain a sequence buffer per neighbor so as to keep track of the unusual sequences of packets incoming to the host that could cause huge difference in the sequence number. The reason behind this could be due to regeneration or overflow of the sequence number variable causing wrap-around case. Whenever any relevant packet arrives, the entry of the neighbor is detected in the run time neighbor nodes list. If the entry exists, the corresponding sequence number in the packet is compared with that stored in the sequence buffer of the node entry. This is done to find out the nearest smaller sequence number, provided that the difference is less than tolerance limit. If such entry exists, the corresponding sequence number is replaced with the current sequence number and the corresponding insertion time *Vtime* of the sequence number is updated. If the required entry is not found, the sequence number is added into the buffer with inserted time in the time attribute. The maintained buffer is used for checking against further arrivals of packets and is refreshed periodically. As the instances of such unusual variation in sequence numbers are not frequent, the size of the buffer remains small without having impact on system performance. The link failure repository maintains the information about failure over the links in the network. The run-time processing unit accesses the neighbor table maintained by the routing protocol in every HELLO interval in order to determine the neighbor list detected at the instant. As shown in Figure 3, the output parameter comprises of real time packet and message analysis as well as their run time averages as observed at the current node upon which the monitoring is taking place. Thus, these components allows users to observe the traffic flows and the overall characteristic from different aspects which is useful for predicting the prevailing conduct in the emergency network and for improving its performance in real time.

Run Time Packet Analysis: This section provides information on link status that includes *link failure* over individual link from the current node, *packet loss*, *packet loss rate* each observed with respect to the corresponding neighbor node on the link. It also provides *the node status* indicating whether this neighbor node is detected in the neighbor list or not at the instant. Thus, the user can observe the latest status per each neighbor that is updated at real time reflecting the changing scenario.

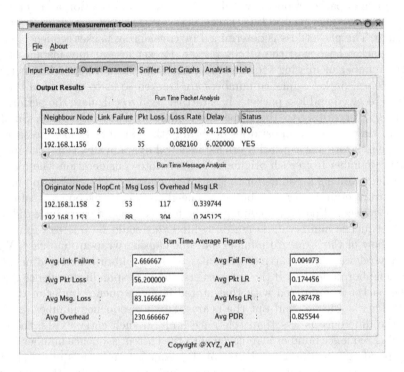

Fig. 3. Performance Parameters with Run Time Average

Run Time Message Analysis: OLSR routes messages generated from the originator nodes in the network by encapsulating them inside OLSR packets. This section shows the list of nodes originating the OLSR messages which are received by the current node. Besides, it also gives real time updates of the corresponding *message loss, message loss rate, hop count* to reach that originator and *control overhead*, where these parameters are determined corresponding to each originator.

Run Time Average Figure: Previous sections provide information on per neighbor or per originator basis. However, from the user perspective, they would also like to know the performance observed by the node on average at any instant. The section determines the average value among all the nodes and shows the average figures observed at the run time. It includes *Average link failure, Average Packet loss, Average Message Loss, Average Overhead, Average packet delivery ratio, Average Packet Loss Rate, Average Message Loss Rate* and *Link*

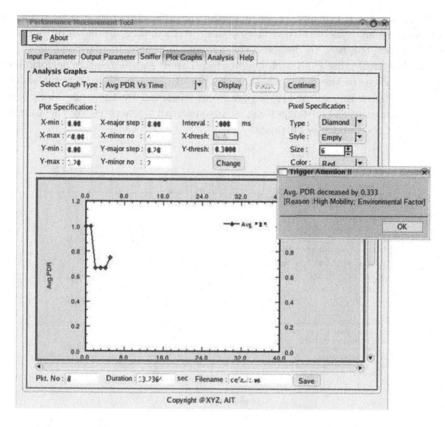

Fig. 4. Graphic Display with Run Time Trigger

Failure Frequency determined as discussed earlier. Therefore, as the network scenario varies, the corresponding performance results experienced by the node in summarized form are depicted dynamically.

To enable the network operators to comprehend the real-time information during an emergency situation, our system has put a strong emphasis on visualization with a graphical presentation which allows user to visualize the network performance graphically at real time. When a user clicks the *Display* button, the corresponding plot is drawn at run time along with the respective legends, type of graph and axis leveling that can be resize as shown in Figure 4. The user can suspend or continue the real time plot at any instant by clicking *Pause* or *Continue* button and save the image. The system constantly monitors the variation in the performance of the network when traverse through various circumstances. Whenever an abrupt change in the performance is detected exceeding the threshold limit preset by the user, the system automatically alerts the user with the corresponding trigger notification. In the Figure 4, the system triggers the user when the packet delivery ratio decrease suddenly exceeding the threshold limits 0.3 as set by the user.

When an event triggers for an attention, RTPMt provides the user with a comparative analysis of the ongoing network performance, as shown in Figure 5, which assists the user to diagnose the network behavior in real-time. It shows the packet traffic rate from each neighbor and analyzes the relative performance with respective to the other whether the performance is high, average or low. Figure 5 shows the log of the trigger event observed by the node along with the possible cause. The trigger log is automatically generated by the tool for subsequent post analysis purposes.

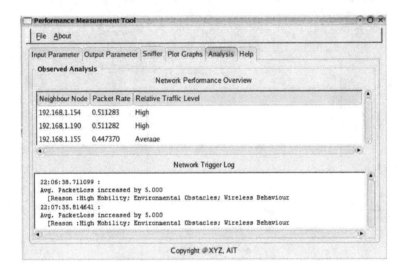

Fig. 5. Analysis Section

5   Tool Evaluation and Experiments

For validation purposes, we first compare our tool with Ethereal to validate its functions. The test-beds were setup within the AIT campus periphery where mobile nodes were distributed within certain area and performance measured by the tool were observed on varying time factor, distance between the nodes, node mobility and increasing the node density, detail description can be found in [10]. From these experiments, it was shown that, with the real time measurement, we could observe the dynamic affect of the changing environments and topology at the instance.

5.1   Comparison with Ethereal

The most commonly used tool considered for the passive approach of performance measurement is the industry standard tool ethereal. In order to evaluate our tool, qualitative and quantitative evaluation was done through multiple tests on the performance of the routing protocol using both RTPMt and Ethereal.

Both tools were deployed in real test-bed environment where its behavior was observed under different criteria. The tests were performed to determine the variation of the different performance parameter on varying four constraints: time, distance, mobility and node density. For the measurement purpose, we have considered all the parameters as discussed in section 4. An example test result is shown in Figure 6 that shows the variation in packet delivery ratios (PDR) measured by our tool and Ethereal versus increasing number of mobile nodes. The corresponding parameters of interest were calculated from the offline analysis of the traces collected from the ethereal during the tests. On comparing the real time results from RTPMt and that calculated from Ethereal, comparable results were obtained with small deviations. The maximum deviation in performance is shown up to 0.1 which is highest in case of testing in mobility environment in account to the multiple failure instances.

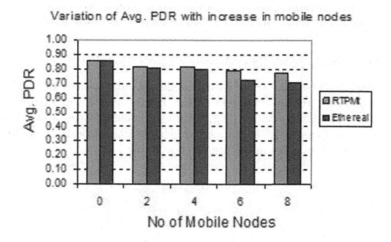

Fig. 6. Comparison of variation of PDR between RTPMt and Ethereal

The variation has been apparent due to the introduction of real time processing in RTPMt that introduces some overhead. Besides, RTPMt also isolates the system scope to the MANET protocol which avoids the processing of the un-necessary information. Due to this, the frequency of the packet captured is found to vary from each other leading to the variation in the two results. In the real time approach, different repositories information and buffers has to be maintained for temporary processing. In order to optimize the memory usage, all these information has to be updated to keep the fresh information. Due to this, certain packet information may be considered obsolete and hence removed. But in case of offline approach, it dumps all the captured data that can be processed later offline. However, the introduction of real-time approach with the acceptable deviation shows the feasibility of the system to be implemented for the real time performance measurement in mobile ad-hoc network environment.

Despite the real time processing, the developed system is found to be efficient with the reduction of 54.79% and 33.05% in CPU and memory utilization as compared to Ethereal. This is due to the requirement of the tools like ethereal to deal with multiple protocols with excessive detailing, increasing the complexity and processor overhead. It has been optimized in our system by avoiding unnecessary information processing and reducing the memory usage by timely refreshing of information based on the validation time period, allocated for each entity. Moreover, the storage requirement of the huge traces for the analysis is reduced significantly by 98% in average on using the system as compared to ethereal. The difference is found to be more significant with increase in the node density and test duration that shows the ability of the system to be implemented for long duration test under highly dense network even in the resource constraint situation. This is achieved by customizing the approach to keep the calculated parameters instead of dumping whole packet information. However, this would not provide user with all the detail packet information as from offline approach which can be considered as tradeoff with memory exploitation issue.

5.2   Experiments with RTPMt

An example test-bed was setup with 6 nodes (4 laptops and two PCs with external wireless card) in a wireless ad-hoc mode as shown in Figure 7. The area consists of buildings, car parking, dormitories, and forest near by. Here, the arrow sign shows the nodes to be moving with normal pedestrian speed. The configurations of the nodes in use are given in Table 1.

Table 1. Node configuration

Node	IP address	OS	Wireless chipset
A	192.168.1.170	FC5	Intel-PRO/Wireless 2200BG
B	192.168.1.52	FC6	Atheros Chipset
C	192.168.1.154	FC6	Atheros Chipset
D	192.168.1.153	FC6	Atheros Chipset
E	192.168.1.130	XP/Cygwin	Linksys
F	192.168.1.150	XP/Cygwin	Linksys

The nodes were allowed to move randomly in the area and the approximate movement boundary of the nodes is represented by the GPS measurement location. The test was conducted for 400secs duration where nodes were moving and getting dispersed at pedestrian speed. For the real time experimentation, the performance is observed in Node A.

In the first test, the packet loss ratio was observed at real time. Initially, the nodes were moving together and though the packet loss was observed, it was not so much considerable. As, a result of which, the loss rate was found to decrease and was below 0.1, till the 170secs duration. Then, the nodes started to move actively and dispersed gradually which showed significant increment in the loss

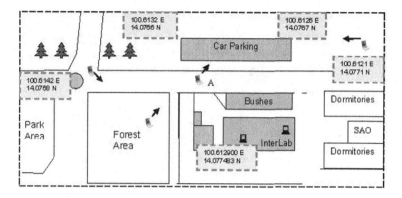

Fig. 7. Node Distribution Scenario

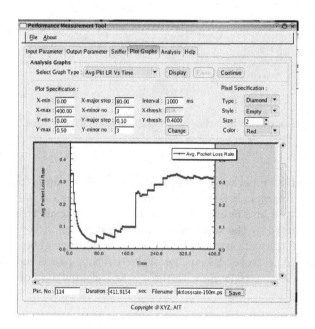

Fig. 8. Observation of the variation in average packet loss rate on node A

rate reaching to the maximum of 0.32 at 285secs duration from start of the test. Then the results remained almost comparable afterwards. The real time graph plotted snapshot is shown in Figure 8.

In the second test, we made observation of the accumulated packet loss in the node A. Initially, all nodes were distributed in static position in the network. Then a node A is moved away towards the dormitory area as shown in Figure 7 and the corresponding impact was shown in real time. The average accumulative packet loss was observed to increase gradually as shown in Figure 9 where the

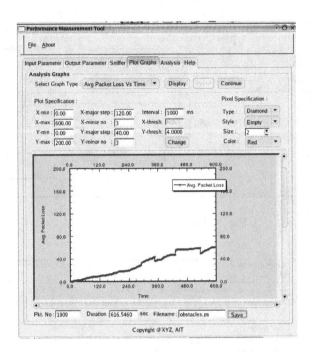

Fig. 9. Observation of the variation in average accumulative packet loss on a moving node A

average accumulative packet loss figure at 600secs duration is found to be 60.0. Due to the environmental factors like trees, car parking, dormitories building, people around, the interference was found to be significant that increased the packet loss observed by the node. Sometimes, decrease in packet loss is observed which is due to introduction of new nodes on its detected neighbor list causing the average figures to decrease. A snapshot of the real time plot is shown in Figure 9. Similar observations were found with the average accumulated of control packets overhead.

6   Conclusion and Future Work

In this paper, we have presented a prototype tool RTPMt developed for the real time performance measurement in MANET operating in an emergency environment. It is capable of detecting and monitoring traffic flows in such networks, providing user with useful information including metrics and statistics dynamically. The tool was validated against measurements from conventional tool *ethereal* and tested over an experimental test bed where it was found to be capable of reflecting dynamic impact of the changing environments and network topology at real-time, effective to identify the reason for deviation that can be valuable to establish a robust network. Though RTPMt was developed OLSR protocol but it can be easily extended for other MANET protocols in the future. Results obtained form the different evaluations demonstrated that RTPMt is easy to use with efficient memory and CPU consumption, time.

Acknowledgements

We would like to thank Dr. Poompat Saengudomlert for his valuation suggestions throughout the work. We would also like to thank interLab researchers for their feedbacks and all the AIT friends and students who helped us with full enthusiasm to perform the real bed tests.

References

1. Clausen, T., Jacquet, P., Laouiti, A., Minet, P., Muhlethaler, P., Qayyum, A., Viennot, L.: Optimized Link State Routing Protocol (OLSR), IETF RFC 3626 (2003)
2. dSniff, http://www.monkey.org/~dugsong/dsniff/
3. Ethereal - Network Protocol Analyzer, http://www.ethereal.com/download.html
4. GTK+, The GIMP Toolkit, http://www.gtk.org/
5. Kanchanasut, K., Tunpan, A., Awal, M.A., Das, K.D., Wongsaardsakul, T., Tsuchimoto, Y.A: Multimedia Communication System for Collaborative Emergency Response Operation in Disaster-affected Areas, Interlab Technical Report TR 2007-1
6. Karygiannis, A., Antonakakis, E.: mLab: A Mobile Ad Hoc Network Test Bed. In: 1st Workshop on Security, Privacy and Trust in Pervasive and Ubiquitous Computing in conjunction with the IEEE International Conference in Pervasive Services (2005)
7. Marques, P., Castro, H., Ricardo, M.: Monitoring emerging IPv6 wireless access networks. Wireless Communication, IEEE (2005)
8. Measurement Tools Taxonomy, http://www.caida.org/tools/taxonomy
9. MRTG - The Multi Router Traffic Grapher, http://oss.oetiker.ch/mrtg/
10. Shakya, S.: Development of automated real time performance measurement and visualization framework for real mobile ad-hoc network. Thesis Report, Asian Institute of Technologies, AIT (May 2007)
11. TcpDump Network Monitoring Tool, http://www.monkey.org/~dugsongtcpdump.org/
12. Unik Olsr Implementation, http://www.olsr.org

A Role-Based Peer-to-Peer Approach to Application-Oriented Measurement Platforms

Kenji Masui and Youki Kadobayashi

Nara Institute of Science and Technology
8916-5 Takayama, Ikoma, Nara 630-0192, Japan
{kenji-ma,youki-k}@is.naist.jp

Abstract. The importance of large-scale measurement infrastructures for grasping the global state of the Internet is recently strongly emphasized. However, a fundamental analysis of these infrastructures has not yet been conducted. In this paper, we highlight the formation of measurement networks and provide a first look at measurement activities performed on those networks. We also propose a scheme for constructing a measurement network, which divides the measurement agent's roles into core agent and stub agent. This scheme entails only simple adjustment for changing the formation of the measurement network. Through the transition from a centralized system to hybrid and pure peer-to-peer networks, we visualize the flow of measurement procedures and explore the factors that have an influence on the overall performance of measurement systems.

Keywords: peer-to-peer network, network measurement platform.

1 Introduction

Large-scale network systems that include an overlay network application and a distributed computing environment have not yet fully succeeded in obtaining network characteristics on the Internet. Network characteristics are necessary information for sustaining and scaling the services of these systems. For example, an IP-level topology and round-trip time (RTT) information between two nodes are used as the metrics of the proximity among overlay nodes, and overlay network applications perform their optimization procedures based on these metrics. However, due to the complicated procedures of measurement and data processing, network characteristics are not yet widely utilized by the applications.

Given this situation, application-oriented measurement services [1,2,3] have been appearing. In these systems, measurement procedures are typically packaged into one independent network service, and applications need only issue a request to the systems in order to obtain network characteristics. Monitoring nodes are located in multiple administrative domains, and the systems manage and control them to obtain the requested data. These systems have emerged as a way for the applications to grasp the global state of the Internet.

S. Fdida and K. Sugiura (Eds.): AINTEC 2007, LNCS 4866, pp. 184–198, 2007.

This tendency has also brought a radical shift in the architecture of measurement systems. Traditional measurement infrastructures generally prepare a central management plane. In such systems, respective monitoring nodes perform measurement independently or according to the decision made by a central control plane. Then the system aggregates collected data in the central storage. This scheme worked well within the statistical observation of the Internet for mid-to-long-term. In the case of application-oriented measurement, measurement targets (e. g., nodes and links) disperse widely and change dynamically depending on the structure of application networks. In addition, collecting a large number of network characteristics with one control point causes a heavy load on specific nodes. For these reasons, the architecture of measurement systems has become more decentralized, and measurement methodologies performed in a decentralized manner have been studied. Some of these measurement methodologies are called "cooperative measurement," [4,5] in which a monitoring node shares collected network characteristics and/or communicates with other agents for more efficient collection of network characteristics.

Though a variety of measurement systems has been proposed, and these systems focus on the sorts of network characteristics that they can collect, their architectures are yet to be sufficiently explored. We do understand the superficial indices, such as the capability and efficiency of measurement methodologies, that are implemented on the systems; however, we do not know which aspects of the architectures bring such results and how they influence actual deployment. This problem cannot be left unsolved before a large-scale measurement service is widely deployed, because such analysis could reveal fundamental drawbacks and advantages of the measurement infrastructures.

In this paper, we focus on the structure of a measurement network as one aspect of the architecture. The measurement network is a network in which measurement procedures are performed and measurement-related information is managed. One of the structures focused on is a centralized structure, where a specific management node manages all of the management information and controls the other monitoring nodes. Another is a pure peer-to-peer structure, where all of the monitoring nodes take partial charge of the management node's tasks. Moreover, we propose a hybrid structure, where some of the nodes work as management nodes and the others work as ordinary monitoring nodes. We explain how the respective measurement networks and the monitoring nodes in the networks actually work, and we investigate their basic characteristics related to their responsiveness and load distribution.

The rest of this paper is organized as follows: Section 2 describes measurement network models including a centralized model, a pure peer-to-peer model and our proposed hybrid model. We describe the experiment in Section 3, and in Section 4, we look into the experimental results and investigate the basic characteristics of the respective measurement networks. Section 5 presents a discussion on application-oriented measurement services and the formation of their networks, based on evaluation in the previous section. We refer to related work in Section 6, and finally conclude this paper in Section 7.

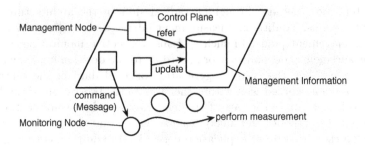

Fig. 1. Components in the measurement network and relationships among them

2   Measurement Network Models

In this section, we first define the components of a measurement network and how they work and interact with other entities. In Section 2.2, we describe two existing models of measurement networks — centralized and pure peer-to-peer models. We also refer to a hybrid measurement network model in the same section. Finally in Section 2.3, we propose a methodology to allow shifting a measurement network between these models, and we describe its implementation on an actual measurement system.

2.1   Components of the Measurement Network

A measurement network is a network in which measurement procedures are performed according to predefined sequences. Here we define the entities that appear in a measurement network and its operation.

The first entity is a "monitoring node," which performs measurement procedures in order to collect network characteristics. The second entity is a "management node," which is responsible for coordinating other entities so that the intended measurement can be performed. For example, the management node inspects and updates "management information," such as the list of monitoring nodes, and commands some of the monitoring nodes to perform measurement procedures. Collectively, we call a system that is composed of management information and management nodes a "control plane." A control plane is, so to speak, an entity where decisions for measurement procedures are made. "Control messages" are exchanged among the monitoring and the management nodes to achieve the intended measurement features. The control messages include a measurement command to the monitoring nodes and the node list in the measurement network, but do not contain the network traffic derived from the measurement procedures themselves. We note that one physical node may simultaneously play the roles of both management and monitoring. Figure 1 shows the relationship among the entities described in this paragraph.

2.2   Three Types of Models

Existing measurement networks are categorized mainly into two models — centralized and pure peer-to-peer models. In the centralized model, one management node or a cluster of replica nodes manages all of the management information and issues control messages to the monitoring nodes. On the other hand, in the pure peer-to-peer model, all of the nodes take the roles of both monitoring and measurement. Therefore each node has to maintain the measurement network and has also to perform the necessary measurement procedures. The merit of the centralized model is that the responsibilities of the respective nodes are clear, and it is easy to follow the sequence of measurement operations. At the same time, a central management node has to tolerate a heavy load caused by all the management operations, otherwise the measurement system will not function. In the pure peer-to-peer model, we can distribute such loads to all nodes; hence this model is considered appropriate for a large-scale measurement system. However, a frequent change in the state of the measurement network, such as nodes joining and leaving, will result in poor stability of the control plane. These trade-offs are also discussed as a general problem existing between centralized and peer-to-peer systems.

As a middle course between these models, we now consider a hybrid measurement network model. In the hybrid model, management operations are divided among some management nodes, while other nodes behave as monitoring nodes. The difference between the hybrid model and the centralized model is that, in the hybrid model, multiple management nodes each perform a different management operation, whereas the management operations are not clearly divided in the centralized model even if there are multiple management nodes. By adopting this model, we can expect to moderate both the load concentration and the instability of the measurement network, which are the problems in the first two models. This model is similar to that of the Kazaa [6] network, in which stable nodes (called "super nodes") construct an overlay network in a peer-to-peer manner, and ordinary nodes join the overlay network through the super nodes.

2.3   N-TAP and Its Extension

N-TAP[1] [7,8] is a distributed measurement infrastructure that provides an application-oriented measurement service. In N-TAP, a program called an "N-TAP agent" performs measurement procedures. The N-TAP agents also construct a pure peer-to-peer measurement network (called the "N-TAP network") that is based on the technique of Chord [9]. In the context of Section 2.1, the N-TAP agent corresponds to a node that works as both a monitoring node and a management node. The management information in N-TAP is stored and shared in a shared database that the N-TAP agents construct upon their peer-to-peer network. Besides the nodes (agents) list being maintained in the shared database as the management information, collected network characteristics are

---

[1] Available at http://www.n-tap.net/

also stored in the same database so that the agents can share them in cooperative measurement. The N-TAP agents decide measurement tactics according to the "local-first and remote-last" rule, which improves the responsiveness to measurement requests from applications. In order to create a situation of a hybrid measurement network on an actual measurement system, we made some modifications on N-TAP.

The key idea of the extension to N-TAP is the division of the agent's roles into core agent and stub agent. The core agent, which corresponds to the management node, constructs the measurement overlay network, called the N-TAP network, as conventional agents did: it maintains its own routing table in the Chord ring and stores some of the shared data in a local database as a part of the shared database. The core agent also performs measurement as a monitoring node if necessary. The stub agent, which is equivalent to the monitoring node, does not perform the operations related to the construction of the N-TAP network. For joining the N-TAP network, the stub agent inserts its information in the shared agent list so that other agents can find it. It performs measurement only when a core agent sends a request to it or when it knows that the measurement procedures that are requested directly from applications should be done by itself. In the case that the stub agent needs to do the operations related to the N-TAP network, it sends a request to one of core agents, and the core agent responds to the request. For example, suppose that a stub agent wants to find a core agent that is responsible for a specified ID in the Chord ring so as to retrieve a shared data entry that has this ID; the stub agent asks a core agent to find the responsible agent, and the core agent performs the procedure of finding it. After the core agent obtains a result, it sends the result to the stub agent. In this way, even a stub agent, which does not perform the management procedures for the N-TAP network, can know the state of the N-TAP network.

By adopting the scheme of core and stub agents, we can also easily form the centralized and pure peer-to-peer measurement networks. Figure 2 shows the transitions of measurement networks according to the allocation of the respective numbers of core and stub agents. Now we have N agents, and C of N agents are assigned as core agents; i. e., $S (= N - C)$ agents are stub agents. The N-TAP network where $C = 1$ is equivalent to a centralized measurement network because all of the management information is concentrated in one core agent. If we take the value of $C = N$, all of the agents are core agents; therefore the N-TAP network in this situation is a pure peer-to-peer network, which is same as the conventional N-TAP network. In case of $C = i \, (2 \leq i \leq N - 1)$, we can regard the N-TAP network as the hybrid measurement network.

As described in this section, we can now have three types of measurement networks on the actual measurement system. In the following sections, we investigate the basic characteristics of these measurement networks.

3 Experiment

For this experiment, we used 128 homogeneous nodes in StarBED [10], which is a large-scale network experiment facility. Each node had an Intel Pentium III

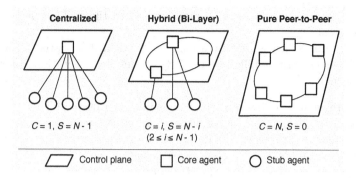

Fig. 2. Measurement network formations with the scheme of core and stub agents ($N = 6, i = 3$)

1 GHz CPU, 512 MB memory and a 30 GB ATA hard drive. These nodes were connected through 100 Mbps Ethernet links in the same network. The Debian GNU/Linux operating system with the 2.6-series kernel was installed on each node.

We had one N-TAP agent run on each node; therefore we constructed a measurement network with 128 agents (i. e., $N = 128$). An N-TAP ID, which puts an agent in the Chord ring, was randomly assigned to each agent with no overlaps. The reason we chose random IDs was to distribute the load derived from maintaining the N-TAP network among the core agents in the hybrid and pure peer-to-peer measurement networks. After the N-TAP network was constructed, we ran a client program on one node that is in the same experimental network and did not have an agent. The program sequentially issued 2000 requests to one of the core agents for the RTT information between two randomly chosen experimental nodes. The program also issued the same number of the requests to one of the stub agents if the N-TAP network had stub agents. The request messages were exchanged based on the XML-RPC protocol between an agent and the client program. We note that an N-TAP agent usually tries to reuse RTT data previously collected and stored in the shared database if a client program specifies the request on the freshness of the RTT data. However, for simplicity in this experiment, we forced the agents not to reuse the RTT data but to perform the actual measurement. The agents logged their operations with time stamps, and N-TAP related packets were captured on the nodes, so we were able to analyze the behavior of the measurement network. We selected the values of 1, 2, 4, 8, 16, 32, 64 and 128 for C (the number of core agents) to shift a measurement network from the centralized one to the decentralized one. For convenience, we numbered the respective agents from 1 to 128 according to the following rules: (a) The first agent was a core agent that accepted and processed the above requests. (b) If there were other core agents, they were numbered from 2 to C. (c) If there were one or more stub agents, we set a stub agent that accepted and processed the above requests as the 128th agent. (d) If there were other stub agents, they were numbered from $C + 1$ to 127. Also note that the 128th stub agent was configured to issue a request related to the N-TAP network to the first core agent.

The procedures carried out by a core agent when it accepted an RTT measurement request are as follows (see [7,8] for detailed operational flows on an N-TAP agent):

1. The core agent searches the source node in the requested RTT measurement. In this procedure, the core agent issues a request to find a core agent that is responsible for storing the data entries on the source node in the shared database. After it finds a responsible agent, it asks the agent to send the information on the source node (for instance, whether the source node is alive or not).
2. If the source node is alive (this condition is always true in this experiment), the core agent asks the source node to measure the RTT. Then the source node sends the measurement result to the core agent.
3. On receiving the result, the core agent responds to a client program with this result.
4. The core agent stores the collected RTT information in the shared database. It finds another core agent, one that is responsible for storing this data entry, and sends the entry to the responsible agent.

In the case of a stub agent, a control message to find a responsible agent was always sent to a specific core agent because the stub agent did not have a routing table in the N-TAP network but only knew the core agent that bridged between the N-TAP network and the stub agent itself. Apart from this messaging manner, the stub agent behaved in a same way as a core agent.

After the experiment, we confirmed that no measurement error had occurred and that all of the N-TAP related packets had been correctly captured during the experiment. The evaluation carried out in the following section is based on the recorded behavior of the agents after the measurement network became stable, i. e., no change in the agents' routing tables were made.

4   Evaluation

In this section, we investigate the basic characteristics of the respective measurement networks shown in Section 2. Our focus is the load distribution and the responsiveness to a measurement request in measurement networks.

4.1   Load Distribution

First we investigate the flow of control messages in the N-TAP network. Since the N-TAP agents have to carry out procedures according to the control messages, we can determine the distribution of loads among the agents by seeing this flow. Figure 3 depicts the distribution of exchanged control messages among the agents. Its horizontal axis denotes the assigned numbers of source agents in control messages, and the vertical axis denotes the assigned numbers of destination

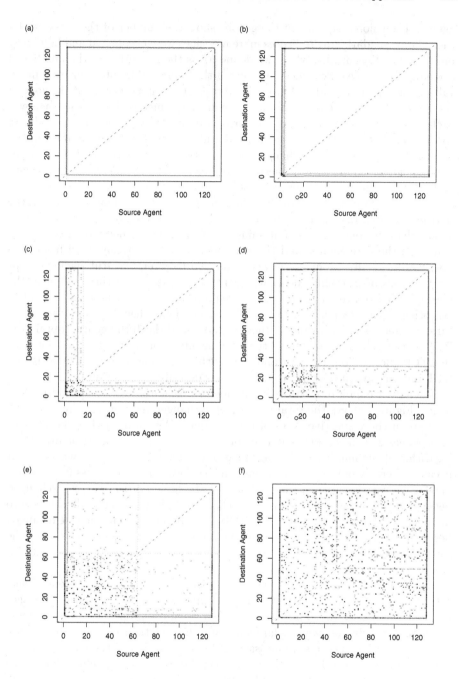

Fig. 3. Distribution of exchanged messages among 128 N-TAP agents where (a) $C = 1$, (b) $C = 4$, (c) $C = 16$, (d) $C = 32$, (e) $C = 64$, and (f) $C = 128$

agents. The colored squares in the graphs show the number of the messages by their darkness: dark gray indicates more messages were exchanged and light gray means fewer. Specifically, where we define M as the logarithm of the number of exchanged messages, we divide the zone of the values of M into four even intervals and assign four shades of gray to the respective intervals so that the zone of the largest value of M is the darkest; a white area means that no message was exchanged between the agents. The horizontal and vertical dotted lines indicate the borders between the core agents and stub agents; therefore the bottom-left area shows the messages exchanged between two core agents, the bottom-right and top-left areas are for the messages between a core agent and a stub agent, and the top-right area is for the messages between two stub agents.

In any case, we can confirm that the squares are plotted more densely in the bottom-left area than in other areas, and the grays there are mostly dark. This shows that the burden of maintaining the measurement network was concentrated on the core agents, and the stub agents were relatively freed from such tasks. Additionally, no message was exchanged between two stub agents except for the cases of involving the 128th agent. The reason why the number of the messages to/from the first and 128th agents is large is that these agents had to ask other agents to perform the RTT measurement when they accepted measurement requests. For example, these agents asked the 10th agent to obtain the RTT between the 10th agent and the other agents. Moreover, after they obtained the RTT information, the first and the 128th agents had to store the measured RTT information in the shared database, as described in Section 3.

Secondly, we look into the exact number of exchanged messages and its tendency. Figure 4 shows the total number of exchanged messages during the 4000 requests in the respective cases of the C values. We can find that the number of messages exchanged between two core agents increases proportionally as the logarithm of the number of core agents grows. This number is zero where $C = 1$ because there is only one core agent and it does not need to issue a control message to another core agent. Meanwhile, the number of messages exchanged between a core agent and a stub agent changes slightly, though it becomes zero in the case of no stub agent ($C = 128$). The number of messages exchanged between two stub agents decreases as the number of stub agents decreases. The total number of messages tends to be larger as the number of core agents increases.

From these tendencies, let us see the number of messages that an agent of each role has to process as a metric of loads. It appears that the number of messages that one core agent has to process is reduced when the proportion of core agents to the total number of agents is large, because the growth order of the summation of the core-core and core-stub messages is lower than that of the number of core agents. On the other hand, when this proportion of core agents is large, the number of messages that one stub agent has to process increases but is still smaller than the number of messages that one core agent has to process.

These facts indicate that the scheme of core and stub agents works just as we had intended, that is, that the loads should be distributed among the core agents,

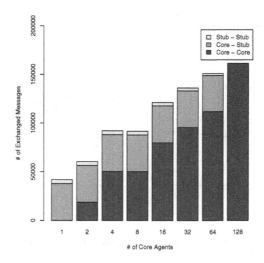

Fig. 4. Number of exchanged messages

and the stub agents should have less burden. The maintainer of the measurement network can easily adjust the load distribution with the proportion of core agents as he or she intends.

4.2   Responsiveness

Next we compare the responsiveness to a measurement request in the cases of a request to a core agent and to a stub agent. Responsiveness is an important factor as an application-oriented measurement service, because it has an effect on optimization procedures performed by emerging applications that need network characteristics. In Figure 5, the boxplots that represent the distribution of the turn-around time for a measurement request are depicted. The left graph represents the turn-around time in the case that a client program issued requests to a core agent, and the right graph represents the turn-around time in the case of issuing requests to a stub agent. In both graphs, the horizontal axis denotes the number of core agents and the vertical axis denotes the turn-around time for one request. In the case of sending a request to a stub agent, the boxplot where $C = 128$ is not given because we have no stub agent in the measurement network.

We can find that, in both cases, the turn-around time where we adopted the centralized model is shorter than the turn-around time with other models. The difference between the centralized model and other models is that the agent that accepts a request must perform the procedures for finding a responsible agent, retrieving the information on agents in the N-TAP network from the shared database, and requesting other core agents to store the collected data as an entry in the shared database. Inspecting the log files of the agents that accepted measurement requests from a client program, we calculated the mean of required

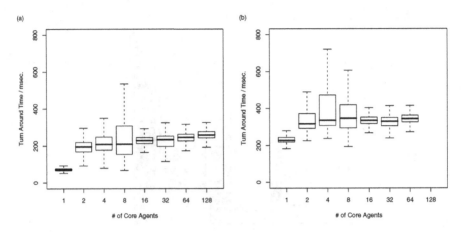

Fig. 5. Turn-around time for a measurement request to (a) a core agent / (b) a stub agent

time for each procedure, and the result is shown in Table 1. From this table, we see that, between the centralized model and the other models, a considerable difference of the time required for a measurement request is dominated by the time required for these procedures. The time required for finding a responsible agent is expected to increase linearly depending on the logarithm of the number of core agents. This is because, given the nature of Chord, the number of times a control message to find a responsible agent is forwarded among the core agents is proportional to the logarithm of the number of core agents. In Table 1, the required time for finding a responsible agent seems to follow this expectation. On the other hand, the required time for the database-related procedures would not significantly change while the size of local databases in respective core agents is small, and we can confirm such a tendency from the table. We also note that the distribution of the core agents' IDs also has an effect on the topology of the measurement overlay network, which results in the fluctuation of the required time, as in the above table. In this experiment, the IDs were randomly assigned; therefore we suppose that the required time for these procedures is almost the same among the agents.

The required time for finding a responsible agent in the case of sending a request to a stub agent is longer in the order of a few milliseconds than in the case of sending a request to a core agent. This can be explained by considering that a stub agent first needs to send a control message to a core agent, while a core agent can send a message directly to the next hop's agent in its own routing table. We can suppose that this additional procedure for a stub agent increases the required time in the case of sending a request to a stub agent.

According to the discussion in this section, a measurement network with the centralized model is superior to one with the hybrid or the pure peer-to-peer model in its responsiveness to a measurement request. In this experiment, communication delay between the agents is short enough to be ignored, however,

Table 1. Required time for the procedures (in milliseconds)

The number of core agents ($= C$)	2	4	8	16	32	64	128
Find a responsible agent (core)	1.0	2.5	6.2	4.8	6.4	7.5	7.8
Retrieve from the shared DB (core)	5.5	5.3	7.6	3.5	3.4	3.0	3.0
Store in the shared DB (core)	52.7	53.7	49.4	58.2	55.5	60.5	62.6
Find a responsible agent (stub)	2.1	7.1	9.6	8.3	9.8	11.2	—
Retrieve from the shared DB (stub)	10.0	9.1	9.7	5.5	5.2	4.6	—
Store in the shared DB (stub)	56.5	58.5	55.0	60.3	56.4	61.5	—

the communication delay will range approximately from tens to thousands of milliseconds when the measurement network is deployed in a wide-area network. This will have significant influence on the measurement network with the hybrid or the pure peer-to-peer model because a larger number of control messages must be exchanged through networks in these measurement networks. However, the centralized measurement network always has to struggle with load concentration at a core agent. These factors should be considered in constructing a measurement network.

5 Discussion

So far we have described the trade-offs among measurement networks with three different models based on the agents' behavior in respective networks. The centralized measurement network can get the best responsiveness in exchange for the heavy loads, which may bring a decrease in responsiveness. In the hybrid measurement network, we can select multiple core agents according to our purposes, and the processing loads can be distributed among the core agents. The load on one core agent will be the minimum on an average in the case of the pure peer-to-peer measurement network. However, in the hybrid and pure peer-to-peer measurement networks, the responsiveness will go down depending on the size of the control planes of these networks.

The ease of adjusting the formation of a measurement network will be important in the actual deployment of a measurement service. In this paper, we first proposed the scheme of core and stub agents in a measurement network. With this scheme, we can easily shift the measurement network among the centralized network, the hybrid network and the pure peer-to-peer network by adjusting the proportion of core and stub agents. In the case that we can control a measurement network (e. g., when we monitor network facilities with such measurement systems), administrators should design the measurement network to meet their requirements. They will benefit from the ease of adjustment to the measurement network. In the case that we cannot know beforehand what types of agents will join a measurement network, we cannot create a clear plan for constructing the network. One of the cases is that the agents run on the same nodes as the applications (an overlay network application, etc.), whose nodes will arbitrarily join and leave. Even in such cases, role-based adjustment will work with the application nodes. For example, in order to improve the responsiveness to a measurement request, we would choose agents that are connected with a high-speed link and have high performance as core agents. Other metrics, like the continuous running time of nodes, will also be helpful in constructing the desired measurement network.

Focusing on the application-oriented measurement service, quick responsiveness to a measurement request is indispensable in a measurement system. To improve the responsiveness in a hybrid or a pure peer-to-peer measurement network, some possible refinements of a measurement system can be pointed out. One is to let an agent cache the results of finding a responsible agent so as to decrease the number of exchanged control messages. From the results in Section 4.2, in a large-scale core network, we can expect that the required time for finding a responsible agent will become dominant in the turn-around time for a measurement request. Caching the results of this procedure will improve the responsiveness, but the agents will need to handle the inconsistency between the cache and the actual topology of a measurement network, and we will pay a waiting time penalty when such inconsistency occurs. Moreover, as described before, choosing core agents based on the capability of agents will also be effective. In the case of choosing core agents dynamically, we will also have to handle the migration of key-value pairs in a distributed hash table (DHT), which is expected to be a considerable burden.

6   Prior Work

Some application-oriented measurement systems have been proposed. The S^3 [2]'s network is similar to our hybrid measurement network in terms of having multiple roles for the entities in its network. On the other hand, considering that these entities are connected in a peer-to-peer manner, the S^3 network can be regarded as a pure peer-to-peer measurement network. iPlane [3] forms a centralized measurement network and provides a variety of network characteristics including an IP-level topology, packet loss rate and available bandwidth. pMeasure [1] leverages the technique of Pastry [11] to form its own pure peer-to-peer measurement network and manage monitoring nodes in this network. In application-oriented measurement, the responsiveness to a measurement request is emphasized. To improve the responsiveness in these systems, an inference algorithm for network characteristics is sometimes utilized instead of performing actual measurement procedures. For example, iPlane estimates the RTT between two nodes based on an AS path. Alternatively, research efforts have produced effective measurement methodologies in large-scale networks called "cooperative measurement." As one example of the cooperative measurement methodologies, Vivaldi [4] lets us calculate the RTT between two nodes from their locations and distance in Euclidean space. Some researchers have adopted an approach of optimizing overlay networks for a specific measurement purpose. For example, MIND [12] focuses on the indexing and query processing in order to make its overlay network suitable for the distributed monitoring of anomalous traffic.

Other measurement infrastructures, e. g., DIMES [13] and NETI@home [14], whose main purpose is the statistical analysis of network characteristics, basically construct centralized measurement networks. They aggregate the collected data to a central server for performing their own analysis. These infrastructures do not need to consider responsiveness as strictly as application-oriented measurement services do. Hence the simple formation of a centralized measurement network seems to be suitable for analyzing the collected data.

In a hybrid peer-to-peer network, each overlay node is assigned one or more node roles and is managed in a hierarchical structure as described already in this paper. Kazaa [6], a peer-to-peer file sharing application, utilizes this scheme to connect between its unstructured peer-to-peer network and ordinary nodes. Though the details of its protocol and structure are not officially unveiled, some measurement-based work [15,16] has already been done. The extension to N-TAP that we have added in this paper is unique in applying this scheme to a structured measurement overlay network in which measurement procedures different from the ones of ordinary file sharing applications are performed.

7   Conclusions

Analysis of the behavior and characteristics of measurement networks was an unexplored field. In this paper, we proposed a methodology for constructing a measurement network, which can easily change its network formation, alternating between centralized, hybrid and pure peer-to-peer models. By adopting this scheme and modifying an existing measurement agent, we investigated the operational flow in each of the measurement networks. As a result, we were able to confirm that exchanging control messages through networks has an appreciable effect on the turn-around time for a measurement request in the hybrid and pure peer-to-peer measurement networks. At the same time, the processing loads were successfully distributed among core agents in these networks. The consideration of such trade-offs is important in constructing a desired measurement network.

More measurement networks of a decentralized type will appear, and their importance will grow in the future, as large-scale network services and emerging applications are developed in the Internet. In further research and development of the N-TAP project, we aim to construct a practical measurement network that can provide network characteristics indispensable for these applications.

References

1. Liu, W., Boutaba, R., Hong, J.W.K.: pMeasure: A Tool for Measuring the Internet. In: E2EMON 2004. Proceedings of the 2nd IEEE/IFIP Workshop on End-to-End Monitoring Techniques and Services (October 2004)
2. Yalagandula, P., Sharma, P., Banerjee, S., Basu, S., Lee, S.J.: S^3: A Scalable Sensing Service for Monitoring Large Networked Systems. In: INM 2006. Proceedings of the ACM SIGCOMM Workshop on Internet Network Management (September 2006)

3. Madhyastha, H.V., Isdal, T., Piatek, M., Dixon, C., Anderson, T., Krishnamurthy, A., Venkataramani, A.: iPlane: An Information Plane for Distributed Services. In: OSDI 2006. Proceedings of the 7th USENIX Symposium on Operating Systems Design and Implementation (November 2006)

4. Dabek, F., Cox, R., Kaahoek, F., Morris, R.: Vivaldi: A Decentralized Network Coordinate System. In: Proceedings of ACM SIGCOMM 2004 (August 2004)

5. Donnet, B., Raoult, P., Friedman, T., Crovella, M.: Efficient Algorithms for Large-Scale Topology Discovery. In: Proceedings of ACM SIGMETRICS 2005 (June 2005)

6. Kazaa: http://www.kazaa.com/

7. Masui, K., Kadobayashi, Y.: N-TAP: A Platform of Large-Scale Distributed Measurement for Overlay Network Applications. In: DAS-P2P 2007. Proceedings of the Second International Workshop on Dependable and Sustainable Peer-to-Peer Systems (January 2007)

8. Masui, K., Kadobayashi, Y.: Bridging the Gap between PAMs and Overlay Networks: a Framework-Oriented Approach. In: PAM 2007. Proceedings of the Eighth Passive and Active Measurement Conference, LNCS, vol. 4427, pp. 265–268. Springer, Heidelberg (April 2007)

9. Stoica, I., Morris, R., Liben-Nowell, D., Karger, D., Kaashoek, M.F., Dabek, F., Balakrishnan, H.: Chord: A Scalable Peer-to-peer Lookup Service for Internet Applications. IEEE Transactions on Networking (TON) 11(1), 17–32 (2003)

10. Miyachi, T., Chinen, K., Shinoda, Y.: StarBED and SpringOS: Large-scale General Purpose Network Testbed and Supporting Software. In: VALUETOOLS 2006. Proceedings of the First International Conference on Performance Evaluation Methodologies and Tools (October 2006)

11. Rowstron, A., Druschel, P.: Pastry: Scalable, distributed object location and routing for large-scale peer-to-peer systems. In: Guerraoui, R. (ed.) Middleware 2001. LNCS, vol. 2218, Springer, Heidelberg (2001)

12. Li, X., Bian, F., Zhang, H., Diot, C., Govindan, R., Hong, W., Iannaccone, G.: MIND: A Distributed Multi-Dimensional Indexing System for Network Diagnosis. In: Proceedings of IEEE INFOCOM 2006 (April 2006)

13. DIMES: http://www.netdimes.org/

14. Simpson Jr., C.R., Riley, G.F.: NETI@home: A Distributed Approach to Collecting End-to-End Network Performance Measurements. In: Barakat, C., Pratt, I. (eds.) PAM 2004. LNCS, vol. 3015, Springer, Heidelberg (2004)

15. Leibowitz, N., Ripeanu, M., Wierzbicki, A.: Deconstructing the Kazaa Network. In: WIAPP 2003. Proceedings of the 3rd IEEE Workshop on Internet Applications (June 2003)

16. Liang, J., Kumar, R., Ross, K.W.: The KaZaA Overlay: A Measurement Study. Computer Networks (Special Issue on Overlays) 49(6) (October 2005)

Gap Analysis in IP Multicast Dissemination

Hitoshi Asaeda[1] and Bill Manning[2]

[1] Graduate School of Media and Governance
Keio University
5322 Endo, Fujisawa
252-8520 Kanagawa, Japan
asaeda@wide.ad.jp
[2] Information Sciences Institute
University of Southern California
4676 Admiralty Way
Marina del Rey, CA 90292
bmanning@karoshi.com

Abstract. IP multicast is advantageous for high quality streaming applications and future needs in the Internet. However, it is generally recognized that IP multicast requires significant routing coordination and configuration, and hence its routing protocols are non-scalable. Recently, Source-Specific Multicast (SSM) has been standardized and proposed as the deployable IP multicast communication architecture. SSM basically works for the one-to-many communication, and eliminates many of the complexities the traditional many-to-many multicast communication has. While SSM gives advantages for the IP multicast deployment, there is still a gap between what is reported as the state-of-the-art in the literature and what could be implemented in practice.

In this paper, we analyze the deployment barriers SSM creates, and consider how we can ease some of the barriers. To define the possible approaches, we discuss the functions SSM requires, and the necessary components network operators and application developers need to know for fulfilling the demand.

Keywords: IP multicast, SSM, multicast deployment.

1 Introduction

IP multicast is designed to distribute data to a large number of receivers in the Internet. It is advantageous for high quality streaming applications and envisioned future needs in the Internet. In contrast, although there is much research work related to IP multicast technologies and most router vendors already support basic IP multicast routing protocols, IP multicast has not fully deployed in the Internet yet. One of the main reasons is that it is generally recognized that IP multicast requires significant routing coordination and configuration, and hence its routing protocols are fairly complex and non-scalable, and network administrators and application developers believe that IP multicast requires additional maintenance and operational costs.

S. Fdida and K. Sugiura (Eds.): AINTEC 2007, LNCS 4866, pp. 199–212, 2007.

Recently, Source-Specific Multicast (SSM) [1] has been proposed as the deployable IP multicast communication architecture. SSM basically works for the one-to-many communication in which a single data sender transmits data to multiple receivers, and eliminates many of the complexities the traditional many-to-many multicast communication has. Moreover, IP multicast technology has been rapidly increasing in perceived importance and growing due to the emergence of IPTV services (in the broad sense) these days. SSM ideally fits an IPTV's communication style, and the IP multicast deployment should have been accelerated. However, the situation was not drastically changed. One of the reasons is that the alternative approaches like Application Layer Multicast [12] or P2P multicast can work well in the current Internet without requiring significant protocol change. But the fundamental point is that, regarding the IP multicast and SSM deployment, there is still a big gap between what is reported as the state-of-the-art in the literature and what could be implemented in practice.

In this paper, we analyze some of the deployment barriers SSM creates, and discuss how we can ease the barriers and grow SSM use. To define the possible approaches, we discuss the functions SSM requires, and the necessary components network operators and application programmers need to know for fulfilling the demand. In fact, there are many alternative approaches, like ALM and overlay multicast [13], that support data distribution to multiple receivers without using IP multicast. Knowing these technologies is important, but showing the future direction toward the IP multicast deployment is the main aim of this paper, and the discussions related to these alternative approaches are out of scope of this paper.

The remainder of this paper is organized as follows: Section 2 briefly explains the SSM architecture and its functions. In this section, we describe the advantages of SSM and the required protocols to make the SSM communication viable in operations. Obsolete protocols that are not used in SSM networks are also mentioned to contrast prior multicast efforts. By showing the statistical trends measured in the target networks, most applications used in the Internet would be able to work on SSM only multicast networks. Section 3 analyzes the gap between the SSM deployment scenarios or strategies and the unsolved issues remaining in the SSM architecture. Note that some issues are very broad and are not completely solved with the current stage. This paper clarifies the points we need to discuss and gives the first steps toward the future solution. Section 4 concludes the discussions and describes the points as the future work.

2   Source-Specific Multicast

2.1   Concepts

Multicast communication has run into barriers to its wide-scale deployment. Mainly, these barriers are rooted in the problem of building efficient multicast routing trees for dynamic group memberships [16]. More precisely, a PIM-SM protocol [2] provides many-to-many communication by using a Rendezvous Point router (RP) and maintaining a shared-tree called a Rendezvous Point Tree (RPT). After PIM routers construct an RPT, they discover the source address whose data is transmitted along the RPT, and switch to the optimal source-rooted Shortest-Path Tree (SPT). Since the routing states between RPT and SPT may be frequently changed, the router procedures require complex algorithms and do not scale well. In addition, in order for an RP to notify information about active sources in a local PIM domain to other domains, Multicast Source Discovery Protocol (MSDP) [3] cooperates with PIM-SM. MSDP provides a mechanism to connect multiple PIM domains by managing multiple RPs in the entire Internet, yet it introduces extra message handling and burden in routers.

On the other hand, in a one-to-many communication environment, each receiver can notify interesting source address(es) with group address to the upstream router on the same LAN as group membership information upon request. In this communication architecture called Source-Specific Multicast (SSM) [1], a multicast data receiver specifies both source and group addresses for his join or leave request. The collaborative effort with source and multicast address specification eliminates the source address discovery procedure from multicast routing protocols. Furthermore, in this communication, a multicast router can eliminate the process of coordinating and maintaining a shared-tree because it can directly construct a source-based tree from its initial protocol phase. At the protocol level, PIM-SM working on SSM solely maintains an explicit source-based SPT. As the result, an RP can be eliminated from any PIM domains in this communication, and hence the scalability problem (mainly caused by RP-to-group mapping) is effectively reduced from the multicast routing protocol.

2.2   Protocols

The multicast protocol architecture works with a common set, including a data sender, a data receiver, and a multicast router. Host-to-router communication is provided by the Internet Group Management Protocol (IGMP) for IPv4 and Multicast Listener Discovery (MLD) for IPv6. When a data receiver wants to join or leave multicast sessions, it notifies the multicast group address by sending an IGMP/MLD join or leave message to the upstream multicast router.

In an SSM environment, a data receiver must send an IGMP/MLD join or leave message that specifies the source address(es), as well as the multicast address, referred to as (S,G) join/leave message to its upstream router. This host-side extension to send a join or leave message with the pair of interesting source and group addresses is done using IGMP version 3 (IGMPv3) [5] for IPv4 and MLD version 2 (MLDv2) [6] for IPv6.

As well, it is indispensable that every receiver site router must support IGMPv3 and MLDv2 protocols in order to recognize the (S,G) join/leave messages sent from the data receivers. Since SSM is a subset of a PIM-SM routing

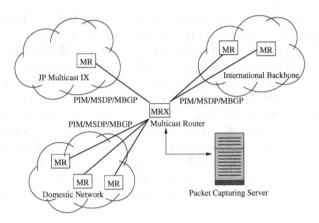

Fig. 1. Network and server configuration

protocol, it is not necessary for PIM-SM to add special functions to support SSM. Oppositely, there are unused protocols or router functions that are not necessary to be used in the SSM communication. Since an RP is not used in SSM, clearly MSDP is not needed if the network works with an SSM only network.

2.3 Statistical Trends

We obtained experimental data through our operational experience and analyzed the statistical trends in international multicast backbones using the following measurements to understand the current situation and future needs of IP multicast services [16].

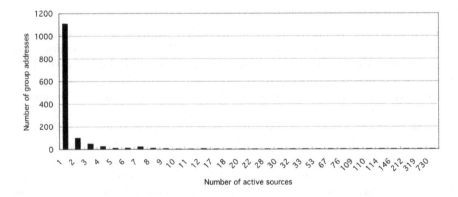

Fig. 2. Number of active data sources per multicast session

Figure 1 shows the topology of the target networks. The Japanese multicast backbone is known as "JP Multicast IX", which was previously established for multicast data exchange over MBone. The "Domestic Network" is a network to which the WIDE project [27] and other Japanese research communities are connecting. The "International Backbone" is the connection to Abilene [28] via TransPAC [29]. Our multicast router (MRX – Juniper M20 with JUNOS 5.7) was connected to six multicast routers (MRs) using Gigabit Ethernet interfaces. These routers used PIM-SM, MSDP, and MBGP [4] to exchange each routing information required for IPv4 multicast routing. The "Packet Capturing Server" was a PC (Dell PowerEdge 2650 with FreeBSD 5.1) equipped with 2 GB memory and 160 GB hard-disk. It was used to collect routing information from our multicast router MRX. It ran a program that logged into the router to extract the MSDP and MBGP routing information at eight-hour intervals from Feb. 28 to Mar. 13, 2004.

From the extracted data, distribution of the number of senders per group was obtained. Figure 2 shows that more than 90% of the multicast sessions were categorized as one-to-many communication, in which a data sender is only one node in a multicast session and the number of the data receivers is many, although the network infrastructure supported traditional many-to-many communication, in which both of data receivers and data senders are potentially many. This fact indicates that currently many-to-many communication is not widely used from the viewpoint of multicast service providers. In other words, one-to-many communication does not interfere with the steady deployment of IP multicast, and hence we believe there should be no problem in replacing the many-to-many communication with the one-to-many communication in IP multicast. In fact, a few multicast sessions were advertised from a large number of senders (e.g. 212, 319, and 730). Yet, they were used for the multicast session announcement by the SAP [15] protocol, which requires multicast data senders send announcement messages to the corresponding multicast addresses.

3   Gap Analysis

3.1   Operational Considerations

Network operations have not embraced IP multicast in any of its forms outside of what might be considered a single broadcast domain. This may be due to the fact that multicast inherits many of the same attributes of its predecessor, broadcast. In essence, multicast "floods" a network with a packet that must be replicated so as to reach all the nodes in a group. This behavior leads to the first operational consideration; Router design. All known routers are designed and optimized to handle unicast packet forwarding. The upshot of this implementation choice is that the multicast handling is pushed to high-overhead systems, usually in general purpose CPU and software. As a result, network operators find multicast processing to be slower than unicast and to consume more infrastructure resources in the form of CPU cycles and memory consumption. In fact, SSM routers need to maintain the routing entries that are composed of complete source-group address pairs (known as "channels" as explained in the next section) in their routing tables. Since it is currently impossible to aggregate the routing entries, network operators may concern that SSM much consumes router memory and does not improve the deployment condition.

A second consideration is that by its design, multicast does not have the functional equivalent of an External Gateway Protocol (EGP) like the unicast Boarder Gateway Protocol (BGP) [19]. For operators, this means that multicast must be artificially constrained or allowed by packet filtering or access controls at the unicast policy edges, where one network interconnects to another. Each of these considerations may be considered a gap in the roadmap to effective, wide-scale deployment of IP multicast or even SSM. Neither is further considered in this paper.

Lack of effective monitoring tools also limits the IP multicast deployment activities on an operator side. While lightweight multicast monitoring tools, like mtrace2 [20] and ssmping [21], have been recently proposed in the IETF MBONED working group, these tools may be too simple and difficult to satisfy to monitor any kind of situation.

3.2   Multicast Address Assignment

According to an IP multicast addressing architecture, a transient multicast address is dynamically assigned to a multicast session for its entire duration. Traditionally, there had been issues how the multicast address is uniquely assigned in the entire Internet and proposals to address the issues [30,31]. Yet, these proposals require that hosts (or applications) access to the address allocation servers that are well coordinated in the entire networks, where this requirement is difficult to be implemented with scalable manners.

Instead, GLOP [24] and EGLOP [25] for IPv4, and unicast-prefix-based IPv6 multicast addresses [26] have been commonly used. GLOP is the standard definition that describes an experimental policy for use of the IPv4 multicast address range by mapping 16 bits of Autonomous System (AS) number into the middle two octets of 233/8 to be uniquely assigned to that ASN. While this technique is simple and successfully used, the assignments are inefficient because of the cases in which users do not have its own AS or have ASN longer than 16 bits. Therefore EGLOP can be used as the extension of GLOP. In the absence of an assigned ASN, the sites then use private ASN. Unicast-prefix-based IPv6 multicast addresses is straightforward, since the source address prefix is inserted (embedded) in the IPv6 multicast address (FF3x::/32, where "x" is any valid scope value) used by the source.

SSM solves the addressing problem, because a "channel" is identified not only by the group address but also by the source address (i.e. (S,G) pair). Since the unique channel is composed of both the multicast address and the source address, the multicast address does not longer have to be globally unique. Hence, in SSM, multicast address allocation is not a global issue but rather a local decision (e.g. by an Internet Service Provider's policy).

However, SSM highlights another contradiction in the IPv4 addressing schema. SSM addresses are allocated in the special SSM range of 232/8 for IPv4. This means that the SSM sources cannot interoperate with GLOP/EGLOP addressed targets. Of course, it is not disallowed to create a multicast channel with non-SSM address range, network administrators or application developers may confuse or conflict in their thoughts.

3.3 Session Information Announcement

Due to the multicast addressing schema, a multicast data receiver needs to resolve a multicast address of the session whenever he joins the session. However, a traditional multicast session and address announcement architecture does not support access control methods to provide the session information including data sender address only to the legitimate members, and hence any user can get multicast session information by accessing a public session directory, e.g., *sdr*.

There would be two possible solutions to resolve a multicast address: one is the use of an address discovery mechanism, and the other relies on an address announcement model. The former model can use the Session Invitation Protocol (SIP) [14] and the later model can use the Session Announcement Protocol (SAP) [15]. In SIP environment, since the inviter must know the unicast addresses of all possible participants beforehand, it is not suited to large multicast sessions. On the other hand, SAP multicasts session information to keep all the session directory instances synchronized. However, such periodic session announcement to whole network not only brings a scalability problem, and is not appropriate to limit the user access nor to bring the privacy and secrecy of a user, in order to advertise private sessions only to the legitimate user.

SAP has several major limitations including scalability problem as explained in [17]. The biggest issue here is that SAP relies on the many-to-many multicast communication model, since every SAP instance can send announcements in the SAP announcement group. For instance, to receive SAP announcement messages for the global scope IPv4 multicast sessions, all clients must join session 224.2.127.254 [15] (without specifying any source address). This is another major limitation of SAP since some Internet Service Providers (ISPs) may want to provide only SSM multicast routing. We believe that a versatile announcement protocol must not rely on any specific routing architecture. the user would get only the available session information individually, and moreover the network administrator or the data sender can avoid bogus join request.

One of the possible idea is to use a distribute session directory system, like Channel Reflector [18]. It aims to provide a concrete implementation that enables the announcement of multicast session parameters. It could handle current and future needs, in particular when considering the scalability in terms of session announcements, the need for policy and scope control mechanisms, and the support of any group communication system, including SSM scheme.

3.4 Multicast Security

We know that security threats against IP multicast would have a catastrophic effect on IP multicast deployment in the Internet. For the clarification, IP

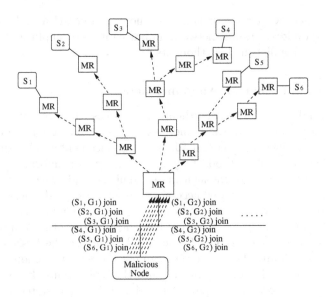

Fig. 3. Receiver-based attack

multicast security should be categorized into three points; (1) infrastructure protection, (2) contents protection, and (3) privacy. In this section, we mainly discuss infrastructure protection, and introduce some activities for contents protection. Privacy issue is skipped as the future issue.

Regarding the infrastructure protection, as described by Savola et al. of the IETF MBONED working group document [32], the security threats are categorized into "source-based" and "receiver-based" attacks. In short, the former is a DoS attack against the multicast networks, in which data is sent to numerous and random group addresses, and the latter is a DoS attack against multicast routers, in which innumerable IGMP/MLD joins are sent from a client.

In terms of multicast routing stability, source-based attacks are very serious. Generally, the data sender will keep streaming data even if there is no data receiver for the data. To make things worse, multicast routers, including first-hop routers, do not recognize or cannot reject these packets. In fact, MSDP has caused When a data sender starts sending data, the RP in the sender's PIM domain forwards Source Active (SA) messages to each MSDP neighbor router (peer), and the SA messages are forwarded hop-by-hop. SA messages used in MSDP are easily flooded throughout the PIM domains. This situation has induced denial-of-service (DoS) attacks, like *Ramen Worm* [22] and *Sapphire* [23]. These DoS attacks presumed on the MSDP architecture and overwhelmed the multicast infrastructure. However, these kinds of attacks do not affect SSM, in which the first-hop router can discard multicast data packets that do not have a corresponding routing entry.

On the contrary, SSM is not robust against receiver-based attack. In the many-to-many communication, a PIM-SM router initially constructs an RPT in order to find available sources for requested multicast address, and switches to each SPT for active sources. This behavior implies that a PIM-SM router working with the many-to-many communication model does not voluntarily construct a *non-active* SPT.

On the other hand, an SSM capable router constructs an SPT with no shared tree coordination. Thus, even if a host triggers invalid or unavailable (S,G) joins, the upstream router starts establishing all SPTs with no intellectual decision (Figure 3). This attack not only largely increases the router's routing table size and its memory by an unlimited number of malicious (S,G) joins, but also affects a large number of multicast routers along the invalid routing paths in the entire Internet. What is worse is that these multicast routers cannot recognize the original router that is attacked and cannot stop the attack itself. By using some timer mechanism to monitor the data flow, it would be possible to prune unavailable (S,G) entries from the routing table. But it is neither a great deal of the solution for tens of thousands of bogus requests.

In summary, because there is no channel validation mechanism in a router side working in the SSM communication, SPT coordination triggered by (S,G) join request may bring another security concern. In addition, current IGMPv3 and MLDv2 do not have a standard mechanism to validate requested joins. It is necessary to propose some mechanism that recognizes and notifies valid join requests to these protocols or routers.

Regarding contents protection, the IETF MSEC working group has been working to standardize protocols by which only legitimate members will have access to contents. The major issues focused on the MSEC working group are related to the group key management architecture [33] and has proposed corresponding protocols [34,35]. These architecture and protocols are necessary components, but more appropriate security model should implement the access control mechanism by the session announcement level. As the beneficial approach, the multicast session announcement scheme is included in the multicast security architecture that authenticates and authorizes legitimate users before giving the session information. Securing the session directory architecture provides security at each level of interaction with users; thus it guarantees privacy and secrecy for any members who join to multicast sessions.

3.5 Filter-Mode Operation

IGMPv3 and MLDv2 implement INCLUDE and EXCLUDE filter-modes that are introduced to support the source filtering function, as well as a source address specification function. If a host wants to receive from specific sources, it sends an IGMPv3 or MLDv2 report with specifying the source addresses and the filter-mode set to INCLUDE. If the host does not want to receive from sources, it sends a report with specifying the source addresses and filter-mode set to EXCLUDE.

The INCLUDE and EXCLUDE filter-modes are also defined in a multicast router to process the IGMPv3 or MLDv2 reports. When a multicast router receives the report messages from its downstream hosts, it forwards the corresponding multicast traffic by managing requested group and source addresses.

The INCLUDE filter-mode is necessary to support SSM by specifying interesting source addresses. However, practical applications do not use EXCLUDE mode to block sources very often, because a user or application usually wants to specify desired source addresses, not undesired source addresses. Even if a user wants to explicitly refuse traffic from some sources in a group, when other users in the same shared network have an interest in these sources, the corresponding multicast traffic is forwarded to the network.

There is a proposal of the simplified versions of IGMPv3 and MLDv2, named Lightweight IGMPv3 (LW-IGMPv3) and Lightweight MLDv2 (LW-MLDv2) [8], in which EXCLUDE filter-mode is eliminated. Not only are LW-IGMPv3 and LW-MLDv2 compatible with the standard IGMPv3 and MLDv2, but also the protocol operations made by data receiver hosts and routers or switches (performing IGMPv3/MLDv2 snooping) are simplified in the lightweight protocol, and complicated operations are hence effectively reduced. Since LW-IGMPv3 and LW-MLDv2 are fully compatible with the full version of these protocols (i.e., the standard IGMPv3 and MLDv2), hosts or routers that have implemented the full version do not need to implement or modify anything to cooperate with LW-IGMPv3/LW-MLDv2 hosts or routers.

In fact, the aim of LW-IGMPv3 and LW-MLDv2 is not only for contributing to the implementation or reducing the memory size on a host. One of the big advantages is that it highly reduces the processing cost on upstream routers by eliminating the EXCLUDE filter-mode operations. If both INCLUDE and EXCLUDE filter-mode operations are supported in the networks, the routers need to maintain all source addresses joined from end hosts. Even if an SPT is well coordinated by (S,G) joins given by SSM-capable receivers, the routers need to refresh (and re-generate) some or all of the corresponding routing paths including the RPT whenever the downstream host requests EXLUDE filter-mode join. According to this unwilling scenario, LW-IGMPv3 and LW-MLDv2 that disable EXCLUDE filter-mode operations are further encouraged to grow SSM only networks.

3.6 Application Development

When a multicast application requests a new (S,G) join, it uses embedded Application Program Interfaces (APIs) to control socket operations. For the SSM communication, Multicast Source Filtering (MSF) APIs for `setsockopt()`, `getsockopt()` and `ioctl()` are defined [7]. These APIs are classified to the "IPv4 MSF API" and the "Protocol-Independent MSF API". In an IPv6 application, the Protocol-Independent MSF API is used.

As another taxonomy, the "Basic API" and the "Advanced API" are available to provide independent usage for each API. The Basic API uses `setsockopt()` and `getsockopt()` functions and can minimize changes needed in existing multicast application source code to add the source address filtering operations. The following example shows a part of a multicast application, which uses the Basic API of the IPv4 MSF API.

Usage-1: IPv4 Basic MSF API

```
bcopy(&in_grp, &ims.imr_multiaddr, sizeof(in_grp));
bcopy(&in_src, &ims.imr_sourceaddr, sizeof(in_src));

if (setsockopt(socket, IPPROTO_IP, IP_ADD_SOURCE_MEMBERSHIP,
    (char *)&ims, sizeof(ims)) < 0)
        perror("cannot listen group");
```

This application first copies the multicast address (in_grp) to ims.imr_multiaddr and a source address (in_src) to ims.imr_sourceaddr respectively. And then it calls setsockopt() function with IP_ADD_SOURCE-_MEMBERSHIP operation defined as the Basic API for the INCLUDE (S,G) join request.

The example using Protocol-Independent MSF API for IPv6 is as follows:

Usage-2: IPv6 (Protocol Independent) Basic MSF API

```
bcopy(&grp, &gsr.gsr_group, grp.sin6_len);
bcopy(&src, &gsr.gsr_source, src.sin6_len);

if (setsockopt(socket, IPPROTO_IPV6, MCAST_JOIN_SOURCE_GROUP,
    (char *)&gsr, sizeof(gsr)) < 0)
        perror("cannot listen group");
```

As shown above, it is easy to adapt MSF APIs to existing applications. The biggest concern is to recognize which APIs can be used on your OS. For instance, Windows XP only supports IPv4 MSF API, and Windows Vista supports both IPv4 and Protocol-Independent MSF APIs (i.e. Basic APIs), but non of them supports Advanced APIs. The latest Linux supports all MSF APIs in definition. Current BSD OSes and MacOS X do not officially support any MSF API, while we have provided LW-IGMPv3 and LW-MLDv2 kernel patches [9,10], which supports Basic APIs. According to this scenario, cross platform compatibility is sacrificed because of incompatible APIs, and therefore, application developers who need to support various OSes should insert procedures to check whether the OSes support SSM and which API can be used in the source codes.

We definitively need the guideline mentioning the newly developed applications should use either IP_ADD_SOURCE_MEMBERSHIP or MCAST_JOIN_SOURCE_GROUP, because these commands are supported by both IGMPv3/MLDv2 and LW-IGMPv3/LW-MLDv2 implementations, and simply request the SSM communication by invoking INCLUDE mode (S,G) join. And also, using IP_BLOCK_SOURCE and MCAST_BLOCK_SOURCE on an IGMPv3/MLDv2 capable host is harmful, because these commands invoke EXCLUDE filter-mode operations and request to construct an RPT to the upstream routers as described in Section 3.5.

4 Conclusions and Future Work

Source-Specific Multicast (SSM) is designed as the deployable IP multicast communication architecture, and the demands of IP multicast technology have been rapidly increasing in perceived importance and growing these days. However, it still requires operational functions and application development manners for its smooth deployment. In this paper, we analyze the deployment barriers resided in IP multicast or SSM deployment, and consider how we can ease some of the barriers. We also discuss the functions SSM requires, and the necessary components network operators and application developers need to know for fulfilling the demand.

As well as addressing remaining issues aforementioned in this paper, we would like to propose much robust routing technology that creates robust routing paths. There has been recently proposing various ways to fulfill the demand like [36], and we believe it is the indispensable research topic.

Multicast AAA should be separately discussed from multicast security. Although the IETF MBONED working group has been trying to standardize AAA frameworks for common multicast services, providing the scalability and combining group key management architecture sec:msec are vital. We definitively need the concrete implementations and must verify the integrated behavior.

As another issue, multicast Quality-of-Service (QoS) is also the sensitive requirement especially for service providers who want to make accounting to their customers. It is a challenge to guarantee the contents quality at a reasonable level, and it would be the hot research topic for the Internet communities.

References

1. Holbrook, H., Cain, B.: Source-Specific Multicast for IP. RFC4607, August (2006)
2. Fenner, B., Handley, M., Holbrook, H., Kouvelas, I.: Protocol Independent Multicast - Sparse Mode (PIM-SM): Protocol Specification (Revised). RFC4601 (August 2006)
3. Fenner, B., Meyer, D.: Multicast Source Discovery Protocol (MSDP), RFC3618 (October 2003)
4. Bates, T., Chandra, R., Katz, D., Rekhter, Y.: Multiprotocol Extensions for BGP-4, RFC2283 (February 1998)
5. Cain, B., Deering, S., Kouvelas, I., Fenner, B., Thyagarajan, A.: Internet Group Management Protocol, Version 3. RFC3376 (October 2002)
6. Vida, R., Costa, L.: Multicast Listener Discovery Version 2 (MLDv2) for IPv6, RFC3810 (June 2004)
7. Thaler, D., Fenner, B., Quinn, B.: Socket Interface Extensions for Multicast Source Filters, RFC3678 (January 2004)
8. Liu, H., Cao, W., Asaeda, H.: Lightweight IGMPv3 and MLDv2 Protocols. Internet Draft (work in progress), draft-ietf-mboned-lightweight-igmpv3-mldv2-01.txt (June 2007)
9. LW-IGMPv3 Host-side Implementation for NetBSD, http://www.sfc.wide.ad.jp/~asaeda/LW-IGMPv3

10. LW-MLDv2 Host-side Implementation for NetBSD, http://www.sfc.wide.ad.jp/~asaeda/LW-MLDv2
11. Casner, S., Deering, S.: First IETF Internet Audiocast. ACM SIGCOMM Computer Communication Review 22(3), 92–97 (1992)
12. El-Sayed, A., Roca, V., Mathy, L.: A Survey of Protocols for an Alternative Group Communication Service. IEEE Network 17(1), 46–51 (2003)
13. Wang, W., Helder, D., Jamin, S., Zhang, L.: Overlay Optimizations for End-host Multicast. In: NGC 2002. Proc. Int'l Workshop on Networked Group Communication, pp. 154–161 (October 2002)
14. Rosenberg, J., Schulzrinne, H., Camarillo, G., Johnston, A., Peterson, J., Sparks, R., Handley, M., Schooler, E.: SIP: Session Initiation Protocol, RFC3261 (June 2002)
15. Handley, M., Perkins, C., Whelan, E.: Session Announcement Protocol, RFC2974 (October 2000)
16. Asaeda, H., Suzuki, S., Kobayashi, K., Murai, J.: Architecture for IP Multicast Deployment: Challenges and Practice. IEICE Trans. on Communications E89-B(4), 1044–1051 (2006)
17. Asaeda, H., Roca, V.: Policy and Scope Management for Multicast Channel Announcement. IEICE Trans. on Information and Systems E88-D(7), 1638–1645 (2005)
18. Asaeda, H., Pokavanich, W., Yamamoto, S.: Channel Reflector: An Interdomain Channel Directory System. IEICE Trans. on Communications E89-B(10), 2860–2867 (2006)
19. Rekhter, Y., Li, T.: A Border Gateway Protocol 4 (BGP-4), RFC1771 (March 1995)
20. Asaeda, H., Jinmei, T., Fenner, B., Casner, S.: Mtrace Version 2: Traceroute Facility for IP Multicast. Internet Draft (work in progress), draft-asaeda-mboned-mtrace-v2-00.txt (July 2007)
21. Venaas, S., Santos, H.: ssmping Protocol. Internet Draft (work in progress), draft-ietf-mboned-ssmping-01.txt (July 2007)
22. Rajvaidya, P., Ramachandran, K., Almeroth, K.: Detection and Deflection of DoS Attacks Against the Multicast Source Discovery Protocol. In: Proc. IEEE INFOCOM 2003 (March 2003)
23. Rajvaidya, P., Ramachandran, K., Almeroth, K.: Managing and Securing the Global Multicast Infrastructure. Journal of Network and Systems Management (JNSM) 12(3), 297–326 (2004)
24. Meyer, D., Lothberg, P.: GLOP Addressing in 233/8, RFC3180 (September 2001)
25. Meyer, D.: Extended Assignments in 233/8, RFC3138 (June 2001)
26. Haberman, B., Thaler, D.: Unicast-Prefix-based IPv6 Multicast Addresses, RFC3306 (August 2002)
27. The WIDE Project, http://www.wide.ad.jp/
28. Abilene Backbone Network, http://abilene.internet2.edu/
29. The TransPAC2 Project, http://www.transpac.org/
30. Hanna, S., Patel, B., Shah, M.: Multicast Address Dynamic Client Allocation Protocol (MADCAP), RFC2730 (December 1999)
31. Radoslavov, P., Estrin, D., Govindan, R., Handley, M., Kumar, S., Thaler, D.: The Multicast Address-Set Claim (MASC) Protocol. RFC2909 (September 2000)
32. Savola, P., Lehtonen, R., Meyer, D.: Protocol Independent Multicast - Sparse Mode (PIM-SM) Multicast Routing Security Issues and Enhancements, RFC4609 (October 2006)

33. Baugher, M., Canetti, R., Dondeti, L., Lindholm, F.: Multicast Security (MSEC) Group Key Management Architecture, RFC4046 (April 2005)
34. Baugher, M., Weis, B., Hardjono, T., Harney, H.: The Group Domain of Interpretation, RFC3547 (July 2003)
35. Arkko, J., Carrara, E., Lindholm, F., Naslund, M., Norrman, K.: MIKEY: Multimedia Internet KEYing, RFC3830 (August 2004)
36. Arberg, P.: High availability multicast delivery in IPTV networks, http://www.nanog.org/mtg-0706/arberg.html

Can Forwarding Loops Appear When Activating iBGP Multipath Load Sharing?

Simon Balon* and Guy Leduc

Research Unit in Networking
EECS Department- University of Liège (ULg)
Institut Montefiore, B28 - B-4000 Liège - Belgium
Simon.Balon@ulg.ac.be, Guy.Leduc@ulg.ac.be

Abstract. We analyse the possible consequences of activating iBGP multipath load sharing in a given domain (or AS), which allows for load balancing over multiple exit routers. It has been stated that interdomain routing loops may appear in this case. We show that under reasonable assumptions (which reflect commercial relationships between ASes) such routing loops cannot appear. Furthermore we show that even if theses assumptions are not met, routing loops can only be transient.

Keywords: iBGP Multipath Load Sharing, Traffic Split, Traffic Engineering, Forwarding Loops.

1 Introduction

Traffic Engineering in OSPF/ISIS networks consists in finding the best possible set of link weights ([5]). The routing scheme resulting from this link weight setting should reflect Traffic Engineering goals, i.e. good user performance and efficient use of network resources. Typically link weights optimizers use ECMP (Equal Cost Multi-Path) to split the traffic on multiple paths between one ingress node and one egress node. Using ECMP has multiple advantages. For example ECMP can be used to improve IP restoration ([9]). It is also a flexible routing technique and usually allows a good engineering of the network.

While it is considered valuable to split traffic on multiple paths inside a domain, splitting traffic on multiple interdomain paths is rarely envisaged. Indeed BGP typically chooses one (and only one) path among its multiple available ones. Although in an AS some destination prefixes are reachable via only one egress point, it is frequent that most of the prefixes (typically provider prefixes) are reachable via multiple BGP-equivalent routes (for example if the AS has multiple links connecting its providers). Using classical BGP one of these routes is chosen via the Hot-Potato criterion or a tie-break at a later stage of the BGP decision process. But it is also possible to configure BGP to allow the network operator to split traffic amongst multiple BGP-equivalent routes. This could move

---

* S. Balon is a Research Fellow of the Belgian National Fund for the Scientific Research (F.N.R.S).

S. Fdida and K. Sugiura (Eds.): AINTEC 2007, LNCS 4866, pp. 213–225, 2007.
© Springer-Verlag Berlin Heidelberg 2007

the horizon of traffic engineering possibilities back, allowing an optimizer to take these traffic splits into account to better engineer the network, even allowing it to engineer the interdomain links ([2]).

But the situation is not as beautiful as it seems. Indeed splitting traffic amongst multiple available BGP-equivalent routes which may have a different AS-level paths can cause problems as explained in [8]. In that paper the authors state that forwarding loops could appear and they propose a solution. In this paper we show that contrary to what can be thought at first glance and under reasonable assumptions, forwarding loops should not appear in any case. These assumptions are based on the BGP router configurations that typically reflect commercial relationships.

The paper is organized as follows. In section 2 we introduce BGP basics and how iBGP multipath load sharing works. We also briefly describe why forwarding loops could appear with iBGP multipath load sharing. Section 3 presents the BGP configuration we assume in this paper. These are natural BGP configurations that should be respected in all the ASes. We show in section 4 that if these assumptions hold, no forwarding loops can appear. In sections 5 and 6 we analyse what happens if the assumptions we made about BGP are not respected. Indeed even if these should be respected in all the ASes it is impossible to be sure of that. We show in section 5 that even in this case no forwarding loops can appear when activating iBGP multipath load sharing. These can only appear at a later stage if the BGP configuration of an AS is changed. We show in section 6 that even in this case forwarding loops are only transient. Section 7 concludes the paper.

2   Routing Principles, iBGP Multipath Load Sharing and Forwarding Loops

We will explain the basic intradomain and interdomain routing principles on the example topology of figure 1. Routers R_0, R_1, R_2 and R_3 are part of the Engineered AS. This AS has two neighbouring ASes : AS_1 and AS_2. We consider

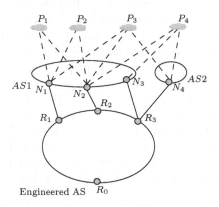

Fig. 1. Example Topology

four IP prefixes (P_1 to P_4) which are joinable through interdomain paths that are depicted by dashed lines. These are possible paths advertised by BGP.

Each packet sent on the Internet follows a path which is defined by routing protocols. The exterior gateway protocol (EGP) defines the path at the network level. This path is called the AS path[1]. The EGP used in the Internet is BGP (Border Gateway Protocol). In each AS the path from each ingress router to each egress router is defined by the interior gateway protocol (IGP). The IGPs that are generally used in the Internet are OSPF and ISIS.

In an AS the path between ingress and egress routers are computed by a Shortest-Path algorithm based on the link weights. If ECMP is enabled, several equal shortest-paths can be used simultaneously to evenly split the traffic among them, by using a hash table that maps a hash of multiple fields in the packet header to one of these paths, so that all packets of a flow will follow the same path with limited packets reordering (see [4] for a performance analysis of hashing based schemes for Internet load balancing). Figure 2 shows an example of ECMP inside an AS. This figure assumes that there are two equal cost paths from R_0 to R_1.

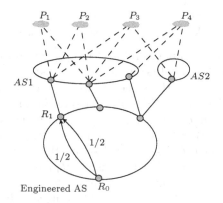

Fig. 2. Intradomain Equal Cost Multipath (ECMP)

BGP allows routers to exchange reachability information between neighboring ASes ([11]). Each AS is connected to several neighboring ASes by interdomain links. Depending on the connectivity of the network and on the destination of the packet, one or several neighboring ASes can be chosen to forward the packet to the destination. The choice of the BGP next-hop (i.e. the egress router in this AS or the border router in the next AS, that will relay the packet toward the destination) is based on the information exchanged with neighbors and on a local configuration implementing its routing policy.

There are two types of BGP sessions that are used to exchange routes between routers. eBGP sessions are used between routers in different ASes, while iBGP

---

[1] AS stands for Autonomous System. In the paper we use domain and AS interchangeably.

sessions are used between routers in the same AS. When a router receives a route on a iBGP or eBGP session, this route has to pass the input filter to be eligible in the BGP decision process that selects the best route(s) toward each destination prefix. The best route(s) selected by this process is(are) then announced on other BGP sessions after passing through an output filter.

The BGP route selection process, implementing routing policies, is made of several criteria ([3,6]):

1) Prefer routes with the highest local preference which reflects the routing policies of the domain;
2) Prefer routes with the shortest AS-level Path;
3) Prefer routes with the lowest origin number, e.g., the routes originating from IGP are most reliable;
4) Prefer routes with the lowest MED (multiple-exit discriminator) type which is an attribute used to compare routes with the same next AS-hop;
5) Prefer eBGP-learned routes over iBGP-learned ones (referred to as the eBGP >iBGP criterion in the sequel);
6) Prefer the route with the lowest IGP distance to the egress point (i.e. the so-called hot-potato, or early exit, criterion);
7) If supported, apply load sharing between paths. Otherwise, apply a domain-dependent tie-breaking rule, e.g., select the one with the lowest egress ID.

Consider the network of figure 1. Suppose that routes to P_1 are announced by N_1 to R_1 and N_2 to R_2 on eBGP sessions. Suppose that the routes announced by these two routers have the same attributes (i.e. local-preference, AS-path length, origin number and MED) after passing the input filters of routers R_1 and R_2 (this is very frequent in practice for routes that are received from the same neighboring AS[2]). Suppose also that these two routes are announced by R_1 and R_2 to R_0 on iBGP sessions. Usually the attributes are not changed when forwarding routes on iBGP sessions. So R_0 has two routes to reach P_1 and these two routes are equivalent w.r.t. criteria 1 to 4. Both are received on iBGP sessions so are also equivalent w.r.t. the 5th criterion. In this case R_0 will use its IGP distance to R_1 and R_2 to select the best route toward P_1. We say that this route is chosen using the hot-potato criterion by router R_0. Note that R_1 and R_2 will directly forward traffic toward this prefix on their interdomain link using the eBGP>iBGP criterion.

Now if R_1 and R_2 are at the same IGP distance from R_0, the 7th criterion will be used. By default only one next hop can be chosen and a tie-break selects the best route. But it is also possible to enable iBGP multipath load sharing [3,6] and balance the load on both paths. As for intradomain ECMP, a hash table is used to select the particular route of a packet. Figure 3 supposes that iBGP multipath is activated and that R_1 and R_2 are at the same distance from R_0. In this case the traffic going from R_0 to P_1 will be split evenly on both paths. Figure 4 presents the combined use of ECMP and iBGP multipath load sharing.

---

[2] For the case study in [2] we have shown that 97.2% of the prefixes have multiple BGP-equivalent (w.r.t. criteria 1 to 4) egress points, which amounts to 35.6% of the traffic on average.

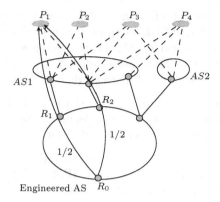

Fig. 3. iBGP multipath load sharing

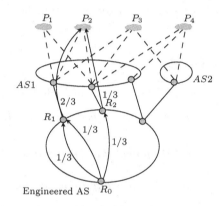

Fig. 4. ECMP + iBGP multipath load sharing

Note also that BGP ([11]) includes a loop prevention mechanism. When an AS receives a route whose ASPATH contains its AS number, it discards the route. This supposes that the ASPATH contains a full list of all the ASes along the path used to forward traffic toward this destination. If part of the ASPATH information is lost, this mechanism does not work anymore.

In [8] we can read that *Most of the current BGP implementations upon receiving multiple equal cost BGP routes from different peers can insert all of them (or a subset depending upon the local policies) in their forwarding table. This can be done to locally split the traffic across several paths. However, because BGP in its current state can only advertise one path to its peers, an implementation MUST choose from one of the best paths that it is using for the advertisement. This has implications for the BGP peers that receive such advertisements from ECMP capable BGP speakers. In the worst case it can lead to potential loops if the entire path information is not advertised to the peers.*

In [8] the authors present a first method to avoid forwarding loops using BGP AS_SET and AS_SEQUENCE. In next sections we analyse what happens if this method is not used and only one ASPATH is announced to other ASes. Contrary to what can be thought at first glance, we show that forwarding loops should not appear when using iBGP multipath on different ASPATH routes.

Definition 1. *A packet is trapped in a forwarding loop if there is a cycle of routers such that each router on the cycle forwards the packet to the next router on the cycle, leading the packet to be infinitely forwarded on the cycle.*

Of course forwarding loops should be avoided in practice. Note also that in IP networks, the time to live (TTL) field of the IP header will force routers to drop a packet which is trapped in a forwarding loop.

Definition 2. *A provider loop (for a particular destination prefix) is a cycle of ASes such that each AS on the cycle is the provider of the next AS.*

Note that a provider loop is also a customer loop if the cycle is analysed in the opposite direction.

3   BGP Model Used

In this paper we consider the following common BGP configurations.

Assumption 1. *We consider import/export rules which state that ([10], [7], [1]):*

- *an AS does not export to a provider or peer routes that it learnt from other providers and other peers;*
- *an AS can export to its customers any routes it knows of.*

This assumption (1) reflects that an AS does not want to provide transit services between its providers and peers.

Assumption 2. *We consider that routes learnt from customers should be preferred to routes learnt from either providers or peers, leaving ASes latitude to assign relative preferences among customer routes, and among peer and provider routes.*

This assumption (2) is the preference rule suggested in Guideline A of Gao and Rexford [7]. This is a logical assumption for commercial relationships. Indeed an AS earns money for the traffic it sends on its customer links while it does not earn money for the traffic it sends on its peer links and it pays for the traffic it sends on its provider links. So it should always prefer to send traffic to its customers than to its provider when it has the choice.

Our last assumption is the following (this is also assumed in [7]).

Assumption 3. *We assume that there is a hierarchical customer-provider relationship among ASes.*

This is equivalent to saying that there is no provider loop in the AS-level topology.

4   When Do Routers Use BGP Loop Prevention Mechanism?

The BGP loop prevention mechanism implemented in a BGP router consists in discarding routes whose ASPATH contains the AS number of the router[3] ([11]). When and how does this situation happen?

For this situation to happen, we have to be in the case of figure 5. AS_X receives a route for a destination prefix from AS_1. It announces this route to AS_2. Later AS_X receives back this route from AS_3 and discards the route because its AS number appears in the ASPATH.

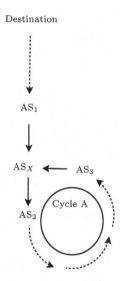

Fig. 5. AS topology

We will demonstrate that this situation never happens if Assumptions 1, 2 and 3 are respected. We divide the problem into different cases, depending on the commercial relationship between AS_X and its neighbouring ASes for the particular destination prefix we consider. Note that applying this reasoning to each prefix known by AS_X allows us to generalize our result.

4.1 AS_1 Is a Provider or a Peer of AS_X

AS_X has received the route from a provider or peer. So AS_X will export this route to AS_2 only if AS_2 is one of its customers (applying Assumption 1). Following the same reasoning the route is announced from AS_2 hop by hop to AS_3 and

---

[3] Note that this loop detection can also be performed on the sender-side. In this case a BGP router will not announce a route to a neighboring router if its AS number is in the ASPATH of this route.

finally back to AS_X if all these links are provider to customer links. If it is not the case the route is stopped before coming back to AS_X. So AS_3 is a provider of AS_X and cycle A is a provider loop. This situation should not happen as we assumed in section 3 that there is a hierarchical customer-provider relationship among ASes (Assumption 3).

Now if cycle A is a provider loop (meaning that Assumption 3 is not respected), a forwarding loop could appear if AS_3 is preferred to AS_1 which are both providers. In this case BGP loop prevention mechanism will discard the route from AS_3 which could be chosen if this mechanism were not present.

4.2 AS_1 Is a Customer of AS_X

As AS_1 is a customer, AS_X can announce the route on all its BGP sessions (Assumption 1). So AS_2 can be a customer, a peer or a provider of AS_X. We consider all these cases.

AS_2 is a customer of AS_X. In this case, following the same kind of reasoning as in section 4.1, the route will come back to AS_X only if all the links from AS_2 to AS_3 and back to AS_X are provider to customer links. So this implies that cycle A is a provider loop (meaning that Assumption 3 is not respected).

The situation is a little bit different than in section 4.1, because anyway, if this situation happens, AS_X will always prefer the route from AS_1 which is a customer when compared to the route from AS_3 which is a provider (Assumption 2). In this case Assumptions 1 and 2 are sufficient to guarantee the absence of forwarding loops.

AS_2 is a provider of AS_X. In this case AS_2 has received the route from AS_X which is one of its customers and so it can announce it on all its BGP sessions (Assumption 1). Thus AS_3 can be a customer, a peer or a provider of AS_X. We consider all these cases.

a) AS_3 is a provider or a peer of AS_X In this case, AS_X will prefer the route coming from AS_1 (which is one of its customer) to the new route coming from AS_3 (which is a provider or a peer) (Assumption 2).

In this case Assumptions 1 and 2 are sufficient to guarantee the absence of forwarding loops. Note also that this (non-problematic) situation may happen without provider loop.

b) AS_3 is a customer of AS_X For AS_3 to announce the route to AS_X (which is its provider), it must have received this route from one of its customers (applying Assumption 1). By extending this reasoning we can deduce that the route has been propagated hop-by-hop on customer to provider links from AS_2 to AS_3. Otherwise the route would have been stopped between AS_2 and AS_3. In this case cycle A is also a provider loop and this should not happen (Assumption 3).

Note that if this situation happens (meaning that Assumption 3 is not respected), a forwarding loop could appear if AS_3 is preferred to AS_1 which are both customers (which respect Assumption 2). In this case BGP loop prevention mechanism will discard the route which could be chosen if this mechanism were not present.

AS$_2$ is a peer of AS$_X$. In this case AS$_2$ will announce this route only to its customers (Assumption 1). So the route will be announced hop-by-hop on provider to customer links to AS$_3$ and then to AS$_X$ (Assumption 1). AS$_3$ is a provider of AS$_X$ and thus AS$_X$ will prefer the route from AS$_1$ which is one of its customer to the route from AS$_3$ which is one of its provider (Assumption 2).

The conclusion is the same as in preceding paragraph labelled a).

4.3   Summary

Table 1 presents all the possible router configurations that result in AS$_X$ receiving a route whose ASPATH contains its AS number. In all other router configurations it is not possible for AS$_X$ to receive such a route.

Note that only two of these configurations could result in forwarding loops if BGP prevention mechanisms were not enabled. These two configurations are the lines marked with the label "No if BGP prevention" in the "Potential Forwarding loop" column (lines 1 and 5). Note that these two configurations imply that a provider loop is present in the network, which was supposed not to happen as stated in Assumption 3. Thus we can say that the BGP loop prevention mechanism is a kind of watchdog avoiding forwarding loops in misconfigured networks (i.e. networks which do not respect our Assumptions).

Anyway we cannot be 100 % sure that our assumptions are respected in the whole Internet. This is why the BGP loop detection check is still useful in today networks. In the next sections, we will analyse what happens if our assumptions are not respected and what is the impact of this point on the activation of iBGP multipath load sharing.

Table 1. All possible configurations (referring to fig. 5) leading AS$_X$ to receive a route advertisement whose ASPATH contains its own AS number

Line	AS$_1$	AS$_2$	AS$_3$	Provider loop	Potential Forwarding loop
1	Provider	Customer	Provider	YES	No if BGP prevention
2	Peer	Customer	Provider	YES	NO[4]
3	Customer	Customer	Provider	YES	NO
4		Provider	Provider or Peer	NO	NO
5			Customer	YES	No if BGP prevention
6		Peer	Provider	NO	NO

---

[4] This is due to the fact that usually routes received from peers are preferred to routes received from providers even if this is not included in our assumptions. If we do not assume this preference rule, line 2 should just be merged with line 1.

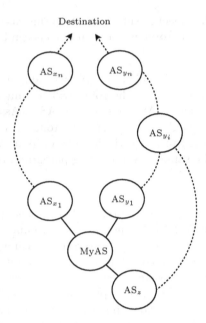

Fig. 6. iBGP mutipath AS topology

5   No Forwarding Loop When Activating iBGP Multipath Load Sharing

In this section we would like to analyse whether activating iBGP multipath load sharing can result in a forwarding loop or not. Indeed a BGP router which activates iBGP multipath on multiple routes will announce only one of these routes to its neighboring ASes. If later on, one AS on one route that has not been announced receives back this route, its BGP loop detection mechanism will be unable to detect the loop[5]. For such a situation to appear we have to be in the case of figure 5 in which one of the routers between AS_2 and AS_3 on cycle A enables iBGP multipath on at least two routes, one going to the destination via AS_X and another route in which AS_X is not present. Such a general topology is depicted on figure 6, where AS_{y_i} is the AS_X of figure 5, $AS_{y_{(i+1)}}$ is AS_1, cycle A is AS_{y_i} ... AS_{y_1} MyAS AS_z ... AS_{y_i} and MyAS is the AS on cycle A which enables iBGP multipath load sharing on multiple available routes : AS_{y_1} ... AS_{y_n} and AS_{x_1} ... AS_{x_n} which does not contain AS_{y_i}. We will show that even with such a topology no permanent forwarding loop can be installed. As this topology is built to reflect all the possible topologies that can lead to a permanent forwarding loop, this will imply that no forwarding loops can be created when using iBGP multipath load sharing. Note that optionally AS_{y_i} could be merged with AS_{y_1}

---

[5] Of course this can only happen if at least one of our assumptions is not respected, as it has been shown in section 4.

and/or AS_z. Our reasoning can also be applied if iBGP multipath load sharing is used on more than one additional path to the destination in which AS_X is not present.

Suppose that at time $t = t_0$ iBGP multipath load sharing is not activated in the network and that MyAS has two BGP-equivalent routes w.r.t. criteria 1 to 6 whose ASPATH are $AS_{x_1} \ldots AS_{x_n}$ and $AS_{y_1} \ldots AS_{y_n}$. One of the two available routes is chosen with some tie-break and this route is announced to AS_z. Suppose now that at time $t_1 > t_0$ we do activate iBGP multipath load sharing on these two routes and that we continue to announce the same route to AS_z. We will show that in this case no forwarding loop is created at time t_1. Indeed the route that was announced at time t_0 was either the route received from AS_{y_1} or the route received from AS_{x_1}. If it was the route received from AS_{y_1} no forwarding loop can be created because AS_{y_i} will see its AS number in the ASPATH received from AS_z. If it was the route received from AS_{x_1}, a forwarding loop cannot be created at time t_1. Indeed the route announced to AS_z is the same at time t_1 than at time t_0. So if AS_{y_i} prefers the route coming back from MyAS via AS_z to the route received from $AS_{y_{(i+1)}}$, it would already have chosen this route at time t_0 and the route with ASPATH $AS_{y_1} \ldots AS_{y_n}$ would not have been available at MyAS.

6   Anyway Forwarding Loops Can Only Be Transient

Now suppose that in the preceding example, at time $t_2 > t_1$, the route selected by BGP at router AS_{y_i} changes. There are two possibilities. Either both routes are used by activating iBGP multipath load sharing at router AS_{y_i} or the route selected by BGP is now the route received back from MyAS via AS_z instead of the route received from $AS_{y_{(i+1)}}$. We will analyse both cases separately.

6.1   Both Routes Are Selected and Used

We will see that this situation is impossible. Indeed this implies that at time t_2, AS_{y_i} activates iBGP multipath load sharing and splits its traffic on its two available routes (the route received back from MyAS via AS_z and the route received from $AS_{y_{(i+1)}}$). But iBGP multipath load sharing cannot select these two available routes as these do not have the same ASPATH length ($|AS_{y_i} \ldots AS_{y_n}| \leq |AS_{y_1} \ldots AS_{y_n}| = |AS_{x_1} \ldots AS_{x_n}| < |AS_{y_i} \ldots AS_z \; MyAS \; AS_{x_1} \ldots AS_{x_n}|$[6]). Indeed one condition for iBGP multipath load sharing to be activated on multiple routes is that these routes are equivalent w.r.t. BGP criteria 1 to 6, which implies equality of ASPATH lengths (via criterion 2).

6.2   The Route Received Back from MyAS Via AS_z Is Now the Best Route

AS_{y_i} has to change its BGP policies (i.e. its local pref values) for BGP to select the route received back from MyAS via AS_z as best route instead of the route

---

[6] $|ASPath|$ denotes the number of ASes of $ASPath$.

received from $AS_{y_{(i+1)}}$. Indeed the local prefs are the only way to force BGP to select a route whose ASPATH is longer (see BGP decision process in section 2). In this case a forwarding loop is created. But as AS_{y_i} now has changed its route, it must withdraw the old route and advertise the new one to $AS_{y_{(i-1)}}$ and so hop by hop to MyAS. When MyAS receives the new route, it can detect the loop because its AS number appears in the ASPATH. So MyAS will stop using the route received from AS_{y_1} and the forwarding loop is stopped. Note that at this time the router of MyAS which detects and stops the forwarding loop should alert the network operator that at least one of our assumptions is not respected somewhere. With such an alert the network operator could analyse the situation and look for the cause of the problem. Indeed this means that one of our 3 assumptions is not respected.

7 Conclusion

In this paper we have analysed how forwarding loops can appear in current BGP networks. We have shown that forwarding loops should not appear even if part of the ASPATH information is discarded, which can be the case when using iBGP multipath load sharing for routes with different ASPATH. Indeed we have shown that BGP configurations reflecting commercial relationships ensure that no forwarding loops will appear. Anyway as it is not possible for a network operator to verify the good configuration of all the involved ASes, we have analysed what would happen in this case (i.e. if BGP configuration would not reflect commercial relationships). We have shown that even in this case, a forwarding loop cannot appear immediately after activating iBGP multipath load sharing. The forwarding loop could only appear if in addition to the aforementioned conditions, some ASes change their policies in a particular way. Moreover we have shown that even in this case, if a forwarding loop appears, it is only transient.

This leads us to conclude that activating iBGP multipath load sharing for routes with different ASPATH is not as dangerous as it may seem at first glance.

Acknowledgments

This work has been partially supported by the Walloon Region (TOTEM project). The authors would like to thank P. François and B. Quoitin (Université catholique de Louvain) for their comments on earlier drafts of this paper.

References

1. Alaettinoglu, C.: Scalable Router Configuration for the Internet. In: Proceedings of the 1996 International Conference on Networking Protocols (October 1996)
2. Balon, S., Leduc, G.: Combined Intra- and Inter-domain Traffic Engineering using Hot-Potato Aware Link Weights Optimization (submitted for publication)
3. BGP Best path selection algorithm,
   http://www.cisco.com/warp/public/459/25.shtml

4. Cao, Z., Wang, Z., Zegura, E.: Performance of Hashing-Based Schemes for Internet Load Balancing. In: Proceedings of INFOCOM (2000)
5. Fortz, B., Thorup, M.: Internet Traffic Engineering by Optimizing OSPF Weights. In: Proceedings of INFOCOM, pp. 519–528 (2000)
6. Foundry enterprise configuration and management guide, http://www.foundrynet.com/services/documentation/ecmg/BGP4.html#17143
7. Gao, L., Rexford, J.: Stable Internet routing without global coordination. IEEE/ACM Transactions on Networking, 681–692 (December 2001)
8. Halpern, J.M., Bhatia, M., Jamka, P.: Advertising Equal Cost Multipath Routes in BGP. Internet Draft, Work In Progress (February 2006)
9. Iannaccone, G., Chuah, C.-N., Bhattacharyya, S., Diot, C.: Feasibility of IP restoration in a tier 1 backbone. IEEE Network 18(2) (2004)
10. Sobrinho, J.L.: An Algebraic Theory of Dynamic Network Routing. IEEE/ACM Transactions on Networking, 1160–1173 (October 2005)
11. Stewart, J.: BGP4: Interdomain routing in the Internet. Addison Wesley, Reading (1999)

Quality-of-Service Multicast Overlay Spanning Tree Algorithms for Wireless Ad Hoc Networks

Georgios Rodolakis[1], Cédric Adjih[1], Anis Laouiti[2], and Saadi Boudjit[3]

[1] INRIA Rocquencourt, France
Georges.Rodolakis@inria.fr, Cedric.Adjih@inria.fr
[2] GET/INT Evry, France
Anis.Laouiti@int-evry.fr
[3] Université Paris 13, France
saadi.boudjit@l2ti.univ-paris13.fr

Abstract. In this article, we explore modified versions of Multicast Overlay Spanning Tree algorithms (MOST) to support quality of service for wireless ad hoc networks. These algorithms (Q-MOST) take into account the interferences due to radio transmissions and the residual capacity of the nodes in the network. Different algorithms are compared to the basic MOST algorithm. We show by simulations the ability and superiority of these algorithms to find spanning trees that connect all multicast group members with respect to the bandwidth requirements.

1 Introduction

Mobile ad hoc networks (MANETs) are one of the key research topics of the moment. A MANET can be defined as a set of mobile nodes that communicate using the wireless medium, and does not require any pre-existent infrastructure. The main challenge of MANET research is to offer connectivity between the participating nodes in a multi-hop manner by sharing the same wireless channel. Several unicast protocols have been proposed to address this issue.

However, the wireless medium has limited capacity and is a scarce resource, because it is a shared among nodes within an area. One possibility is the use of multicast, which fits the increase of the popularity of group communication (P2P, Web 2.0, . . .), where several nodes exchange the same data among themselves. With multicast, every transmission from the source(s) will ultimately reach all the multicast group members, and this is achieved by using dedicated multicast structures and protocols that connect a set of nodes. This enables gains by decreasing the number of necessary transmissions. Indeed, for massively dense ad hoc networks and in the same setting as the result of Gupta and Kumar [1], it has been shown that multicast can offer a gain of $\Theta(\sqrt{n})$ over direct unicast to each of n destinations [2].

But decreasing the number of transmissions may not be sufficient since some multicast multimedia applications may also require quality of service guarantees in order to deliver real time data flows within the network. In particular, gains

S. Fdida and K. Sugiura (Eds.): AINTEC 2007, LNCS 4866, pp. 226–241, 2007.

from multicast will delay the apparition of congestion, but might not prevent it in overloaded networks, resulting in packet loss and delays, that will have a negative impact on QoS applications. Avoiding congestion in a wireless ad hoc network is not simple, because of the issues of shared medium and interference. The question is then how to perform multicast in a way that avoids congestion, taking interferences into account.

In this article, we propose some answers to this question: we introduce multicast algorithms that are, first, based on admission control, so that they are able to detect and reject multicast groups that would create congestion, and, second, that can find multicast structures which avoid congested areas, and hence are more likely to be admissible. The multicast structure computed by the algorithms, is a shared multicast spanning tree, which is constructed as an overlay tree linking all group members. This approach has several important advantages. It implies that only nodes interested in taking part in the multicast communication would need to participate in the protocol operation. In addition, the overlay tree approach can offer high robustness and reliability for the multicast service [3]. Finally, when the number of group members is small compared to the network size, multicast overlay spanning trees achieve asymptotically optimal performance [2] and maximize the network capacity. Indeed, the key QoS metric is the capacity: every multicast group has a QoS requirement expressed as a total required bandwidth for the source(s) of the group. The algorithms we propose prevent congestion by considering the channel occupancy on each node on the paths and of other nodes within the interference area of the paths, during the construction of the multicast trees.

The rest of this paper is organized as follows: Section 2 provides background material from related work; Section 3 states the studied problem, and describes formally the QoS interference model; Section 4 introduces the different new algorithms; Section 5 evaluates and analyzes the algorithms by means of simulations; Section 6 discusses protocol aspects and future work; and Section 7 concludes.

2   Related Work

As discussed, our contribution is the introduction of quality of service for multicast in ad hoc networks. In this section, we first focus on quality of service in wireless networks, especially the concept of "residual capacity" of a node; we then detail multicast protocols and QoS for multicast.

Interference and QoS for Unicast in Ad Hoc Networks. Architectures of quality of service involve a complex set of features. They include the *semantics and QoS model* that quantify the performance for some metric of quality of service in some network model and may allow to check whether admitting a flow would result in acceptable performance, e.g. *admission control*. In this article, the focus is on the semantics and QoS model, whose main feature is *interference-awareness*. In wireless ad hoc networks, additional challenges are caused by the distinguishing features of the wireless medium, and a number of adapted QoS solutions have been proposed; see [4] for a recent survey. One of these features is the fact that the network operates on a shared medium, where the number of transmission opportunities should be carefully examined due to the issue of *interferences*. Essentially, two simultaneous transmissions by nearby emitters may interfere with each other, and as a result, may not be correctly received by their intended recipients. A solution is to ensure that no such concurrent transmissions will occur, and thus to avoid the *hidden terminal problem*. The *signal-to-noise ratio* (SNR) may be used to determine whether a set of transmissions may occur at the same time and still be successfully received, but a frequent simplification is to consider that two transmissions may occur simultaneously if the transmitters (and/or the receivers), are sufficiently far from each other [4].

With this assumption, several approaches exist, which we describe from the more complex for the wireless MAC and physical layers, to the less demanding:

• In slotted networks, where the transmission opportunity schedule is predetermined, a reservation algorithm can ensure that two nodes on the same channel and in the same area would never transmit on the same slot, as in [5]. For networks that are not using a slotted MAC layer, such as IEEE 802.11, the constraints of non-interference may still be expressed as conflict graphs, indicating which sets of transmitter-receiver pairs may transmit simultaneously, as in [6]. In both cases, this requires complex synchronization to be effectively implemented.

• Another approach is based on measurements: rather than pre-determining transmissions that would not interfere with each other, the idea is to measure the *medium occupancy* using carrier-sense features, and, based on this information, to accept only new flows for which the measured idle channel time on each node is sufficient, as in [7]. However, in practice the medium occupancy is not readily available for off-the-shelf equipment, hence estimates are often required, as proposed in [8]. As indicated in [8], the medium may be available for two neighbor nodes, but at different times, so in reality, they might not be able to communicate with each other: not only medium occupancy but also scheduling should be considered once again; however it was proposed to estimate the probability that such an event occurs (mismatch of idle medium intervals).

• The last approach is to ignore precise scheduling aspects, which are complexly linked to the wireless MAC and physical layers, and which are not robust with respect to mobility, and to only consider channel occupancy, of a node and of its neighbors. Then the *residual capacity* of a node, is defined as the minimum of the total time for which the channel is not occupied from the point of view of one node and the other nodes in its interference area. It is actually an upper bound of the transmission possibilities with scheduling.

This model can be used as an admission control algorithm: if there is not enough residual capacity, given the flows that are already present, a new flow is not accepted. [9] had shown that this admission control decision is an NP-complete problem, but [10] introduced efficient heuristics. This is the model and admission control that we use in this article, see Section 3.1 for details. Under a similar model, an entire QoS interference-aware version of the routing protocol

OLSR, was developed in [11], for unicast QoS flows; the channel occupancy is derived from a packet transmission counter of each node, and transmitted as an extension of OLSR messages. The soundness of the approach is validated in practice by simulations in [11] and experiments on real test-beds [12].

Multicast routing - Multicast & QoS.   Many protocols have been proposed for multicast routing in mobile ad hoc networks. These protocols can be classified into two categories: tree based and mesh based protocols. While mesh based protocols use a single structure for each multicast group, tree based protocols can either use one tree per multicast group (shared tree) or create a separate one for each tuple (source, multicast group). Among the tree based multicast protocols we can cite MAODV [13], MOLSR [14], and MOST [3]. MAODV(Multicast Ad hoc On Demand Distance Vector) is an extension to the routing protocol AODV [15], and is a reactive multicast protocol. MOLSR (Multicast Optimized Link State Routing) is an extension to OLSR unicast routing protocol [16]. MOLSR uses the topology information given by OLSR to build a multicast tree for each tuple (source, group). MOST (Multicast Overlay Spanning Tree) [3] builds a shared overlay spanning tree between the members of the multicast group. As an example of mesh-based routing protocols, we mention On-Demand Multicast Routing Protocol (ODMRP) [17].

Multicast algorithm design for ad hoc networks is a complex problem in itself. One must take into account the characteristics of these networks such as the sensitivity of the shared wireless medium and the dynamicity of the nodes within the network. The main goal of the multicast protocols is to save bandwidth from unnecessary data transmissions. But maintaining a multicast structure implies additional overhead, and decreases the overall reliability. Using the same tree to forward multicast data for all the group members means that when a multicast packet is lost (notice that a multicast packet is not acknowledged by the receiver(s)) or when a link fails, a subset of the tree is prevented from receiving the multicast data. Mesh structures may offer more redundancy in some situations to cope with this problem. Multicast overlay structures use unicast tunnels and are less sensitive to packet loss than the basic multicast trees or meshes.

Most multicast protocols deal with multicast structure building, some of them try to improve the reliability, but only few of them are addressing the QOS requirements like QAMNET[18], QMR[19]. The basic idea of QAMNET is to extend existing approaches of mesh based multicasting and unicast QOS provisioning (the local capacity of a node is calculated as in SWAN [20]). QMR (QoS Multicasting Routing) is also a multicast mesh based protocol coupled with its own mechanism to evaluate the residual capacity locally on each node. In this protocol, nodes have to interact with their MAC layer to estimate the available bandwidth [21]. These protocols build a mesh structure in a reactive manner. Thus, there is no control neither a knowledge of the constructed mesh. In this case, the use of the overall network capacity is not optimized, and new nodes may be prevented from joining the multicast communicating groups. Both protocols try to estimate the residual bandwidth with different mechanisms, but, they do not consider the interferences problem efficiently during the bandwidth reservation. In fact, in QAMNET and QMR, bandwidth reservation is made locally on multicast mesh nodes. The neighboring nodes have to evaluate continuously the available bandwidth on their own, hence, their residual capacity is updated only when the multicast data flows start later on. Nodes transmissions from a same multicast group mesh may interfere in that case.

3   Methodology

In this section, we present the methodology we use to derive efficient algorithms for QoS multicast in multi-hop wireless networks. Our approach is based on the models and heuristics proposed in [9,10] concerning unicast routing. However, we present the models and the problem formulation in a slightly different manner, which allows us to generalize for the case of multicast communication and to propose improvements and performance estimates for the heuristics we consider.

3.1   Network and Interferences Model

As indicated in Section 2, we consider the interferences model that was introduced in [9]. We assume that a transmission from a node i interferes with all nodes within an interference zone, and equivalently, transmissions within this zone interfere with node i. This means that in order for a reception to be successful, it must be ensured that no other node within the interference zone is transmitting at the same time. We denote $\mathcal{I}(i)$ the set of nodes that are within the interference zone of node i. For example, if we assume at most two-hop interferences, $\mathcal{I}(i)$ will comprise the one-hop and two-hop neighbors of i, as well as the node i itself. In general, $\mathcal{I}(i)$ can be any set of nodes containing i. We also denote C_i the residual capacity of node i.

Let us consider two nodes i and j which can communicate directly. We will describe the effect on the residual capacities in the network, when a flow of x units of bandwidth is sent from i to j. All nodes in the interference zone of i will not be able to receive data in the same time that i is transmitting, and if a CSMA MAC protocol is used, such as IEEE 802.11, these nodes will not be allowed to transmit either. The model we consider here is consistent with this constraint, since we make no distinction between receiving and transmitting capacities. Similarly, transmissions from the nodes in the interference zone of node j will interfere with correct reception from j. These nodes will not be able to transmit data at the same time that j is receiving from i. Hence, when the flow x is injected, all nodes k in the interference zone $\mathcal{I}(i) \cup \mathcal{I}(j)$ (including i and j too) will have residual capacities updated to $C_k - x$. We note that our model is symmetric, in the sense that a flow from i to j has the same effect on the residual capacities as a flow from j to i.

Let us now consider a flow of x units of bandwidth following a route $\mathcal{R}$ from a source s to a destination t. We represent the route $\mathcal{R}$ as a set of links, i.e., $\mathcal{R} = \{e_1, e_2, \ldots\}$. We will generalize the previous discussion to describe the residual capacities in this case. For the given route $\mathcal{R}$, we define the coefficients

λ_k corresponding to the number of route links (u, v) where at least one of the nodes u or v are located in the interference zone of node k:

$$\lambda_k = \sum_{(u,v)\in\mathcal{R},\ k\in\mathcal{I}(u)\cup\mathcal{I}(v)} 1 \quad . \tag{1}$$

These coefficients allow us to express the effective bandwidth which a flow x passing through the route $\mathcal{R}$ will consume in node k, due to interferences and/or transmissions by k. The effective bandwidth will depend on the route and, for a node k, it is equal to:

$$x_{\mathcal{R}} = \lambda_k x. \tag{2}$$

As a result, the residual capacities for all nodes in the network, after the flow x is accepted through the route $\mathcal{R}$, will be equal to: $C_k - \lambda_k x$.

3.2   Problem Statement

According to the model presented in the previous section, we can formulate the necessary conditions for the available capacities in the network, in order for a flow to be potentially accepted. Moreover, if a bandwidth reservation mechanism is in use, the effective bandwidth defined in (2) corresponds to the amount of bandwidth that each node would have to reserve for the given flow (we can include a factor to consider the MAC and scheduling overhead, as in [11]).

At first, we consider unicast routing. We present our formulation of the path with Residual Capacity problem (RC), defined and shown to be NP-complete in [9]. The objective is to find a route $\mathcal{R}$ in order to transmit x units of bandwidth from a source s to a destination t. The constraint is that the residual capacity of all nodes in the network must be larger (or equal) than 0. Using the previously presented notation, this can be expressed as follows:

$$\forall k : C_k - \lambda_k x \geq 0. \tag{3}$$

In other words, the capacity C_k must be larger than the total bandwidth which a flow x passing through the route $\mathcal{R}$ will consume in node k.

Using the same notation introduced in the previous section, we can formulate the problem of finding a multicast overlay spanning tree with residual capacity (MOST-RC), as a direct generalization of the previous case, which is obviously NP-complete too. An overlay tree corresponds to a set of routes (tunnels) between the multicast members. So, we can represent it as a set of links $\mathcal{T}$, in analogy to the route $\mathcal{R}$. For instance, a tree consisting of n tunnels $\mathcal{R}_i$ will be represented as $\mathcal{T} = \bigcup_{i=1..n} \mathcal{R}_n$, where the sources and destinations for the tunnels are chosen arbitrarily[1]. The objective is to find such an overlay tree spanning on all the multicast nodes, which can accept a flow of x units of bandwidth. Again, the constraint is that the residual capacity of all nodes in the network must be

---

[1] Due to the symmetry in the interference model, we do not need to consider a particular source in the tree, hence the arbitrary choices concerning the tunnel sources for the definition of the sets $\mathcal{R}_i$.

larger (or equal) than 0, as described in (3). In this case, the coefficients λ_k are defined with respect to a given tree $\mathcal{T}$, instead of a route $\mathcal{R}$, but their definition remains unchanged, *i.e.*, $\lambda_k = \displaystyle\sum_{(u,v)\in\mathcal{T},\ k\in\mathcal{I}(u)\cup\mathcal{I}(v)} 1$.

3.3 Heuristics

Since the problem we consider is NP-hard, we describe some heuristics that can be used in order to compute bandwidth-aware routes and overlay multicast trees. In this section, we provide a general discussion and the motivation for using these heuristics, as well as some arguments concerning the performance that can be achieved. A detailed description of the QoS multicast overlay spanning tree algorithms will be presented in Section 4.

The main goal of the heuristics we will describe is to find a route/tree that satisfies the capacity constraints (3). Moreover, it is desirable to find a solution that does not consume too many resources, so that future flow admission requests can be satisfied too. Hence, the heuristics take into account the available capacities in the network, so that nodes that have higher capacities are preferentially chosen as relays, while nodes that have low capacities are bypassed. We note that, while the heuristics can be used to compute in an efficient way a candidate route/tree, they offer no guarantee or definitive answer on whether a flow can be accepted in the network. Thus, the constraints in (3) must be checked after the computation, to verify whether the flow can actually be accepted.

From the definition of the coefficients λ_k we note that we only need to consider nodes in the route/tree, as well as the nodes in their interference zones. For all the remaining nodes we have $\lambda_k = 0$, and the residual capacities do not change. Hence, (3) is true if and only if:

$$\forall k \in \mathcal{I}(u) \cup \mathcal{I}(v),\ (u,v) \in \mathcal{T} : C_k \geq \lambda_k x, \tag{4}$$

where we took the case of the multicast tree for generality.

We can then write the following equivalent constraint formulation:

$$\min_{k\in\mathcal{I}(u)\cup\mathcal{I}(v),\ (u,v)\in\mathcal{T}} \frac{C_k}{\lambda_k} \geq x \tag{5}$$

According to the previous discussion, a candidate route for satisfying the given constraints will be the route that maximizes the route capacity in the left hand side of (5), or equivalently that minimizes the inverse capacity, *i.e.*,

$$\min \left\{ \max_{k\in\mathcal{I}(u)\cup\mathcal{I}(v),\ (u,v)\in\mathcal{T}} \frac{\lambda_k}{C_k} \right\}. \tag{6}$$

However, such a route may be too long and may consume too many network resources due to interferences. Consequently, the capacity of the network for accepting more flows could be unnecessarily reduced.

A better candidate route/tree can be found by the following heuristic. Each node k is associated with a weight $w_k = \sum_{j \in \mathcal{I}(k)} \frac{1}{C_j}$, *i.e.*, the sum of the inverse capacities of all nodes in the interference zone of k (including k). We can then define the weight of a route/tree as the sum of weights of the nodes in the route/tree. The heuristic consists in taking the route/tree with the minimum weight. Such a minimization can easily be performed with Dijkstra's algorithm or a classic spanning tree algorithm, for a route or an overlay tree respectively. This will result in avoiding nodes which have low capacities, or which interfere with other low capacity nodes. This approach was introduced in [10] for unicast routing, and it was found (via simulations) to achieve the best performance among other proposed approaches. We observe that the route/tree that we compute in this case minimizes the sum: $\sum_{k \in \mathcal{I}(u) \cup \mathcal{I}(v), (u,v) \in \mathcal{T}} \frac{\lambda_k}{C_k}$.

We can propose a variant of this heuristic, by considering weights $w_k = \sum_{j \in \mathcal{I}(k)} \frac{1}{(C_j)^n}$, where n can be any positive integer. We then define the following incremental algorithm: we start with $n = 1$ and if the route/tree discovery fails (*i.e.*, the capacity constraints are not satisfied) the value of n is increased. The procedure is repeated until the flow is accepted, or until n reaches a predefined upper threshold (in this case the flow cannot be admitted). In fact, larger values of n mean that low capacity nodes will have even larger weights and they will be chosen less often. So, we will compute longer routes/trees. As n tends to infinity, the computed route/tree will maximize the minimum residual capacity in all its interfering nodes, since we have that $\lim_{n \to \infty} \left(\sum_k \frac{1}{(C_k)^n} \right)^{\frac{1}{n}} = \max_k \frac{1}{C_k}$.

The above heuristics take into consideration the available capacities in the network, but they ignore the amount of bandwidth that is being requested by the current flow. Although this approach can be effective when the requested bandwidth is small compared to the residual capacities in the network, the performance can be improved by heuristics that adapt the route/tree computation to the particular amount of bandwidth requested each time. In fact, in the case of multicast flows, this adaptation is even more important, since a large number of nodes might be involved, and the flow may have a significant impact on the network conditions. As a result, better performance can be achieved if the node weights are updated during the algorithm execution, according to the new residual capacities. Let us assume that we use a greedy algorithm and the same definition of the node weights as before. If the weights are updated each time a node is added to the route/tree, the algorithm will minimize the sum[2]: $\sum_{k \in \mathcal{I}(u) \cup \mathcal{I}(v), (u,v) \in \mathcal{T}} \sum_{j=0..\lambda_k-1} \frac{1}{(C_k - jx)^n}$. The route/tree we compute will then approach (as n tends to infinity) the route/tree which minimizes the least residual capacity in the network after the new flow has been admitted, *i.e.*, $\max \min_k (C_k - \lambda_k x)$. However, this optimization is achieved at the cost of an increase in the algorithm's running time complexity. In the next section, we discuss how a compromise can be found between the running time and the expected performance, with selective weight updates whenever a multicast node is added to the multicast overlay tree.

---

[2] We take $\frac{1}{C_k - jx} = \infty$ if $C_k - jx \leq 0$.

4   QoS Multicast Overlay Spanning Tree Algorithms

In this section, we present the algorithms which we use to construct multicast overlay spanning trees. All new algorithms are based on the spanning tree algorithm which is in use in the MOST protocol [3], combined with the heuristics we presented in Section 3.3. The performance of all algorithms described here will be compared via extensive simulations in the following section.

Basic MOST Algorithm. The algorithm in the MOST protocol computes a minimum spanning tree over all multicast nodes, by minimizing the size of the multicast tree in number of links/hops. An efficient algorithm for constructing such an overlay tree is presented in [3]. However, this algorithm does not take into consideration the available capacities in the network.

MOST with Unicast QoS. One possibility for improvement consists in taking an overlay tree computed by MOST and using unicast QoS routing independently for each individual tunnel in the overlay tree, as if each tunnel corresponded to a different unicast flow. This means that the overlay tree structure is not dependent on the available capacities in the network, since each multicast node will have exactly the same overlay neighbors as with the basic MOST algorithm. Nonetheless, some optimization is possible since the unicast tunnels will follow more appropriate paths, using the heuristics from [10].

Simple Q-MOST Algorithm. It is possible to construct a better overlay tree, by taking into account the available capacities directly in the computation of the overlay tree structure. This can be achieved by using the defined weights, and by computing the overlay spanning tree that minimizes the sum of these weights. This minimization can be performed with algorithm 1, which is an adaptation of the basic MOST algorithm for our particular context. The difference consists in taking node weights instead of unit edge costs.

We denote $G(V, E)$ the network graph, where V is the node set, E is the edge set. Each node v is associated with a weight $W(v)$. We also denote S the set of multicast nodes. The array d associates each node with a distance to the multicast overlay tree, i.e., $d[v]$ corresponds to the minimum distance of node v to the multicast nodes that are already part of the tree. This distance is initialized to $W[root]$ for the root node and to ∞ for all other nodes. The root node corresponds to the node with the smallest weight. The array *overlaypred* associates each node with an overlay predecessor multicast node. On the other hand, the array *pred* associates each node with its direct predecessor in the multicast tree (which is not necessarily a multicast node). These arrays need only be maintained during the computations, in order to construct the list of overlay routes *routeList*, which represents the complete multicast tree structure. The algorithm manages a set F of multicast nodes that have not been covered yet by the tree, and a min-priority queue Q which includes all nodes, with the priority attribute being equal to their distance d. In each iteration the algorithm chooses a node u with the smallest distance to the overlay tree (step 7), and

---

Algorithm 1: Efficient QoS Minimum Spanning Tree Algorithm

Input: Graph $G(V, E)$, Multicast Node Set S, Node Weight Array W.
Output: Overlay route List $routeList$

1. for all $(v \in V)$ { $d[v] \leftarrow \infty$; $pred[v] \leftarrow NIL$; $overlayPred[v] \leftarrow NIL$;}
2. $root \leftarrow \arg\min_i W[i]$
3. $d[root] \leftarrow W[root]$;
4. $Q \leftarrow V$;
5. $F \leftarrow S$;
6. while $(F \neq \varnothing)$ {
7. $u \leftarrow$ EXTRACT-MIN(Q);
8.   if $(u \in S)$ {
9. $d[u] \leftarrow W[u]$;
10.   DEL(F, u);
11.   INSERT$(routeList, getRoute(overlayPred[u], u)$ }
12.   for each $(v \in adj[u])$ {
13.   if $(d[v] > d[u] + W[v])$ {
14. $d[v] \leftarrow d[u] + W[v]$;
15.   if$(v \notin Q)$ { INSERT(Q, v); }
16.   if $(u \in S)$ $overlayPred[v] \leftarrow u$;
17.   else $overlayPred[v] \leftarrow overlayPred[u]$;
18. $pred[v] \leftarrow u$; }} }

---

checks whether it is a multicast node (step 8). In this case, the node's distance is updated to $W[u]$ (because the node is added to the overlay tree) and it is removed from the set F. Afterwards, for each chosen node, steps 13−18 check its adjacent nodes on whether their distance can be improved, and update the predecessors appropriately, similarly to the basic MOST algorithm (*cf.* [3]).

The node weights are set according to the formula: $w_k = \sum_{j \in \mathcal{I}(k)} \frac{1}{C_j}$ for a node k. We call this algorithm variant *QOSMOSTsimple*. Similarly, we can use the weight definition $w_k = \sum_{j \in \mathcal{I}(k)} \frac{1}{(C_j)^n}$, where n is an integer. In this case, the algorithm is repeated with increasing values of n until the flow is accepted, or until n reaches a predefined upper threshold. This variant is denoted *QOSMOSTsimple-inc*. In the following, we denote N the number of nodes in the network, M the number of links, n the number of multicast members, and D the maximum number of nodes in an interference zone. The time needed to compute the weights for all nodes in the network, is $O(ND)$. Similarly, the complexity for checking whether the residual capacity constraints are satisfied is $O(TD)$, where T is the size of the multicast tree. Once the weights have been computed, the complexity of algorithm 1 is exactly the same as the basic MOST algorithm, *i.e.*, $O(n(N \log N + M))$ in the worst case, and approximately equal to Dijkstra's algorithm on average (*cf.* [3]). Therefore, this particular algorithm has the important advantage of having low running time complexity. Moreover, we note that we do not need to take into account here the amount of bandwidth requested by a given flow. This means that this algorithm can be used to compute bandwidth-aware multicast overlay trees, which can be used regardless of the bandwidth requirements, in a group shared multicast tree protocol.

Improved Q-MOST Algorithm. In case the QoS requirements are stricter, it is beneficial to propose an algorithm which can adapt to the precise amount of bandwidth requested by a given multicast flow. Therefore, an improved version of the Q-MOST algorithm consists in updating the remaining capacities and the node weights whenever a multicast node is added to the overlay tree. More precisely, the following modifications must be made to algorithm 1, after step 11:

1. Update the residual capacities in the network (when the tunnel which connects the newly added multicast node to the tree has accepted flow x);
2. update the weights for all concerned nodes;
3. reset the distances of all nodes in the network to infinity (except multicast nodes that have already been added to the overlay tree).

Again, we define two variants of the improved Q-MOST algorithm, depending on whether we use incremental weights or not: *QOSMOST* and *QOSMOST-inc.* According to the discussion in the previous section concerning weight updates, we note that the incremental algorithm will find an overlay tree which approaches the tree that maximizes the least residual capacity in the network, after the multicast flow is accepted. Hence, we expect to find a suitable multicast tree with respect to a flow request in almost all cases where such a tree exists. This performance gain comes at a (small) extra complexity cost. Once the node weights have been computed, the worst case complexity in both variants of the improved Q-MOST algorithm is $O\left(n(N \log N + M) + TD\right)$, where T is the overlay tree size. However, the average case complexity is also higher due to the fact that the distances must be reset each time a multicast node is added to the tree.

5   Simulations

In order to evaluate the performance of the variants of Q-MOST, we perform extensive simulations, which are detailed in this section. The focus of the Q-MOST algorithm is on wireless ad hoc networks. Such networks have been modeled as *unit disk graphs* of the plane, where two nodes are neighbors whenever their distance is lower than a fixed radio range. The simulator used was self-developed; the simulation parameters are given in table 1. In the simulations, the network considered is a square. The interference area of one node will be considered to be either the one-hop neighborhood, i.e. the area within range ρ; or the two-hop neighborhood (which is an approximation of the area within range $2 \times \rho$).

In the first scenario, 1000 nodes are randomly distributed, the interference area is the one-hop neighborhood, and every node has an initial capacity of 5000 units of bandwidth. The scenario repeatedly attempts to add more multicast trees, with a randomly selected group of 10 members, and each of the trees requiring a capacity of 10 units of bandwidth. The results are shown on Fig. 1 (we omit the plots corresponding to the incremental variants, because in this particular scenario they have exactly the same performance as the non-incremental

Table 1. Basic simulation parameters

Parameter	Value(s)
Network width L	$L = 1$
Number of nodes	200 or 1000
Range ρ	0.2 for 200 nodes, 0.1 for 1000 nodes
Position of the nodes	random uniform i.i.d

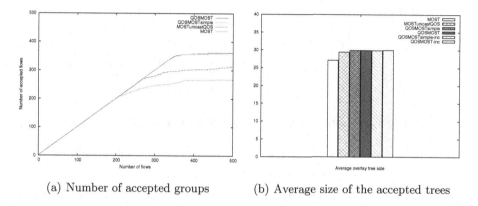

(a) Number of accepted groups   (b) Average size of the accepted trees

Fig. 1. Admission control of 500 successive groups

algorithms). We first see on Fig. 1(a), the evolution of the accepted groups with
the number of groups: on the x-axis, the network starts with 0 groups, and new
groups are created randomly until 500 groups are reached. On the y-axis, the
number of groups that are successfully added is displayed.

As one can see, both the simple Q-MOST and improved Q-MOST perform
very similarly and clearly outperform the basic MOST algorithm and MOST
with Unicast QoS, in spite of all the algorithms being simulated with the same
groups. This result comes from the fact that, when congestion begins, while
minimum spanning trees based on hop-count distances (MOST) are no longer
necessarily accepted, the Q-MOST algorithms are able to find trees with routes
sidestepping from nodes with low residual capacity. MOST with Unicast QoS is
able to do the same to some extent, but its performance on the scenario is only
midway, illustrating that the fact that QoS for multicast is more than multicast
using unicast QoS. Hence, the global optimization in the multicast tree structure
performed by the Q-MOST algorithms implies an important performance gain.
Another interesting point is the sharper plateauing of the Q-MOST algorithms
(after about 350 admissions), showing that almost no group can be accepted
after some congestion level is reached, hinting at the fact that these algorithms
are efficient in finding possible trees when they exist. In Fig. 1(b), the average
size of the final accepted overlay tree is shown for the various algorithms; it is
the average total number of links in the tree. It appears that the size of the
overlay tree of the Q-MOST algorithm is not significantly larger than for basic

MOST; hence, although the heuristics avoid going through and near areas with low residual capacity, this is done in a adequate manner. Notice that using too large trees would have a negative performance impact on Fig. 1(a).

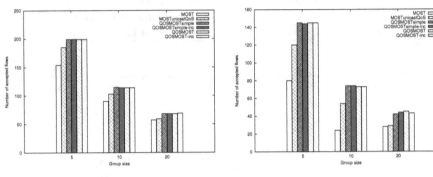

(a) With identical initial capacity   (b) With initial capacity hole in the center

Fig. 2. Admission control of 500 successive groups for all algorithm

The second scenario is similar to the first one, except that the interferences area is the two-hop neighborhood, and that the number of members in each group varies: 5, 10 or 20. The results are represented on histograms in Fig. 2, which indicate the total number of accepted multicast groups after 500 attempts. Fig. 2(a) is for a network where all the nodes have the same initial capacity equal to 5000, whereas in Fig. 2(b), the nodes in a smaller square in the center of edge 0.5 have a halved initial capacity, that is 2500 units of bandwidth.

We see again that all the variants of Q-MOST have a similar performance, considering the number of multicast groups that can be accepted, that MOST performs worse, and that MOST with Unicast QoS has intermediary performance. One significant result here, is comparing Fig. 2(a) and Fig. 2(b), it appears that the benefits of Q-MOST over MOST increase, when the capacity is not uniform (for instance, when there is a capacity hole in the center). This last case corresponds to more realistic cases, where the center of the network is more likely to get congested, or where non-multicast traffic is not uniformly spread.

The last scenario focuses on the impact of the size of requests (requested bandwidth) on the performance. The two base scenarios are: either 1) with 200 nodes, or 2) with 1000 nodes. In addition, two sub-variants are tested, for different initial capacity assignments: 1) in the first, every node has an initial capacity selected uniformly at random in the range of 4000 to 5000 units; 2) in the second, every node has an initial capacity of 5000, except for nodes in the center square, a capacity "hole", which have a random capacity in the range of 2000 − 2500 units. We present here the results when in the first variant we assume one-hop interferences, while in the second variant we assume two-hop interferences. For the four combinations, the scenario simulates the arrival of *one* group with a large bandwidth requirement, with 10 members. The metric

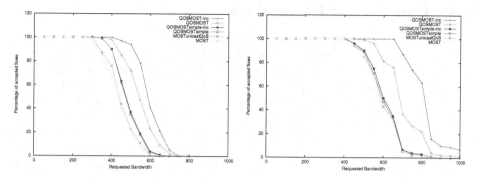

(a) 200 nodes, 1-hop interferences, no capac- (b) 1000 nodes, 1-hop interferences, no ca-
ity hole   pacity hole

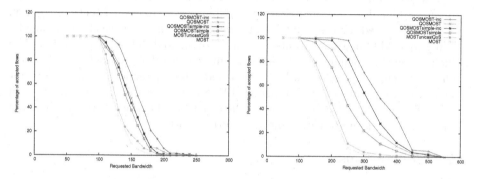

(c) 200 nodes, 2-hop interferences, with ca- (d) 1000 nodes, 2-hop interferences, with capacity hole   pacity hole

Fig. 3. Admission probability w.r.t. requested bandwidth (avg. of 100 requests)

is the average admission rate, based on 100 attempts with randomly selected
members on the same topology and with the same bandwidth requirement. The
results are on Fig. 3.

On these figures, one can see the admission rate: for instance, on Fig. 3(d),
for a requested bandwidth equal to 250 units, the admission probability is 7%
for MOST, compared to 99% for the iterative improved Q-MOST. The results
get better and better when the algorithms are more sophisticated and more interference aware; noticeably, unlike previous results from Fig. 3, this time the
difference of performance between the variants of Q-MOST are more clearly
established: this comes from the fact that only one request is to be satisfied
at a time, hence, algorithms cannot compensate by accepting later "easier" requests. The best Q-MOST variant in all cases is the incremental improved Q-
MOST algorithm, which can nearly accept the double of the requested bandwidth compared to the basic MOST algorithm, in the more critical case of
Fig. 3(d).

6   Protocol and Future Work

In the previous sections, we presented Q-MOST as an algorithm, and evaluated its performance by simulation, assuming all information is available to every node. In practice, one needs to extend the QoS model that is used, in order to create a protocol with proper signaling. In reality, most of the ingredients necessary to construct such an actual protocol already exist, if the OLSR routing protocol is selected as the routing protocol of the ad hoc network: the multicast signaling and network interfacing are available with MOST [3], which in turns reuses implementations and ideas from MOLSR [14] - both have been implemented and tested in real test-beds. Similarly, the mechanisms and protocols for exchanging the necessary information about quality of service and residual capacities have already been designed in a QoS interference-aware version of OLSR [11], implemented, tested and validated on test-beds [12]. The two remaining difficulties are the following: the first one is that consistent information needs to be used for the multicast tree computation; this is easily overcome by using some kind of global counter/timing in order to decide which sets should be included in the calculation. The second is more general: the model only considers channel occupancy and not scheduling as indicated in Section 2, and although it has excellent performance in practice [12], precise probabilistic arguments such as in [8] would be interesting. Lastly, the exact specification of the protocol and its implementation are also subjects of future work.

7   Conclusions

In this article, we presented a family of algorithms, Q-MOST, for multicast in ad hoc networks. The central feature of these algorithms is that they integrate quality of service constraints based on the concept of residual capacity, as well as interference-awareness, with a specific model of interferences. They perform admission control. They essentially compute a multicast tree, linking nodes of the group, satisfying the QoS interference constraint that the residual capacity must never go below zero in the network; in addition, the multicast tree is an overlay tree, hence two neighbors in the tree are linked by reliable multi-hop routes which are themselves interference-aware. The difficulty is that even unicast route calculation is NP-complete within this model, hence we have proposed several variants of the Q-MOST algorithms based on efficient heuristics. We have experimentally shown via simulations the excellent behavior of these heuristics on several scenarios: for instance, compared to the basic MOST algorithm, they allow to admit noticeably more groups. Future work includes considering the impact of scheduling, and developing an actual protocol specification and implementation.

References

1. Gupta, P., Kumar, P.R.: Capacity of Wireless Networks. IEEE Trans. Inf. Theory 46(2), 388–404 (2000)
2. Jacquet, P., Rodolakis, G.: Multicast Scaling Properties in Massively Dense Ad Hoc Networks, SANSO, Fukuoka, Japan (2005)

3. Rodolakis, G., Meraihi Naimi, A, Laouiti, A.: Multicast Overlay Spanning Tree Protocol for Ad Hoc Networks, WWIC, Coimbra, Portugal (2007)
4. Hanzo, L., Tafazolli, R.: A Survey of QoS Routing Solutions for Mobile Ad hoc Networks IEEE Communications Surveys & Tutorials (2007)
5. Lin, C.R., Liu, J.-S.: QoS Routing in Ad Hoc Wireless Networks, IEEE Journal on Selected Areas in Communications, 1426–1438 (August 1999)
6. Gupta, R., Jia, Z., Tung, T., Walrand, J.: Interference-aware Qos Routing (IQRouting) for Ad-Hoc Networks. In: Proc. Globecom 2005, vol. 5 (November 2005)
7. Ge, Y., Kunz, T., Lamont, L.: Quality of Service Routing in Ad-Hoc Networks Using OLSR. In: Hawaii International Conference on System Sciences (January 2003)
8. Sarr, C., Chaudet, C., Chelius, G., Guerin-Lassous, I.: A Node-Based Available Bandwidth Evaluation in IEEE 802.11 Ad Hoc Networks. International Journal of Parallel, Emergent and Distributed Systems (July 2005)
9. Georgiadis, L., Jacquet, P., Mans, B.: Bandwidth Reservation in Multihop Wireless Networks: Complexity, Heuristics and Mechanisms, WWAN, Japan (2004)
10. Allard, G., Jacquet, P.: Heuristics for Bandwidth Reservation in Multihop Wireless Networks, INRIA Research Report RR-5075 (January 2004)
11. Nguyen, D., Minet, P.: Quality of Service Routing in a MANET with OLSR. Journal of Universal Computer Science (JUCS) 13(1), 56–86 (2007)
12. Nguyen, D., Minet, P., Adjih, C.: Quality of service for OLSR: Implementation and Measures on a Real Military MANET, 3rd OLSR Interop, Japan (October 2006)
13. Royer, E., Perkins, C.: Multicast Ad hoc On-Demand Distance Vector (MAODV) Routing, IETF, Internet Draft: draft- ietf-manet-maodv-00.txt (2000)
14. Laouiti, A., Jacquet, P., Minet, P., Viennot, L., Clausen, T., Adjih, C.: Multicast Optimized Link State Routing, INRIA research report RR-4721 (2003)
15. Perkins, C., Belding-Royer, E., Das, S.: Ad hoc on-demand distance vector (AODV) routing, RFC 3561 (2003)
16. Clausen, T., Jacquet, P., Adjih, C., Laouiti, A., Mühletaler, P., Minet, P., Qayyum, A., Viennot, L.: Optimized link state routing protocol, RFC 3626 (2003)
17. Lee, S., Su, W., Gerla, M.: On demand multicast routing protocol in multihop wireless mobile networks, ACM/Baltzer Mobile Networks and Applications (2000)
18. Tebbe, H., Kassler, A.: QAMNet: Providing Quality of Service to Ad-hoc Multicast Enabled Networks, ISWPC, Thailand (2006)
19. Saghir, M., Wan, T.C., Budiarto, R.: Load Balancing QoS Multicast Routing Protocol in Mobile Ad hoc Networks, AINTEC, Bangkok, Thailand (2005)
20. Ahn, G., Campbell, A.T., Veres, A., Sun, L.: Supporting Service Differentiation for Real-Time and Best Effort Traffic in Stateless Wireless Ad Hoc Networks (SWAN), IEEE Transactions on Mobile Computing (September 2002)
21. Saghir, M., Wan, T.C., Budiarto, R.: QoS Multicast Routing Based on Bandwidth Estimation in Mobile Ad Hoc Networks, ICCCE, Malaysia (2006)

Architecture of Satellite Internet for Asia-Wide Digital Communications

Kotaro Kataoka[1], Achmad Husni Thamrin[1],
Kenjiro Cho[2], Jun Takei[3], and Jun Murai[4]

[1] Graduate School of Media and Governance, Keio University
[2] Internet Initiative Japan
[3] Corporate Technology Group, Intel Corporation
[4] Faculty of Environmental Information, Keio University

Abstract. This paper describes the network architecture of an Asia-wide satellite Internet that considers the situations in developing regions. The design considerations for the architecture are costs, effective use of satellite bandwidth, scalability, and routing strategy when combined with terrestrial links. The architecture includes using one-way shared satellite links to reduce costs, IP multicast to leverage the broadcast nature of satellite links, QoS, audio-video application gateway to adapt to the limited bandwidth of satellite links. This architecture is implemented in an operational network testbed connecting 13 countries and supporting a distance learning project.

1   Introduction

1.1   Background and Focus of Research

There are high demands for wide-area Information Communication Technology (ICT) infrastructure in Asia. Human resource development, closing the gap of the digital divide, and communications in emergency situations are among the driver for these demands. Broadband Internet is an infrastructure to give high-speed Internet access to users, but the development in Asia is usually limited within major cities. The characteristics of satellite communications are: (1) wide-area coverage, (2) quick installation, (3) independent from terrestrial infrastructure, and (4) broadcast capability, can be leverage to give broadband access to places where terrestrial infrastructure is still underdeveloped. Therefore, satellite communication is a viable option to build a network in developing regions, such as many parts of Asia.

This paper discusses the architecture of an Asia-wide satellite Internet infrastructure, as an example of how satellite communication can give benefits to the developing Asian regions. Our focus on this research is sharing the technical aspects of networking using satellite link, that we have experienced through design, installation, operation and R&D activities on an on-going satellite Internet in Asia. Hence this paper is expected to give technical suggestions to those who want to join or even launch IP network using satellite communications.

S. Fdida and K. Sugiura (Eds.): AINTEC 2007, LNCS 4866, pp. 242–255, 2007.

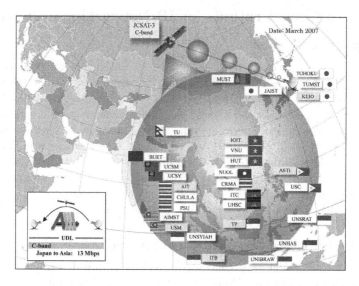

Fig. 1. Satellite UDL in AI³

1.2   AI³ Satellite Network

Asian Internet Interconnection Initiatives (AI³)[6] provides an R&D network in Asia. AI³ network employs several satellite bi-directional links (BDLs) and one satellite uni-directional link (UDL) to interconnect its participating partners as shown in Fig.1. We have been operating AI³ since 1996 as a testbed, and the operation of UDL started in 2000.

AI³ supports School on the Internet Asia (SOI Asia) [11], a project to realize an infrastructure for human resource development by distance education in Asia, where 29 institutes from 13 countries participate as of April 2007. SOI Asia provides its remote lectures over the satellite UDL to share lecture contents, such as video, audio and presentation materials from the lecturer site among the student sites.

AI³ and SOI Asia have been providing mechanisms to enable an Asia-wide satellite network and digital communications. However, the past achievements of these projects have not satisfied the entire requirement regarding the satellite Internet.

1.3   Paper Organization

Section 2 discusses requirements of satellite Internet. Section 3 presents an architecture of satellite Internet, including current challenges, that is used in AI³ and SOI Asia. Section 4 qualitatively evaluates the architecture and achievement discussed in this paper. We conclude this paper in Section 5 with raising issues to conduct for future satellite Internet.

2   Design Considerations for IP Networking over Satellite

2.1   Cost Requirement

The cost of hardware equipments is an issue in satellite communications. Not only that the hardware cost discrepancies between receive-only stations and transmit-capable stations are big, but also transmit-capable stations have to be operated by specialists and usually the government requires a certain license for such stations. Transponder costs may also be an issue, as the costs are much higher compared to the costs of terrestrial links, if such links are available. These costs often make it difficult to install satellite communications for IP networking in spite of their characteristics described in Section 1.1. Therefore, the satellite communication technology selection, including hardware and use of transponder, has to be made in such a way to minimize these costs.

2.2   Effective Utilization of Radio Spectrum

The allocation of radio spectrum and its configuration determines the bandwidth for each satellite link. However, radio spectrum is a limited resource, and is shared among transmitting earth stations and their receivers. Therefore, flexibility is required to make effective use of radio spectrum.

Because various traffics flow on the IP network over satellite, it is important to employ suitable networking technologies such as compressing the traffic, prioritizing one type of traffic over the others, and using IP multicast to take advantage of the broadcast nature of satellite links.

2.3   Scalability for Future Deployment

A satellite radio spectrum can be allocated into bi-directional links, but it will severely limit the bandwidth for each link when the number of users is large. The cost implications will also be huge due to the number of installed transmit-capable stations. Instead, the radio spectrum can be used as a uni-directional link, taking advantage of the broadcast nature of satellite links. In this case the number of installed receive-only stations can virtually be unlimited, and therefore IPv6 is promising as the network protocol for this link as the address space is large. However, the scalability of the network protocol will be an issue when it is implemented on a large-scale uni-directional link.

2.4   Routing Strategy

Internet access using fiber optic cables has not been widely deployed in Asian regions, and dial-up or DSL connections are the major access. When both satellite path and terrestrial path are available between two communicating nodes, it is often the case that the satellite path has larger capacity but with much larger delay than the terrestrial path. Hence path selection needs to take delay and capacity into consideration. Routing strategy on the end node and operational supports in the upstream network is important to optimize the usage of available paths.

Table 1. Components of Architecture

Index	Component	Target Requirements
S1	One-way shared satellite link	R1, R2
S2	IP Multicast	R2
S3	QoS traffic management	R2
S4	Application gateway for video/audio communication	R2
S5	UDL mesh networking	R1, R2
S6	Transition to IPv6 operation	R3
S7	Scalability of UDL	R1, R4
S8	Sophisticated InterAS Routing using Satellite	R5

2.5 Summary

Based on the discussion above, this research raises 5 requirements for implementation of actual IP network using satellite communications as follows.

R1. Cost reduction on installation and operation of satellite communications
R2. Engineering to maximize utilization of radio spectrum
R3. IPv6 to accommodate a large number of connecting nodes
R4. Scalability of network protocols
R5. Routing strategy in the environment where multiple paths are available including a satellite communication

Following sections discuss how we conduct IP networking with satisfying these requirements.

3 Satellite Internet Architecture

There are several technical components for IP communication over satellite. Fig.2 shows the architecture of satellite Internet used by AI[3]. The components of this architecture provide the solutions to meet the requirements set forth in Section2. Table3 summarizes the components and the requirements they will satisfy. Each of these components will be discussed in this paper. S1-S4 have been achieved, and S5-S7 are the current challenges, while S8 is under discussion for the future work.

3.1 One-Way Shared Satellite Link

A one-way shared satellite link can be established using satellite receivers, and is effective for (1) an easy solution for broadband Internet connection in the start-up phase of ICT infrastructure, and (2) deployment of large-scale, wide-area Internet services, and (3) an alternative path for the Internet in emergency situations. Using a one-way shared link (uni-directional link) satisfies R1 and R2.

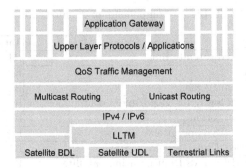

Fig. 2. Technology Architecture

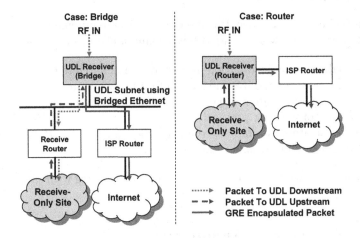

Fig. 3. UDL Receiver Bridge and Router

A receive-only earth station, that does not transmit any carrier to the satellite, is small and inexpensive to install and quick to start operation because it is not necessary to acquire a radio license in many countries.

The current routing protocols on the Internet assume that links have bidirectional communication capability. Therefore, Link Layer Tunneling Mechanism (LLTM) [8] was developed and it provides transparent functionality of routing protocols by emulating a bi-directional, broadcast-capable multiple access link on the UDL.

LLTM specification defines that UDL Feeds and Receivers are routers or hosts. However, AI[3] employs an Ethernet bridge implementation for UDL Feed and Receiver. Fig.3 shows the two cases of UDL Receiver, which is implemented as an Ethernet bridge or a router.

In this figure, UDL Receiver Bridge provides Receive Router with a connectivity to the UDL via Ethernet. UDL Receiver Bridge operates LLTM on behalf of Receive Router that only forwards packet from/to the UDL. This implementation allows using an IP router as Receive Router regardless of its vendor and available routing protocols. On the other hand, UDL Receiver Router has to operate not only LLTM but also routing protocols. However, few router vendors support the functionality of, in the case of UDL Receiver, satellite receiver and LLTM in addition to Internet routing protocols. Also, the available routing protocols may be limited or very slow to support new routing protocols. And this is the major reason why AI[3] employed bridge for UDL Feed and Receiver.

3.2   IP Multicast

Broadcast capability is the most important advantage of satellite communication. IP multicast uses that characteristic, and it delivers a single copy of data to multiple destinations at a time. Therefore IP multicast maximizes the utilization of radio spectrum (R2). A satellite link can work as a large-scale IP multicast overlay network for regions where IP multicast is hardly deployed. We have enabled multicast using Protocol Independent Multicast - Sparse Mode (PIM-SM) [9] in AI[3]'s backbone and the satellite UDL. In order to let multicast traffic flow from its source to the receiver networks via the satellite UDL, the appropriate selection of RP, which is the UDL interface of the upstream router in Feed network, is important in the PIM-SM configuration [12].

3.3   QoS for Classified Traffics

Two limiting factors for satellite bandwidth are satellite bandwidth capacity, including transponder bandwidth, and budget to rent the bandwidth. Therefore, given that the available bandwidth of a link is usually less than the expected amount of the total traffic, we need to prioritize certain types of traffic according to some metrics in order to make effective use of the limited link bandwidth (R2).

AI[3] and SOI Asia have arranged a QoS policy for the UDL usage to support distance education programs. This QoS policy defines the classification of traffic as follows:

1. Control traffic for routing protocols (OSPF, ICMP)
2. Multicast traffic for SOI Asia lectures (Video, Audio, File Transfer)
3. Unicast traffic for terminal access and IRC (SSH, IRC)
4. Transit traffic to the other ASs via receive-only sites
5. Commodity traffic to the satellite UDL prefixes.

To achieve the classification, we have installed the QoS policy using ALTQ[7] HFSC queuing discipline on the upstream network interface of the gateway router to the satellite UDL. Table 3.3 shows the QoS rules for the situations depending whether SOI Asia is having a lecture or not. Each traffic class is guaranteed to a certain rate (denoted as NKbps) and may use a certain percentage of the unused bandwidth. The total bandwidth of the AI[3] uni-directional link is 12.6Mbps.

Table 2. QoS Rules of AI³ Uni-directional Link

Class	Lecture	No Lecture
Control	100Kbps, 1%	250Kbps, 5%
Multicast	4800Kbps, 60%	2000Kbps, 10%
Unicast	—	250Kbps, 5%
Transit	1000Kbps, 25%	3000Kbps, 40%
Commodity	1000Kbps, 5%	1000Kbps, 30%

3.4 Application Gateway for Video/Audio Communication

There are many ways for video/audio applications to be used with the appropriate rate in the satellite Internet with limited bandwidth. For realtime video/audio applications, there are mainly three approaches: (1) transmission of native format without any modification, (2) rate adaptation by an intermediate proxy, and (3) media conversion by an intermediate proxy. Fig.4 shows how the three above mentioned approaches are implemented by the application gateway for SOI Asia remote lectures.

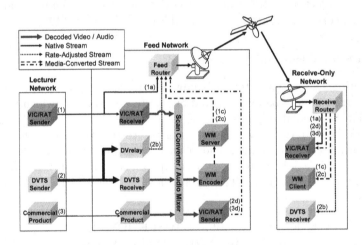

Fig. 4. Application Gateway Overview

Approach (1) uses VIC/RAT to send lecture video/audio, whose transmission rate is already configured to be sent to the UDL without any proxy as (1a) in Fig.4. Approach (2) employs a very high-rate communication such as Digital Vide Transport System (DVTS) [1] whose transmission rate is around 30Mbps. DVrelay[15] reduces the transmission rate to, for example, 6Mbps in realtime before the traffic is forwarded to the satellite UDL as (2b) in Fig.4. Approach (3) uses commercial video conference products such as Polycom or Sony PCS that are available in the lecturer site. Video/audio stream is transferred from the lecturer site to the application gateway, and then the traffic is converted to Windows Media [4] or VIC/RAT multicast stream and transmitted to the satellite UDL as (1c, 2c, 2d, 3d) in Fig.4.

3.5   UDL Mesh Networking

Interconnecting multiple networks using satellite links, there are 3 approaches: (1) Point-to-Point (P2P) mesh, (2) Single Feed (SF) UDL, and (3) UDL mesh[5]. P2P mesh is a topology that uses satellite BDLs to interconnect peer earth stations. SF UDL is a re-definition of the satellite UDL that was discussed in Section 3.1. UDL mesh is a new approach that uses satellite UDLs to interconnect peer earth stations.

In this section, we use "peer" to denote a network that is connected to the mesh network. We also use "feed peer" and "receive peer" to clearly distinguish them in SF UDL.

This paper analyzes these three topologies by the following four aspects; (1) number of required channels, (2) ease of installation, (3) propagation delay, and (4) link bandwidth. UDL mesh requires N channels, where N is the number of peers, to interconnect peers like (c) in Fig.5. And P2P mesh requires $N(N-1)$ channels and SF UDL requires 1 channel like (a) and (b) in Fig.5 respectively.

UDL mesh and P2P mesh require transmission capability to the peering earth station, and in most cases, transmission license, that increases the difficulty to install an earth station. SF UDL requires the earth station with feed peer to have transmission capability and a license. Other peers do not have to acquire any license in most cases, because they only receive a carrier from the satellite.

Propagation delay of UDL mesh and P2P mesh is expected to be one-way delay of a satellite link, which is approximately 250ms. In the case of SF UDL, propagation delay is expected as (1) propagation delay of a satellite UDL from feed peer to receive peers, (2) BDL delay from receive peer to feed peer, and (3) propagation delay of a satellite UDL plus BDL delay from receive peer to another receive peer.

UDL mesh and P2P mesh occupy a dedicated satellite bandwidth, where SF UDL shares a single satellite bandwidth among peers. Therefore, UDL mesh may not satisfy scalability requirement, if a large number of earth station join UDL mesh network to reduce the bandwidth for each link.

The analysis above shows that UDL mesh has advantages and disadvantages compared with the other mesh topology. The biggest benefit is to establish a mesh with direct connections among peers with reduced number of channels and propagation delay. The potential trade-offs are (1) the less scalability of channel allocation, and (2) the less efficiency of link utilization compared with SF UDL, especially when the links of mesh are not fully loaded.

Implementation of the UDL mesh system has been done in the IF environment. Fig.6 shows the system composition of UDL mesh in the peering earth station. UDL mesh bridge is a PC-based system that encodes an Ethernet frame to UDL mesh leaf network into DVB-S format, and reassembles the Ethernet frame

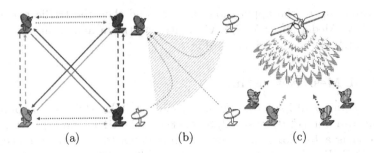

Fig. 5. P2P Mesh, SF UDL, and UDL Mesh

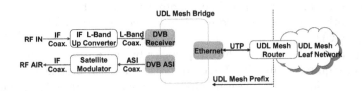

Fig. 6. UDL Mesh System Overview

after decoding receiving carrier from the satellite. AI[3] is installing UDL mesh to evaluate its performance and feasibility using satellite spectrum.

3.6 Transition to IPv6 Operation

We started the operation of receive-only sites using IPv4. Then some sites wanted to extend the network to their campus. With the limited IPv4 address in our hand, we see this as a challenge on how to deploy a network using the new Internet protocol, IPv6. Therefore, IPv4 is not feasible to extend global Internet connectivity to developing regions in a scalable manner where a number of potential sites may come up. This is because IPv4 address space is running out and it is difficult to get enough space for emerging regions. Hence, this research is starting the process to migrate applications and routing protocols for the receive-only sites to IPv6 as shown in Fig.7.

IPv6 has a large address space to accommodate many receive-only sites. The problem is that not all applications support IPv6, even though routing protocols already support IPv6. We have proposed an approach that does not generate IPv4 traffic on the satellite UDL subnet even when IPv6 hosts access IPv4 services as shown in Fig.8.

In this figure, one upstream network and two downstream networks are connected through a satellite UDL. Then, our focus is on (1) web traffic, (2) DNS, and (3) protocol translation for other IPv4 services. For a web proxy, we patched Squid[2], that originally supports only IPv4 in order to process requests IPv6 clients. We installed Trick or Treat Daemon (TOTD) [3] to resolve DNS queries,

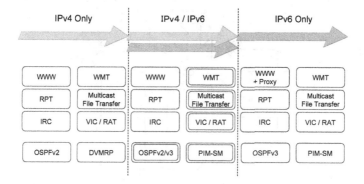

Fig. 7. IPv6 Transition Scheme in SOI Asia

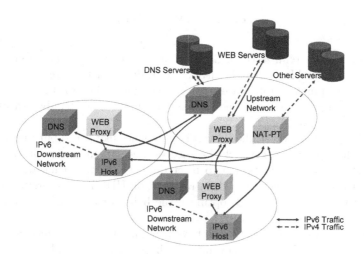

Fig. 8. Host Support in IPv6 Operation

so hosts without any IPv6 address entries in their DNS records will be given fake IPv6 addresses to be used in conjunction with Network Address Translation - Protocol Translation (NAT-PT)[10].

NAT-PT allows IPv6-only nodes to access other IPv4 services until IPv6 is fully deployed. AI[3] is now testing access to the existing Internet applications from IPv6 receive-only sites. We have held hands-on workshop to distribute know-how of IPv6 operation for SOI Asia partners to AI3 and SOI Asia fully transit to IPv6 operation in the very near future.

3.7 Scalability of UDL

LLTM contributes to deploy receive-only earth stations to join the satellite Internet. However, if the number of receive-only earth stations increases, there is an

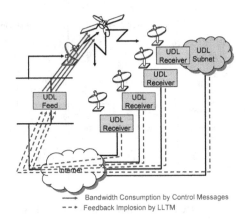

Fig. 9. LLTM Scalability

issue on how to maximize the utilization of UDL bandwidth for service traffics. There are two problems that (1) feedback traffic from UDL receivers implodes at LLTM end point and increase network load, and (2) control traffic caused by network configuration among nodes may consumes UDL bandwidth as shown in Fig.9.

For the solutions, we studied several approaches like (1) to put multiple UDL Feeds with appropriate network distance between them to decentralize LLTM traffic from UDL Receivers, (2) to filter duplicated control messages, such as Multicast Listener Discovery (MLD) Reports, on UDL Feed to prevent forwarding them to the UDL, and (3) optimize the behavior of IP nodes to work in a scalable manner on the UDL.

For the approach (1) and (2), we have been discussing their mechanism to be implemented on a simulator to evaluate their performance. And for the approach (3), we focused on the Prefix Discovery of IPv6 Address Auto-configuration of nodes on the UDL downstream, and have simulated the simple modifications to tune its feedback random back-off timer and the condition that a node may cancel to transmit the feedback message. Also, focusing on scaling multicast sessions, we have been doing efforts to sophisticate such timers and stateful control to suppress the transmission of feedback messages to improve scalability of multicast sessions[14][13].

4   Evaluation

We evaluate our achievement qualitatively by analyzing whether each requirement is satisfied or not and what have been brought through the achievement.

One-way shared satellite link is proved to significantly reduce the cost on installation and operation of satellite link. UDL mesh also exhibited the potential to reduce bandwidth consumption while keeping same information speed as P2P mesh. Therefore, R1 can be said to be met.

The combination of one-way shared satellite link and the deployment of IP multicast on the satellite UDL is the biggest contribution for efficient utilization of radio spectrum. QoS traffic management let prioritized traffic and other traffic coexist by guaranteeing or limiting their bandwidth. The video/audio communication between a very high-speed network and our satellite network can be done by rate adaptation and media conversion using application gateway. Given the situation that SOI Asia lecture can be delivered from the global Internet to Asian regions with as good quality as possible with a very limited bandwidth resource, R2 can be said to be met.

In addition to OSPFv3 and BGP4+ operation in the AI³'s backbone network, transition to IPv6 operation in receive-only network via the satellite UDL will make our entire network ready for IPv6 in both routing and application. Some AI³ partner sites have already completed the transition to IPv6 operation, and R3 is satisfied adequately and to be met completely in the near future.

For the scalability issues of satellite network, our achievement is still partial and does not completely satisfy R4 at this moment, There can be many network protocols to work on a large-scale satellite UDL, and they may suffer from limited bandwidth and long delay of the satellite. Hence we still need much effort to satisfy R4.

As a result, the evaluation can be concluded that the architecture described in this paper has achieved R1, R2 and R3 adequately. However, this architecture is not completed yet for potential large-scale or advanced usage of this network as set in R4 and R5 requirements.

5   Conclusion

5.1   Summary

This paper has described the benefits and concerns, and current challenges for architecture of a wide-area satellite Internet based on our experiences and implementations in AI³ network and SOI Asia.

Although our activity is on-going and needs more evaluation for some parts of the architecture, our architecture can be also applied to establish IP networks on other wireless communications because satellite communication is also a part of them. We are going to continue the operation and deployment of satellite Internet in Asia, research and development on the current and potential challenges on technology to establish a better Asia-wide digital communication infrastructure in the global Internet.

5.2   Future Work in Satellite Internet

Multicast-Only LLTM. Both multicast and unicast packets from a receive-only site to the rest of the Internet are encapsulated using LLTM based on RFC3077. While this method works well with IP multicast packets, the path for unicast packets is not optimal. A unicast packet has to be sent to the UDL Feed

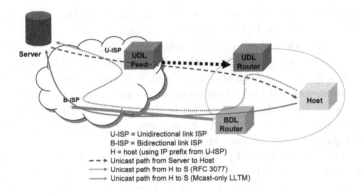

Fig. 10. Unicast on Multicast-Only LLTM

first before being forwarded to its destination, thus creating additional delays. We can alleviate these delays by allowing unicast packets to be forwarded to the destination without undergoing LLTM encapsulation and decapsulation as shown in Fig.10. Multicast packets should be forwarded via RU and encapsulated using LLTM. Thus, this solution preserves the operation of multicast network.

The requirements for this solution are: (1) RO network routes the unicast packets via B-ISP and B-ISP should allow the prefix of the receive-only site, which is assigned from the U-ISP, to pass, (2) LLTM should encapsulate multicast packets and packets for link-local communications to keep the bi-directional emulation of UDL, and (3) multicast routing in the RO network should be separated from unicast routing to allow the normal operation of multicast network.

Satellite Internet for Emergency Situations. In the event of emergencies due to natural disasters, etc., we can make use of the satellite communication links to provide connectivity to the stricken areas. The main issue is how to quickly deploy satellite links using this architecture. An approach for this would be to install a receive-only site with a low-bandwidth wireless link as the uplink. This is still an open research issues to be addressed in the future.

References

1. Digital Video Transport System (DVTS) (April 2007), http://www.sfc.wide.ad.jp/DVTS/
2. Squid Web Proxy Cache (April 2007), http://www.squid-cache.org/
3. Trick or Treat Daemon (April 2007), http://www.vermicelli.pasta.cs.uit.no/software/totd.html
4. Windows Media (April 2007), http://www.microsoft.com/windows/windowsmedia/
5. Ang, W.C., Yusri, N.A., Tan, C.W., Wan, T.C.: Implementation of ip mesh networks using ule protocol over dvb-s links. In: ICOCI 2006. Proceedings Int'l Conference on Computing and Informatics (June 2006)

6. Baba, T., Izumiyama, H., Yamaguchi, S.: Ai3 satellite internet infrastructure and the deployment in asia. IEICE Transactions on Communications E84-B, 2048–2057 (2001)
7. Cho, K.: A framework for alternate queuing: Towards traffic management by pc-unix based routers. In: Proceedings of USENIX 1998 Annual Technical Conference, New Orleans, LA (June 1998)
8. Duros, E., Dabbous, W., Izumiyama, H., Fjuii, N., Zhang, Y.: A Link Layer Tunneling Mechanism for Unidirectional Links, RFC 3077 (March 2001)
9. Fenner, B., Handley, M., Holbrook, H., Kouvelas, I.: Protocol Independent Multicast - Sparse Mode (PIM-SM): Protocol Specification (August 2006)
10. Tsirtsis, G., Srisuresh, P.: Network Address Translation - Protocol Translation (NAT-PT), RFC 2766 (February 2000)
11. Mikawa, S., Basu, P., Tsuchimoto, Y., Okawa, K., Murai, J.: Multilateral distance lecture environment on the internet for asian universities. The journal of Information and Systems in Education (5) (2006)
12. Thamrin, A.H., Izumiyama, H., Kusumoto, H.: Pim-sm configuration and scalability on satellite unidirectional links. In: Proceedings SAINT 2003 Workshops, pp. 27–30 (January 2003)
13. Thamrin, A.H., Izumiyama, H., Kusumoto, H., Murai, J.: Delay aware two-step timers for large groups scalability. IEICE Transactions on Communications E87-B(3), 437–444 (2004)
14. Thamrin, A.H., Kusumoto, H., Murai, J.: Scaling multicast communications by tracking feedback senders. In: AINA 2006, pp. 459–464 (April 2006)
15. Tsuchimoto, Y., Awal, M., Saengudomlert, P., Sanguankotchakorn, T., Kanchanasut, K.: Bandwidth adjustable dvts on the heterogeneous internet environments for distance learning. In: Applications and the Internet Workshops, SAINT Workshops. International Symposium (January 2007)

Author Index

Lecture Notes in Computer Science

Sublibrary 5: Computer Communication Networks and Telecommunications

For information about Vols. 1– 4503
please contact your bookseller or Springer